No Longer Patient

Feminist Ethics and Health Care

Susan Sherwin

Temple University Press

Philadelphia

Temple University Press, Philadelphia 19122
Copyright © 1992 by Temple University. All rights reserved
Published 1992
Printed in the United States of America

The paper used in this publication meets the minimum
requirements of American National Standard for Information
Sciences—Permanence of Paper for Printed Library Materials,
ANSI Z39.48-1984 ∞

Library of Congress Cataloging-in-Publication Data

Sherwin, Susan, 1947–
    No longer patient : feminist ethics and health care / Susan
Sherwin.
      p. cm.
    Includes bibliographical references and index.
    ISBN 0-87722-889-2 (alk. paper)
    1. Medical ethics. 2. Feminism—Moral and ethical aspects.
3. Women—Health and hygiene. I. Title.
R724.S48 1992
174′.2—dc20   91-14499

Chapter 3 is adapted from "Feminism and Moral Relativism," in
Perspectives on Moral Relativism, ed. Douglas Odegard and Carole
Stewart (Toronto and Milliken, Ont.: Agathon Books Limited, 1991).
Chapter 5 is adapted from "Abortion through a Feminist Ethics Lens,"
Dialogue XXX, no. 3 (1991).

For my parents, Ethel and Nathan Sherwin

Contents

Acknowledgments

This book reflects a great deal of stimulation, insight, and help from many valued sources. It is strongly influenced by the work of other feminist theorists and by contributors to the domain of biomedical ethics. It is also very much inspired by the work of feminist activists in the realm of women's health care. I hope that readers will perceive this book as I do, as being part of a larger conversation with others who are concerned with the moral dimensions of health care, especially as they arise in the area of women's health care.

Many people have provided direct help on this project. Perhaps those who are most responsible for the initial conception are the members of the coalition of Halifax women's groups who in 1985 invited me to participate in a panel discussion of the issues surrounding the new reproductive technologies. When they asked me to choose whether I wanted to occupy the feminist or the bioethicist slot on the panel, I realized the degree to which these fields seemed to be separated both in the public mind and in my own professional life. This simple question clearly revealed for me the need to find ways to bridge the gap between the two domains.

My views on feminist ethics have been evolving over several years. They were helped along by a national conference on feminist ethics that was sponsored by the Canadian Research Institute for the Advancement of Women (CRIAW) in 1986. The CRIAW feminist ethics theory group (consisting of Lorraine Code, Maureen Ford, Kathleen Martindale, Debra Shogan, and me) was formed at that time; it met several times over the next three years, and I am very grateful for the many stimulating discussions I had with the other group members.

Various parts of this book were read at a variety of conferences and universities in the last couple of years, and they have been much improved as a result of the feedback received on those occasions. Of particular importance was the criticism received at my own campus, Dalhousie University, where several members of the philosophy and the women's studies departments were especially generous with their advice and assistance. The Canadian Society for Women in Philosophy heard early versions of a number of chapters, and many of its members offered valuable criticism. I also learned a great deal from the students who participated in the class I taught in feminist ethics in 1990.

Financial support for this project was provided by Dalhousie University through the Research and Development Fund of the Faculty of Graduate Studies and by Robert Fournier, Associate Vice President (Research). The sabbatical leave that I was granted at Dalhousie University provided me with the opportunity to get the project underway.

Several chapters have been reworked from essays that were previously published, and I appreciate the cooperation of the editors of *Perspectives on Moral Relativism* (Chapter 3), *Hypatia* (Chapter 4), *Dialogue* (Chapter 5), and the *Canadian Journal of Philosophy* (Chapter 6) for allowing more evolved versions of some earlier ideas to appear in this form.

I also thank my research assistant, Marie Paturel, who helped track down many elusive references, and Ariella Pahlke, who helped in putting the finishing touches on the book. Judith Fox was indispensable throughout, providing assistance whenever needed and ensuring the cooperation of printers, copiers, and couriers at crucial moments. I am grateful to Jane Cullen, who, as editor, recognized the potential in this book while it was still in a very formative stage and provided support and encouragement. I wish also to express my appreciation for the efforts of the referees who reviewed the manuscript and offered useful comments that have helped strengthen the final product.

There have been other important readers whose welcome advice and support must be recognized. I am particularly grateful to Rosemarie Tong and Janice Raymond for their enthusiasm and comments at an early stage of the writing. Robert Martin, Sharon Sutherland, and Leslie Thielon-Wilson were extraordinarily generous with their time, commenting extensively on a later draft. Their feedback was very important to me.

The person to whom I owe the greatest debt is Richmond Camp-bell, who has read and discussed the book with me at almost every stage. He fully appreciated the aims and agenda of this book from the beginning, and his enthusiasm for the project never flagged. His encouragement helped to sustain my own commitment, and his comments and questions were always invaluable. He has succeeded in convincing me that it is possible for men to share feminist goals with women and has demonstrated through his work and his life how men can work, in their own ways, to help bring about the transformations that will lead to an end to women's oppression.

No Longer Patient

Introduction

Over the past thirty years, feminism has undergone enormous growth in every respect: the number of women and men who identify themselves as feminists (or pro-feminism), the geographical and ethnic dispersion of self-proclaimed feminists, the range of views incorporated under the feminist label, and the variety of activities carried out in the name of feminism have all grown dramatically since the mid-1960s. In addition, feminism is responsible for many significant political and legal changes in our world, as well as numerous important personal changes, and it can be credited with some of the most exciting examples of intellectual, artistic, and spiritual creativity of our time. It is a multifaceted and diverse movement, with so many distinct and overlapping dimensions that it has become almost impossible to sum up.

This phenomenal expansion is nowhere more evident than in the area of intellectual pursuits, where feminist theorists have been critiquing old patterns and shaping new ways of thinking. Researchers have brought their feminist consciousness to bear on their respective academic disciplines and have revealed that male bias operates as an implicit element in many traditional lines of thought. In the social sciences, for instance, feminists have shown that male standards have been consistently taken as the norm from which theories are developed and against which they are tested; this has left women in the position of being either ignored altogether or treated as deviant. Hence what has traditionally been referred to as "human" psychology, sociology, history, anthropology, and so on is more accurately described as the psychology, and so forth, of men (and often of white, middle-class, able-bodied Western men). Moreover, feminists have argued, such oversights are seldom benign because such thinking is instrumental in the maintenance of patriarchal arrangements; in other words, this biased intellectual focus is supportive of oppressive practices. More deeply, in several important critiques of science feminists have challenged some of the methodological assumptions and practices that define all of the sciences (for example, Bleier 1984; Harding 1986b; Keller 1983; Longino 1990; Merchant 1980).

Other feminists have established that the humanities too have been committed to exploring the experiences of men and not women. They have observed that the sensibilities of countless generations of students have been shaped by works of art and literature that have been created almost exclusively by men; moreover, the critics who have been recognized as authoritative interpreters of these creations have also been overwhelmingly male. Women, as readers or viewers, have had to learn to perceive through the masculine point of view, because women's specific interests and experiences were seldom considered worthy of serious study in institutions of higher learning.

In discipline after discipline feminists have shown that apparently gender-neutral theories are put forward as if they are, thereby, genuinely universal. It is widely believed that as long as gender is not an explicit topic in a field, there cannot be any bias in its teachings—that provided that the standard formulations of a theory and its methodology do not include actual misogynist statements, the field is free of gender bias. Feminist examination of the foundations of most disciplines, however, has revealed that they contain inherently masculinist presumptions that were previously invisible.

In my own discipline, philosophy, feminist critiques first appeared in the area of social and political thought, where the familiar proposals on such fundamental notions as freedom, equality, and justice were shown to be defined in terms of men's needs and interactions; the specific concerns of women did not appear at all. Although many philosophers became embarrassed by the expressions of woman-hating that pervade the writings of many of the great historical figures, they encouraged their students and readers to ignore these "temporal" biases and to concentrate on the more important theoretical claims of the select "fathers" of philosophy. The absence of female figures of historical significance was (is) explained as a product of local custom in earlier times, whereby women did not pursue philosophic training. Feminists have found, however, that the antiwoman bias in the history of philosophy is more than superficial. They have argued that gender is a factor in many theoretical claims of traditional philosophy; it is not, then, just a matter of "mistaken empirical claims." Indeed, feminists have found gender bias in such abstract areas of philosophy as epistemology, metaphysics, philosophy of mind, and philosophy of science, which are not perceived as culturally specific (Harding and Hintikka 1983; Griffiths and Whitford 1988). Feminist analysis has also questioned the traditional conceptions of ethics (Kittay and Meyers 1987; Hanen and Nielsen 1987; Hoagland 1988); and now we even have a feminist reading of the history of logic, an area of thought that was long prized as immune from bias (Nye 1990).

Curiously, the field of bioethics (also known as biomedical ethics, medical ethics, and health care ethics)[1] has been relatively free of feminist criticism to date.[2] Perhaps this is because bioethics is itself a new discipline of study and has developed through the era of expanding feminist influence. It certainly helps that most writing in the field is free of explicitly misogynist remarks. Many authors in bioethics are sensitive to the importance of using gender-inclusive language, and most strive to accommodate their thinking to the basic injunctions of feminism; for example, they frequently reverse traditional sex-role stereotyping in their choice of case examples. Issues of obvious concern to women, such as abortion and the new reproductive technologies, figure prominently in the literature, and many bioethicists promote positions that defend women's rights to choose in these matters. Nevertheless, as I try to demonstrate in this book, such adjustments are not sufficient.

Much of the work to date in biomedical ethics is problematic in its handling of questions of gender and power. These issues are subtle, however, and problems are unlikely to be discerned unless an explicitly feminist analysis is adopted. To perceive gender bias, we need to examine from the perspective of feminist ethics the sorts of analysis that are generally used in bioethical work. We need also to reflect on the types of problems that are usually pursued in the field. Such investigation reveals that the organization of bioethics reflects the power structures that are inherent in the health care field, which, in turn, reflect the power structures of the larger society. For instance, work in bioethics is largely defined in terms of what may be characterized as the narrower field of medical ethics; attention is focused on the moral dilemmas that confront physicians, and the doctor's point of view is generally adopted. Problems specific to nurses are encountered far more rarely, and those that might be experienced by occupational or respiratory therapists, pharmacists, social workers, technicians, orderlies, or nursing assistants are seldom dealt with at all. These decisions about emphasis reflect and project a belief among bioethicists and their readers that the physician's work is the most difficult, most important, and most worthy of study.

When we examine the sorts of questions that take priority in the field, we find great interest in issues of control and power within the boundaries of the patient–provider relationship: for example, autonomy and paternalism, informed consent, control of information, or euthanasia. Inquiries about relative power within the larger social sphere are seldom pursued, however. On most accounts, all patients are considered equally vulnerable and equally used to expressing their autonomy, although physicians and other health care workers inevitably respond differently to patients who are differently situated with respect to economic class, education, ethnicity, and so forth. Few discussions address the salient connections between individuals' social statuses and their health and health care. Moreover, the complexities and tensions that exist in the lives of the caregivers are not recognized as relevant, although such factors are often significant determinants of the quality of care that is provided.

Feminism has several contributions to make to the field of biomedical ethics. First of all, it should explore whether bioethics is itself an instrument of gender oppression that helps to legitimate existing patterns of dominance and perhaps even introduces some dimensions of its own. Because sexism is often too subtle and pervasive to be recognized without conscious investigation, it is necessary to bring feminist tools to bear on the subject matter of the discipline. That most of the literature in the field of biomedical ethics has been silent on the role medicine plays in the oppression of women is, for example, cause for feminist suspicion.

Feminism directs us to explore the assumptions that are central to a discipline. It asks us to examine which questions get asked and which are ignored.[3] Principal questions to be raised are whose interests are affected by the decisions that have been made and who has the power to control the agenda. In "deconstructing" the discipline and investigating the sites at which male bias may enter, we can begin to understand if and how gender plays a role in structuring the field of bioethics.

Feminism expands the scope of bioethics, for it proposes that additional considerations be raised in the ethical evaluation of specific practices: it demands that we consider the role of each action or practice with respect to the general structures of oppression in society. Thus medical and other health care practices should be reviewed not just with regard to their effects on the patients who are directly involved but also with respect to the patterns of discrimination, exploitation, and dominance that surround them. Feminism urges us to revise the values, perceptions, and concerns that shape how we look at human interactions, so that we may take account of the place of those interactions in the broader set of human relationships.

In addition, feminism encourages us to explore the place of medicine itself in society. Medicine has become one of our most powerful and significant institutions; generally, it is treated as an unqualified good, because it is almost universally regarded as the best instrument for protecting and restoring health. Speaking with the authority of a discipline devoted to improving the human condition, medical practitioners have been granted the status of the new priesthood within secularized Western culture (Raymond 1982). Their view of reality is seldom challenged, even when the subject matter on which they speak extends beyond their scientific evidence. Their attitudes toward the human body have gained preeminence in the culture; medical values help construct people's experience of their own bodies and those of others with whom they interact. Human beings have learned to regard their bodies as potential sites of disease or organ breakdown. Many have appropriated medical views of themselves and see the body as just another machine in the complex technology that surrounds us in postindustrial society; like other machines, one's body is to be delivered to the relevant technicians for monitoring and repair. This perspective changes our experience of ourselves and one another and thus has ethical import.

Scope

It is important to place this discussion in its formative context. My focus is the health care system that is in place in North America in the early 1990s. Most of the issues discussed are common to other developed countries, although specific practices, such as approaches to childbirth, vary in significant ways across nations. When possible, I try to consider aspects of the issues under review that may be significant to the vastly different sorts of health service that are available elsewhere, but I do not attempt a comprehensive global analysis. Further, this book is not meant to constitute a feminist critique of all health care practices.

It should also be noted that the descriptions of patterns of practice that appear throughout the book do not accurately reflect all actual medical interactions. Although some cases exist where medical behavior is worse than anything to which I refer, many particular relationships between health professionals and patients are far better than my discussion here might lead one to believe. Throughout this book I am extremely critical of many aspects of our health care system, and I hold physicians accountable for much that I object to, because they have exerted the most powerful influence on the evolution of health care. This criticism is problematic; I realize that many individual doctors are deeply concerned with the well-being of their patients; most are very interested in ethical matters and are highly motivated to benefit and to avoid harming their patients.[4] Moreover, many physicians are strongly committed to ending sexism. This text should not, then, be interpreted as a direct assault on the motives of practitioners. Unlike some other critics of medicine, I still believe that many medical interactions provide valuable health services to patients. For these reasons, I favor reforming, rather than rejecting, many (although not all) existing health care arrangements, and I believe that the altruistic motives of health practitioners, as individuals, can play an essential role in effecting such reform.

My argument is that the institution of medicine has been designed in ways that reinforce sexism, and the effects of medical practice are often bad for women. Most individual medical actions make sense in the context of medicine as it is currently defined, but we need to step back and examine the cumulative effects of some of its practices. We need to see the patterns of medical values and structures as a whole, in order to identify some of the connections between medical practice and patriarchy; only then can we see the sorts of changes that should be made. As long as we focus on the merely personal—that is, on an individual encounter with a particular doctor—we cannot see the systematic force of sexist assumptions in our health care institutions.

If we are to bring an end to patriarchy and other patterns of oppression, then we need to transform some of our understandings of health and health services. My aim is to identify steps that can be taken in the process of reconceiving some of the relevant notions and rethinking the associated relationships of our health care systems. The ultimate objectives guiding my analysis are to bring an end to medicine's contribution to patriarchy and to help to develop a health care system that is truly beneficial to women as well as men.

Hence this book attempts to deepen common understandings of what considerations are relevant in discussions of bioethics. It is meant to offer a clearer picture of what morally acceptable health care might look like. I argue that a feminist understanding of the social realities of our world is necessary if we are to recognize and develop an adequate analysis of the ethical issues that arise in the context of health care. The specific analyses offered here are not definitive; other feminists would likely emphasize different features. I would expect all to agree, however, that feminist questions should be part of any bioethical investigation. People's lives can be poisoned by oppression as well as by toxins, and both elements merit consideration in moral evaluations of health care practices.

Structure

This book is structured in three parts, reflecting three of the tasks I see as critical to a feminist approach to bioethics. In Part One I set out my conception of the theoretical underpinnings for feminist work in the area of health care. Chapter 1 provides a guide to my understanding of feminism, beginning with evidence for my belief that women are systematically oppressed in multiple, interlocking ways. I address some of the principal reservations many non-feminists have with regard to feminism, and I offer an explanation for my own attraction to feminist analysis. I describe and explain my own negotiated path through the many competing visions of feminism, so that readers can have a clearer sense of what I mean by the term "feminism."

In Chapter 2, I explain what I understand to be constitutive of feminist ethics and show why I find it a more promising approach to ethical reasoning than the proposals offered in traditional ethics. I also distinguish feminist ethics from some recent proposals for an ethics that is explicitly designed to reflect women's apparently distinctive approach to moral reasoning.

Chapter 3 offers a feminist response to one of the classical issues in metaethics: moral relativism. Many feminists distrust all work in theoretical ethics on the grounds that its very need to move to an abstract level of analysis makes it unreliable and dangerous; formal ethics is often seen as an oppressive tool, which mystifies reality and legitimates the power of the dominant group. In examining the strengths and weaknesses of a relativist response to questions about the nature of ethics, it becomes clear that we need to develop a feminist version of moral relativism, and I make my own suggestion for the task.

Part One concludes with a review of what is required to develop a distinctively feminist approach to questions in health care ethics. It compares and contrasts the literatures of feminist ethics and biomedical ethics and concludes that a feminist ethics of health care must be self-consciously oriented to investigating the practices of health care with respect to the overall power structures of dominance and subordination.

In Part Two I move to the analysis of specific problems in the area of ethics and health care, concentrating on some of the questions that are already widely discussed in the bioethics literature. The chapters in this section reflect a feminist re-vision of a few of the problems that are widely discussed in bioethics. I discuss how debate on these matters changes when we adopt the position of feminist ethics that has been outlined in Part One.

The issues of abortion and the new reproductive technologies are predictably prominent in any feminist approach to bioethics because they have been principal concerns for both feminists and bioethicists. These are discussed in Chapters 5 and 6, respectively. In both cases, I argue, feminist ethics yields different analyses, focuses on different problems, and proposes different answers than those that are usually found within the domain of traditional medical ethics.

Chapters 7 and 8 explore the topics of paternalism and research with human subjects. Both issues are widely discussed in the arena of biomedical ethics, but to date they have been largely neglected in the writings of feminist theorists. Here, too, I find that feminist ethics suggests concerns that have been overlooked in the nonfeminist literature and offers proposals that are novel and provocative.

The topics examined in Part Two are meant to be representative but are by no means exhaustive. Further surprises and insights would ensue if other familiar bioethical topics were addressed from the perspective of feminist ethics. Questions about the allocation of resources cry out for feminist exploration: proposals to limit the very old from access to expensive medical technology should be considered in light of the fact that women form a significant majority of the elderly population (Bell 1989). Questions about mental illness and medicine's responses to it demand attention to patterns of power and oppression in society. Investigations on right-to-die issues should reflect on the fact that women's requests have been treated with less seriousness than have men's (Miles and August 1990). Other topics in the area of death and dying might well take a different shape if they were more consciously investigated in the context of life cycles and birthing, experiences that have been significant in most women's lives (for example, Lind 1989).

Part Three is designed to suggest ways in which feminist ethics can broaden our understanding of suitable topics for medical ethics by bringing questions of concern to feminists into the domain of bioethics. It shifts the focus of interest to the structures and organization of health services in the belief that moral concerns should not be restricted to the problems of individual practitioners or those of policymakers.

Chapter 9 considers how medicine constructs a medicalized view of women's experiences and thereby assumes proprietorship over women's lives. In particular, I explore the matter of ascribing illness to women, focusing on whether it is a good or bad thing to accept the label of premenstrual syndrome as an illness; this health question is troubling to feminists but is never addressed in traditional bioethical discussions about the definition of health and illness. Indeed, as I argue, it would not be appropriate to examine this question without adopting an explicitly feminist perspective.

In Chapter 10, I consider how medicine constructs human sexuality, and I explore some of the moral repercussions that follow from its power in this regard. Because sexuality is a matter of significant concern in both personal and public life, medical authority to legislate, interpret, mold, and modify sexuality has much to do with how gender relations are conducted in society. Decisions about whether to medicalize or criminalize (or ignore) rape, for instance, have profound consequences for the lives of women and men, as do medical practices governing the treatment of survivors of child sexual abuse.

In addition, medical pronouncements in support of heterosexuality and against homosexuality provide license for homophobia and so contribute to the oppression of lesbians and gay men. Medical decisions about public health policies in the sexual sphere are important factors in limiting individual freedom of sexual expression.

In the final chapter I explore the significance of gender, race, and class in the organization of health care services. Because the gender, race, and class identity of both patients and providers is a significant feature in the service delivered, moral questions arise about the role of social power in the structure of health care and about the invisibility of these questions in most bioethical discussions. These features define existing dominance relations, and the effects of those dominance relations on the lives and health care needs of persons should be considered in deciding issues of health care policy.

As in Part Two, the topics addressed in Part Three are illustrative rather than comprehensive. Many other ethical questions probing distinct aspects of women's experiences with organized health care await investigation; I am confident that feminist researchers will become increasingly vocal in the area of bioethics and more issues will be introduced.

One of the central insights of feminist work is that the greatest danger of oppression lies where bias is so pervasive as to be invisible. Hence it is necessary to ask questions about all sorts of practices that have heretofore been accepted as normal. Within the fields of both medicine and bioethics, feminism reveals that we need to make conscious efforts to consider what ethical questions may be hidden from view in our ordinary assumptions about health care. This book offers some examples of how we might go about accomplishing that task.

One

Theoretical Beginnings

1

Understanding Feminism

Oppression

Ours is a world permeated by sexism. In virtually every sphere of life, women's interests are systematically subordinated to those of men; and yet, these arrangements are so extensive, so familiar, and so entrenched in our habits of thought that it is possible not to notice them at all. Such all-encompassing exploitation is harmful to women. It is unjust and unacceptable.

Because this discrimination is embedded in the fabric of our culture, special attention must be focused on the details of the many distinctive aspects of women's social, economic, political, and personal positions in society; it is necessary to illuminate the oppression inherent in the specific arrangements of women's diverse lives. "Feminism" is the name given to the various theories that help reveal the multiple, gender-specific patterns of harm that constitute women's oppression. It is also the term used to characterize the complex, diverse political movement to eliminate all such forms of oppression.

Marilyn Frye (1983) has defined oppression as an interlocking series of restrictions and barriers that reduce the options available to people on the basis of their membership in a group. Oppression is often insidious, because the individual practices that make up the system of barriers may look innocent when examined on their own; their role as restraints may be easily obscured. As Frye notes, however, when the various oppressive practices are seen as an interwoven set of institutionalized norms, the pattern of restriction becomes clear.[1]

The most obvious systems of oppression are those maintained by the power of the state through the use of armed force: for example, South Africa's enforcement of apartheid. But other systems of oppression, including sexism, are so well established that they have been internalized by both those who suffer under them and those who benefit from them; they remain invisible to many of the people most directly involved. Many women have learned to accept as natural the socially determined obstacles that they confront and do not perceive such obstacles as restrictive. Feminist consciousness-raising is the process of learning to recognize the barriers of oppression, so that we can begin to challenge and dismantle them.

Although the statistics that document women's oppression are familiar, they bear repeating because some people continue to doubt that women are (still) systematically discriminated against; others, thinking of particular women who do not seem to be oppressed or do not feel oppressed, are inclined to underestimate the seriousness of the problem. I therefore offer a summary of some of the overwhelming evidence that women as a class are oppressed.

In the economic sphere women in North America earn two-thirds of what men earn; they are concentrated in job ghettos, usually in the service sector, where they have access to few benefits and have less job security than do men. Few women hold positions that reflect any degree of authority or political power, and most are in jobs that have no real opportunities for advancement or seniority. Those women who do work in traditionally male professions, such as university teaching, medicine, or engineering, or who hold influential positions in the business world or in politics tend to be concentrated in the lower-paid end of the spectrum for their respective careers. Most are still excluded from the senior positions of their professions by stereotypical attitudes and male-defined norms. For example, working mothers in these fields are hampered in their opportunities for success by expectations that serious professionals should be free to travel frequently, devote more than sixty hours a week to their jobs, and be available for important meetings that may be scheduled during breakfast or evening hours. Less-privileged women who work in factories, hospitals, shops, domestic service, or restaurants often have no control over the shifts they are required to take. In all categories of employment, women are generally treated as the reserve labor pool—the last-hired, first-fired cohort of inexpensive labor to be added to and withdrawn from the labor force according to the economic conditions of the marketplace (Connelly 1978; Phillips and Phillips 1983).

Moreover, women and their children constitute the majority of the poor in the developed world; experts in the field of poverty studies now speak of "the feminization of poverty." Joni Seager and Ann Olson (1986) report: "In the USA, 78 per cent of all people living in poverty are women or children under 18 years old. Statistics from all over the world tell the same story: no matter how poverty is measured, the poor population is largely and increasingly comprised of women and their dependent children" (Seager and Olson 1986, 28). Lenore Weitzman's important study shows the economic vulnerability of women and children in the face of marital breakdown: in the first year after divorce, the average standard of living for men rises 42 percent, whereas for women (and their children) it falls by 73 percent (Weitzman 1985). Furthermore, female poverty is not restricted to young families. Although the financial status of the elderly in the West has improved in recent years, those seniors who are poor are overwhelmingly female.

In many countries of the developing world, women are prevented from owning property or determining what crops should be planted, even though they do most of the labor of working the land. In a Report to the UN Commission on the Status of Women, former Secretary General Kurt Waldheim (a man not inclined to feminist hyperbole) summed up conditions worldwide: "While women represent half the global population and one-third of the [paid] labor force, they receive only one-tenth of the world income and own less than one percent of world property. They also are responsible for two-thirds of all the working hours" (quoted in Morgan 1984, 1). Other UN statistics indicate that approximately 500 million people suffered from hunger and malnutrition in the early 1980s; women and children under five years old are the groups most seriously affected by famine (Morgan 1984). In light of the discriminatory levels of pay, inadequate job protection, and minimal social supports available to working women, it is not hard to see how so many women become trapped in cycles of poverty.

In addition to the economic disadvantages women experience, significant gender injustice exists in the sphere of interpersonal relationships. Even though most women now work outside the home, they are still considered responsible for the demands of household management and child-rearing; such expectations create a double workday for the majority of women. Relatively few have access to affordable, reliable child care; professional child-welfare experts, such as doctors, psychologists, and educators, endorse the conventional social wisdom about the importance of good mothering to healthy child development and thereby foster a perpetual sense of guilt in mothers: mothers are criticized if they work outside the home (for not spending enough time with their children and for not finding good child care while at work) and if they choose to stay at home (for failing to provide adequately for their children and for setting the wrong sort of role model). Here, as elsewhere, the double bind is the common condition of women; no option is available to them that will not provoke criticism and guilt (including the option of having no children).[2]

The traditional sexual division of labor makes women responsible not only for the perpetual grind of meeting daily needs—shopping, cooking, cleaning, tending the sick, organizing, and, in the developing world, collecting and transporting water, fuel, and food—but also for the emotional support of family members and workplace colleagues. Women's customary roles in the bedroom, the kitchen, the hospital, the classroom, and the boardroom require them to be sensitive to others' emotional states and to provide comfort and understanding when things get rough. Women are not usually thanked for their nurturing, because it is accepted as natural to them and therefore not recognized as work. They are, however, blamed and often punished if they fail to deliver.

Moreover, a pervasive pattern of violence and sexual dominance by men over women is, for the most part, tolerated by the various male-controlled legal institutions. On both an individual and a collective basis, men exercise physical and sexual dominance over women. In the United States reports indicate that approximately 93 percent of women experience some degree of sexual harassment or assault, 44 percent of women are subjected to rape or attempted rape, 43 percent of girls experience sexual abuse (and in 16 percent of the cases the abuse is from male family members), at least 30 percent of women are subject to systematic battering in their homes, and up to 70 percent of married women are beaten at some time in their married lives (MacKinnon 1987; Morgan 1984). And this is not a uniquely American problem: a major Canadian study on sexual offenses against children discovered that at some point in their lives, about half of all women have been victims of unwanted sexual acts and about four in five of these incidents first happened to the victims when they were children or adolescents (Badgley et al. 1984, 175). In reports on the state of women's conditions, collected from seventy countries in the early 1980s, Robin Morgan found that nearly every contributor cited the widespread acceptance of woman-beating as a problem in her country (Morgan 1984). Meanwhile, the enormous international profit in pornography reinforces the sexualization of dominance of and violence against women (MacKinnon 1987).

Closely connected with male control of women's sexual lives is men's control over women's reproductive lives. Despite widely diverse social and political systems, powerful men in all nations use their institutional authority in the church, the courts, medical societies, and legislatures to set the rules that limit the control women can have over their own reproduction. In the West male-dominated institutions restrict women's abilities to prevent or terminate pregnancies unless the women are members of a minority race or are poor or mentally disabled, in which cases they are vulnerable to being coerced into sterilization; either way, women are denied the chance to make their own decisions about reproduction. In China women are limited in the number of children they are allowed to produce; in India in 1980 a woman died of septic abortion every ten minutes, and 50 percent of the women who see pregnancies through to term are so malnourished that they gain no weight in their third trimesters (Morgan 1984). The average Soviet woman has six to eight abortions (some have as many as twenty), because contraceptives are virtually unobtainable, whereas in Peru, 10 to 15 percent of women in prison are there for having had illegal abortions (Morgan 1984). Two-thirds of the women in the world have no access to contraceptive information or devices (Morgan 1984).

The subordination of women is a well-entrenched cultural arrangement, which continues to be supported by many of the principal institutions and values of modern society. The major organized religions reinforce male privilege and perpetuate male dominance by treating its exercise as a matter of accustomed norms. In her survey of the concerns expressed by feminists around the world, Morgan found that almost every contributor stressed that the organized religion of her state, be it Christianity, Judaism, Islam, Hinduism, or Buddhism, was repressive to women (Morgan 1984). Within the Judeo-Christian tradition of Western culture, patriarchal structures are promoted as the product of divine will, and spiritual feelings are linked to a duty of submission to one's place in the hierarchy.

Moreover, political and economic ideologies offer further support for the continued subordination of women. In the West capitalist economic and political values uphold a worldview that conceives of humanity as made up of egoistic, competitive beings who are perpetually involved in "natural" power struggles against one another; dominance over others is taken as the measure of individual success rather than as a moral problem in need of rectifying. Women's unpaid role in the reproduction of labor is accepted as an essential element of the system. The state capitalism of the USSR, the People's Republic of China, and Cuba, however, offers no more emancipatory vision of interpersonal interactions. There, too, hierarchical structures support a view of dominance over others as the measure of personal power and success. Developing countries, for their part, are preoccupied with efforts to heal the wounds of their colonial past. They often give priority to revolutionary plans that promise stability and economic viability; frequently, armed struggle among competing forces pushes concern for women's interests to some future agenda.

Women worldwide are excluded from positions of power in a multitude of ways. They may be denied education: although the world's illiteracy rate is dropping, the rate of illiteracy for women, already representing two-thirds of the total, is growing (Morgan 1984). Those women able to pursue an education find that the material they are required to master is thoroughly male-oriented. The academic disciplines of our universities, in theory places for innovative thought, are mired in values that have been developed from a masculine perspective to promote male interests. The insights and interests of women are so effectively repressed that a feminist consciousness may be required to identify the masculine bias of most subjects and to see the role of this body of knowledge in the perpetuation of the sex-gender system.[3] Feminists see that the study of "man" in our academic texts is usually restricted to the study of the dominant male class; they note how, even in abstract areas such as philosophy, women are associated with whatever is defined as negative (the irrational, the chaotic, the partial, and the amoral), whereas men are associated with whatever is valued in the field.[4] The scientific values of our age promote disinterested, rational, human control over the forces around us, but they fail to acknowledge that our understanding of science and the organization of scientific institutions rest on an implicit commitment to the value of dominance.[5] Yet feminist critiques of these important and powerful institutions are usually labeled as biased and distorting, and those who offer such critiques are caricatured as "shrill" and excessively angry (that is, unfeminine).

The values that dominate our cultural institutions are male ones, and at least until very recently, women's work has been ignored and recognition of it suppressed. The literature studied, the music performed, and the works of art revered as "master"pieces are almost always the works of men. Historically, women's work has been invisible, ridiculed, or discounted. In the popular media the images presented of women are usually stereotypically limited and restrictive. Sometimes feminist rhetoric is taken over and transformed in such ways that its meaning is lost, as when a packaged image is offered of the "new, liberated" woman who must meet high standards of achievement at both work and home. In such promotions the contradictions and stresses of the "new woman's" life are trivialized, while the old norms in which women are valued for their nurturing work and their appearance remain intact.

There are differences in the expectations held and treatment received by men and women in every aspect of their lives. Some of these differences are dramatic, such as the incidence of violence against women; others may seem minor or accidental, such as differences in fashion and constraints on appearance.[6] Feminism is the recognition of the pattern that runs across these diverse social arrangements and connects the various manifestations of sexism; it is the perception of the power relations that structure gender relations. A feminist consciousness allows us to see the multiplicity of these layers and leads us to identify the pattern as unjust; the political arm of feminism focuses on securing the means necessary to eliminate such hierarchical structures.

Critiques of Feminism

Despite the obvious injustice documented by these statistics, not everyone accepts feminist analyses. Some remain oblivious to the evidence, others deny that these gender-based inequalities constitute oppression. The most virulent forms of antifeminism come from people who believe that male aggression toward and dominance over women is biologically determined, hence inevitable, and hence acceptable. Such critics of feminism muster scientific evidence to show that male dominance is a biological feature shared with many other species. Ultimately, these sociobiological arguments founder. Their proponents tend to select only the sociobiological examples that serve their political agendas and to ignore the evidence that still other species do not seem to organize according to male dominance. They fail to establish sufficient reason to believe that humans are genetically similar to the selected species with regard to male dominance, while the two species differ greatly in so many other respects. As a result, their examples do not establish that male dominance is "natural" for humans. Moreover, they ignore the fact that humans have the intelligence to create social structures that allow us to modify much of the "purely biological" programming to which we may be subject; therefore, even if antifeminist sociobiologists could establish that patterns of gender dominance are "natural," they cannot prove that these patterns are inevitable. Thus they cannot demonstrate that these so-called biologically determined patterns are acceptable.

Some conservative critics insist dogmatically that the patterns of patriarchy are divinely willed, and they cite scripture to establish their claims authoritatively. Such arguments, however, rest on an acceptance of a patriarchal god, a selective reading of the relevant authoritative texts, and a reliance on self-interested, male interpreters of those texts. These are not particularly effective arguments outside of the circle of those who are already converted.

Other critics assume a more benign, open-minded response to feminist documentations of the patterns of women's subordination in society but still resist drawing feminist conclusions. Some grant that many, perhaps most, women are oppressed, but they protest that these statistics do not accurately reflect the whole picture. They note that many other women can be identified who seem to be free from oppressive forces in their lives; further, many men do not seem to fit the role of oppressor. Feminists recognize that many women do not consider themselves to be oppressed by men; many do not recognize their experience as that of oppression, especially if they are young and privileged (for example, many women who attend university in an apparently democratic environment). The suffering of middle-class, white, Western women, imperceptible as it is to many of them, does not seem to belong on the same scale as the suffering of those involved in genocidal wars, of tortured political prisoners, or of victims of famine. Moreover, women who are members of an ethnic minority, disabled, or poor may well see their victimization because of this latter aspect of their identity as far more severe than any discrimination they experience as women, and they may be right in this perception.

As we have seen, however, part of the force of women's oppression is that it has been legitimized and entrenched in the prevailing cultural values to such a degree that the structure of oppression is obscured. The conditions of dominance are so pervasive, so much the normal state of things, that one needs to acquire a feminist consciousness to perceive the patterns of the discrimination. Until one collects the statistics that document the instances of rape, wife-battering, and female poverty, those who have escaped these particular harms may feel insulated from them, and some who have experienced them may even believe that their falling victim to abuse is attributable to bad luck or personal failure. The cultural myth of individualism—wherein heroic tales of self-determined success in the face of overwhelming odds are regularly reported and celebrated—teaches that we are responsible for our own success and, conversely, for our own misfortune.

Moreover, psychologically it may be more comfortable to reject the patterns of victimization of women that feminists pick out. The feminist interpretation is frightening. Some women (and those who care for them) cling to the hope that they can avoid attack if they sensibly avoid dangerous situations, because it is disturbing to think otherwise. That may explain why sexual assault is commonly treated as anomalous or deviant: for instance, as an event provoked by a foolish, seductive woman who encounters a sex-crazed psychopath while traveling alone at night. Nevertheless, such analyses cannot account for the fact that the majority (83 percent) of rapes are performed by men that the victims knew and may have trusted (Russell 1984) or for the fact that rape victims include not only attractive young women but also infants, elderly women, and hospitalized patients recovering from surgery.[7]

Although feminism values the authority of personal experience, many feminists do not accept that a woman's denial that she has experienced oppression refutes the reality of that oppression. As the background condition of women's lives, oppression is often hidden in the norms of a culture that accepts male dominance as a natural ordering. Many feminists have themselves experienced the dramatic shift in perceptions that occurs when they acquire a feminist consciousness,[8] and they remember their earlier unconscious acceptance of oppressive patterns. The subordination of women is different from other forms of oppression: whereas racism and classism are often maintained through mechanisms of segregation, most women live in intimate relationships with men. The sexual, domestic, public, and working lives of most women are intertwined with those of men, and women often have their deepest emotional ties to men. In a culture that devalues women, many women have learned to dislike other women and to find men more interesting. Male approval is emotionally and professionally vital to many women, even to many feminists. Many women fear that a feminist consciousness will cost them their important relationships with men; they believe that accepting feminism will lead them to hate the men they now love and admire, and they do not relish the prospect of this transition. They may gain confidence, however, if they understand that feminism requires opposition to male power; this need not involve the rejection of all actual men. It is dominance and its ties to masculinity that must be eliminated, not the individuals in whom such norms are internalized.[9] Learning to value women does not require that one learn to hate men.

Those women willing to engage in feminist analysis learn that the objectification of women in pornography includes their own objectification and that often rapists and batterers attack women qua women; those who happen to be spared the actual attack might best think of it as a matter of luck rather than an absence of danger. A feminist consciousness helps women see that restrictions on abortion and manipulation of the process of childbirth affect their options, whether or not they ever become pregnant. They learn that although oppression is experienced differently by different individuals, it is aimed at women collectively as a class.

Feminists can acknowledge that some women manage largely to escape being personally affected by the system of interlocking, harmful practices that constitutes male dominance. Some women manage to accumulate a great deal of personal power and hardly seem to suffer from their membership in an oppressed group.[10] The good fortune of a few successful, powerful women, however, does not establish that women as a class are not discriminated against; it shows only that discrimination can be varied and uneven in its effects.

Another reason many people resist feminism is that they perceive it as guilty of perpetuating the same mistake that they object to in sexism. Because feminists criticize the use of gender as the basis for discriminatory treatment where it ought to be irrelevant (for example, in terms of different economic opportunities, different levels of personal safety, and predetermined stereotypical responsibilities in the household), the proper solution would seem to be to disregard people's sex and treat them as individuals. Feminists insist that we continue to pay attention to the gender of individuals and single out women for special attention and consideration because of their sex. They tend to support programs, such as affirmative action, that give preferential treatment to women, although others may see these programs as being no more than "reverse discrimination." Some critics are concerned that this reinforces sex as a significant difference between people and continues to make it the relevant criterion in determining how an individual should be treated.

The special interest that feminists take in women's concerns, however, is not parallel to the sexist's privileging of men. The difference lies in how women and men are situated in the existing patterns of oppression. Under sexism, men are already dominant (on the unjust basis of their sex), so sexism grants them yet greater power and privilege. Under feminism, women are seen as unjustly oppressed, so they must be allowed the means to free themselves from their subordinated position. Because gender is the basis of women's subordination, feminists believe that their oppression cannot be ended without attending to matters of gender. They realize that as long as women are oppressed because of their sex, to disregard the significance of gender and treat everyone simply as "an individual" is to perpetuate women's oppression; the forces of oppression are complex and systematic, and they will continue to operate until they are dismantled. Therefore, feminists argue, we cannot act in accordance with the ideal of sexual equality until that equality is itself a reality. Attending to the needs and perspectives of women is essential to achieving that end.

Men

It must also be added that there are forms of oppression other than gender oppression (for instance, class, race, or religious persecution). Clearly, some men are victims of these other sorts of oppression, and many suffer profoundly as a result. More-

over, men and boys may suffer some of the same harms as women;
they too may be sexually abused. (It is significant, however, that in
the majority of cases this sexual exploitation is at the hands of men,
not women.[11]) Individual men also suffer from countless kinds of personal tragedies.

Although suffering is not a condition restricted to women, the suffering that constitutes oppression is of a particular sort. It is connected with a pattern of hardship that is based on dominance of one
group by members of another. The dominance involved in oppression is rooted in features that distinguish one group from another; it
requires that existing differences be exaggerated so that supremacy of
the dominant group can be claimed over the other(s). The pain this
process produces in members of the subordinate group is not a product of mere individual misfortune. Sexism is undoubtedly harmful to
men as well as to women, because it puts men into the dominant
role, encourages them in unhealthy behaviors, and deprives them of
the opportunity to develop valuable skills and traits that have been
associated with the feminine. Nevertheless, it would be a mistake to
call this harm to men oppression; it is more a form of alienation from
authentic self-development for men. Although sex roles restrict the
options available to both men and women, the system of restraints
serves men's overall material interests (power, domestic and sexual
service, freedom from many emotional responsibilities) at the expense
of women's, and this is a fundamental difference in how these restraints affect each group. As Marilyn Frye observes, "The woman's
restraint is part of a structure oppressive to women; the man's restraint
is part of a structure oppressive to women" (Frye 1983, 15).

In feminist accounts it is often difficult to know where to cast
blame. An account of oppression implies that someone explicitly
takes on the role of oppressor; it suggests a conscious, malevolent
purpose on the oppressor's part. Most people can confidently identify
individual men who fit this pattern, whose behavior reflects a deliberate intention to dominate and repress women (for instance, rapists,
pimps, pornographers, and sexual harassers). Many other men, however, do not seem to hate or exploit women; when they discuss their
attitudes toward women, they sincerely report themselves as admiring
women and enjoying interactions with them. Many men are involved
in strong, loving relationships with women. These men generally abhor the violent behavior of other men toward women. It seems per-

verse and unfair to describe these men in language that labels them as oppressors.

There is a conceptual difficulty here; when oppression is pervasive, it can be quite unconscious. This subtlety may make the offense of many forms of sexist practice invisible in the perspective of nonfeminists; thus some manifestations of oppressive behavior may be nonintentional and excusable in some sense.[12] Nevertheless, I believe there is a degree of responsibility that attaches to all men.

Regardless of whether they choose their position within the dominant group, all men benefit from the privileges that attach to being male in a culture where men are permitted (and encouraged) to exercise power over women. Some men opt for the role of protector and guard particular women against the violence of other, more dangerous men; in doing so, they are likely to earn the naive gratitude of those women just because they have refrained from exercising their male power.[13] Most men also benefit from women's training in the virtues of femininity, for these are the virtues of subordination through which many women learn to be sensitive and responsive to the interests and needs of others, to be pleasing and conciliatory.

Ours is a society where women are taught to measure their worth in terms of male approval, where women do most of the domestic labor, and where men are considered the likely candidates for positions with high salaries, good benefits, and the most authority. Men who take on an equal share of household duties or who support women's equal treatment in the workplace earn credit simply for being fair. Hence whether individual men wish it or not, a system where women are universally perceived as inferior, dependent, and vulnerable to male violence serves the interests of even those men who do not choose to exercise their male power.

It is not enough, then, for men simply to condemn the harm that other men do; men who care about women (or justice) must also act to transform the social relationships that permit violence against women in all its forms—physical, emotional, economic, or institutional. Unless they engage in demolishing patriarchal structures, they are complicit in the maintenance of those structures. Because sexism gives men the option of exercising the unjust power they retain over women, men who are committed to gender equality must do more than refrain from using that option; they should take steps to eliminate the residual power that attaches to them by virtue of being male.

They can, for example, join women in subverting the sex-gender domination system by challenging the social tolerance of pornography and sexual harassment, by learning to employ gender-neutral language, by attending specifically to the experiences of women, and by rejecting jokes and stories that humiliate and devalue women. Further, they can challenge assumptions of male dominance when they encounter them and demonstrate their commitment to making unacceptable the subordination of women in all its manifestations.[14] It follows, then, that men who do not actively involve themselves in dismantling patriarchy permit continued injustice.

Agency and Oppression

Nevertheless, I caution against reading the language of oppression in such a way as to conclude that the situation of the oppressed is entirely outside of their control. Most women are not helpless, passive victims of the forces of sexism. Although sexism is undoubtedly debilitating—and in many of its manifestations, it can be devastating—women need not accept the role of mere victim, with no room for agency under the circumstances of oppression. Women can and do find ways to resist and deflect the hostility directed at them. They learn survival skills and how to fight against the forces of oppression. On the other hand, I do not mean to imply that continued oppression is women's fault or to suggest that it could be eliminated by a simple act of a woman's will. Sexism is a product of social construction, not a straightforward biological fact (as the anti-feminists would have it). As such, it can be socially changed, but this cannot be achieved by isolated individuals; it requires widespread, collective efforts.

Neither helpless victim nor complicit agent is the appropriate image of women's role in patriarchal structures. Women do not have to accept their assigned position in the hierarchy; they can and do challenge the legitimacy of the hierarchy and seek ways of organizing social structures that are not based on dominance and control. That is the political agenda of feminism, and it takes a great deal of individual and collective work to make such significant transformations in society. Feminists believe in the possibility for resistance and change. By recognizing the patterns of oppression and working collectively to overturn them, feminists can reject the dichotomies of oppressor/victim, master/slave, or dominator/subordinate on which patriarchy rests. Through working and talking together, we can discover and pursue other models of relationships, building on our strengths and connections to create social systems that are free of patriarchal oppression.

Feminists seek ways of empowering persons to pursue nonexploitative relationships. Contrary to popular misapprehensions, feminists are not interested in creating a world structured on hierarchies where women dominate; they are interested in ways of organizing our world that would free it from dominance structures altogether. They want power for women as well as for men, but the power that is sought would be enabling and emancipatory; it is not power over others, as is the common understanding of power relations in the hierarchical thinking of patriarchy.[15]

Varieties of Feminism

Once one accepts the value of feminist analysis in explaining the different opportunities and barriers facing women and men, the question arises of which feminist analysis should be chosen. Feminism is far from monolithic, and there is room for a great deal of disagreement among feminists about the explanation of sexist structures and the changes that should be pursued. The range of views considered under the name of feminism has become so extensive and diverse that sometimes there appears to be little territory common to all. To help situate my position and its implications for the study of ethics generally and health care ethics more specifically, I shall spell out what I consider to be the minimal claims necessary to constitute a core version of feminism.

Several taxonomies have been proposed for distinguishing among various theoretical conceptions of feminism, using such labels as liberal feminism, socialist feminism, cultural feminism, or postmodern feminism.[16] Such distinctions help to identify differences in understandings and commitments, although they often exaggerate disagreements over emphasis and raise these to the level of substantive political conflicts, in order to establish boundaries. Competition for political correctness can interfere with effective communication; it is important to remember that most forms of feminism still share many principal values.

My approach is an eclectic one. In this book I include insights that are commonly associated with different formulations of feminist theory. Thus I pursue a loosely defined characterization of a feminism that is not ideologically bound to any exclusive theoretic definition (although I recognize that this, too, is a theoretical stand that many feminists will reject).[17] The ambivalence of perspective I offer is meant to reflect the respect I feel for the range of directions encompassed by feminist thought.

Liberal feminism is probably the most common variety of feminist thought; it represents a set of views that are widely held in Western society. Derived from the more general political theory of liberalism, liberal feminism is committed to making the formal legal and political changes necessary to guarantee women rights that are equal to those of men, including rights to education and to all opportunities.[18] Although a rights-based theory can readily be distorted to protect the interests of the most privileged members of society against the demands of the disadvantaged,[19] I believe that the concept of human rights can still be a potent tool for protecting the interests of those people who are most likely to be overlooked in formal political and interpersonal contexts. Therefore, I support liberal campaigns to establish wider definitions and greater protection of the rights of women, and I cautiously accept reliance on the state to enforce some of these rights (for example, through programs of affirmative action, equal pay for work of equal worth, equal opportunity, and so forth). I believe that feminism remains an emancipatory movement, committed to increased—or perhaps, more accurately, better distributed—freedom for persons; such ends can only be achieved with the destruction of oppressive patterns, and I believe that wary attention to claims of equal rights can, to a significant degree, help accomplish this goal.

I do not, however, consider myself to be a liberal feminist; I do not think the liberal strategy of fostering equal rights is sufficient for a feminist transformation. I fear that liberal feminism places too much emphasis on the individual and relies too heavily on legal and political solutions to correct the abuses of complex, interpersonal power differentials. It does not provide sufficient scope to correct the ways in which groups, rather than individuals, are victims of oppression. Liberal feminism also is not sufficiently critical of the dangers of (bourgeois) individualism, and it fails to pay adequate attention to the significance of economic and social structures in the patterns of oppression.

Therefore, I find that my feminism must be strengthened by appeal to some of the insights of socialist feminists (for example, Jaggar 1983), who have insisted that we attend to the structures of economic organization in oppression. Socialist feminists have shown that capitalism and patriarchy are interdependent forms of oppression in the West, which must be attacked jointly. Feminists have good reason to be critical of the selfish values of capitalism, which support competitive individualism while denying individual and collective responsibilities for the welfare of others. Economic domination of some over others (whether we speak of persons, genders, races, or nations) is connected with other forms of domination, and universal freedom cannot be achieved as long as economic exploitation is tolerated. As a feminist concerned with the interests of all women, I consider democratic socialism to be preferable both to a capitalism driven by the interests of giant, multinational corporations and to the corrupt bureaucracy of the forms of state capitalism/socialism that characterizes most communist countries.[20]

I also share with socialist feminists their critique of the common liberal feminist view that persons, considered in some abstract, ideal form, should be regarded as the basic units of political and moral analysis (Scheman 1983). On the socialist feminist view persons and their relationships are understood to be socially constructed. They exist in specific circumstances at specific times and places, and therefore sweeping generalizations about generic, ahistorical persons are problematic.

Socialist feminists argue that it is important to look for the historical roots of the oppression that women now experience. They recognize that the particular form that oppression takes may vary widely from one society to the next and from one segment of society to another; therefore, it is important to detail explicitly the forms of oppression that are being challenged by a particular feminist action. Socialist feminists have been particularly conscientious to make the analysis of other kinds of oppression (in addition to the oppression of women) significant in their task, and they have been sensitive to the fact that women's specific experiences of oppression vary with their race and class.

I have difficulties with some formulations of socialist feminism, however. In particular, I find that most socialist feminists do not pay enough attention to the sexual nature of women's oppression.[21] On many socialist feminist accounts sexual exploitation and abuse is more likely to be addressed as a symptom than as a causal factor or prominent feature of women's oppression. Economic, rather than sexual, exploitation remains the principal focus of such accounts, and many socialist feminists seem insufficiently critical of the cultural norms of heterosexuality (for example, Segal 1987).

Therefore, I find myself persuaded by many of the theorists who are usually pegged as radical feminists.[22] In particular, I agree with radical feminist analyses that suggest that sex differences function explicitly as power differences under sexism. Marilyn Frye (1983), for instance, argues that in a sexist society a person's biological sex is always relevant to how that person is treated; sex identification (the process by which we sort people into categories of male and female) is made an obsession. Because dominance structures demand dichotomies, natural differences are exaggerated and embellished; this allows the more powerful group to distinguish itself from the other, claiming not only difference but superiority and hence a legitimate right to dominate. To justify the hierarchy, differences must be established and emphasized.

It follows, then, that a principal function of establishing sex differences is to structure dominance relations. One of the prominent areas of difference between the sexes is the domain of sexuality. Sexuality is socially constructed and also constructing—that is, we are taught specific patterns of sexuality according to our culture, and in learning them we shape ourselves to certain social expectations. Under sexism, sexuality is made to serve the pattern of dominance by making hierarchy erotic and turning women into sexual objects. It is, then, not an accident that male violence against women is endemic in our society: in our cultural consciousness, "woman" means sex, and "sex" means dominance (MacKinnon 1987).

It is, therefore, important to include criticisms that lesbian feminists offer of the compulsory nature of heterosexual norms in our culture. They are correct to insist that we examine the role that heterosexuality plays in reinforcing the sex-gender system. Lesbian independence from male-oriented relationships gives lesbian feminists a unique and vital perspective on feminist debates; they have a particular standpoint that should be heard on all feminist issues. All feminists must support lesbians in their sexual choices and recognize that the sexual freedom of every woman is tied to the sexual freedom of lesbians; that is, physical love of men cannot be a free choice for women unless lesbianism is a genuine (safe) option as well. Unlike lesbian separatists, however, I do not advocate abandonment of all heterosexual relationships. I do not think feminism demands the exclusive lesbianism of all its proponents.

In addition, I agree with feminists of color that we must recognize the vast differences among women and the variety of ways in which the oppression of women can be manifested (for example, hooks 1984; Lugones and Spelman 1983). To speak as if there were a single, universal class of women who all experience sexism in the same way and who are all oppressed to the same degree is distorting and biased. Women of color must often remind others that membership in a dominant group affords one the luxury of ignoring one's own race or class. Members of dominant groups tend to presume that their own identification defines the norm; they are inclined to believe that their own race, class, or gender is not a significant factor in the discussion. Women of color, working-class women, disabled women, immigrant women, and lesbians are sometimes described as speaking from a "special" perspective, whereas the rest often carelessly presume to speak as generic women. Too often it has been left to multiply oppressed women to remind middle-class, Western, white women such as me to avoid this error in theorizing.[23] It is important, then, that both author and reader be sensitive to the distinctiveness of my perspective on women's oppression(s) and critical of generalizations that imply that my experience is typical of all women.

There are further reasons for addressing race and class privilege in feminism: many women are themselves complicit in the various forms of oppression. Feminists must come to terms with the fact that some women exercise dominance over others. Women often embrace their class, religious, national, and political identities and are understandably inclined to take advantage of whatever privileges may be provided by such affiliations. In addition, women often assume the role of conservators of tradition and may work to perpetuate existing sex-role standards within their own class, thereby serving as the instruments of oppression for their own daughters.[24] Feminists, too, have grown up in societies that promote sexist and racist practices, and they must attend to their own parts in maintaining the ongoing systems of oppression.

There are many more debates within feminist theory. Cultural

feminists, for instance, presume that there is an essential female nature common to all women, which should be identified, developed,
and celebrated; others, such as socialist feminists, reject the notion of
a universal nature shared by all women that is anything more than
their subordinated position in a sexist society; still others, such as
some postmodern feminists, doubt that there is any such thing as the
category "woman."[25] In addition, ecofeminism introduces important
concerns about the connections between the domination and exploitation of women and the domination and exploitation of nature
(Plant 1989). Proponents of psychoanalytic feminism, feminist spirit-
uality, and feminist aesthetics focus on other relevant dimensions. It
is not possible even to name all the variants of feminism in a brief
chapter. Feminism is a rich, complicated field, and no brief survey
can do it justice; I hope, however, that this brief review offers some
guidance for those who want to locate within the complex terrain of
feminism the views that shape this book.

Eclectic Feminism

The various feminist theories that have been es-
poused reflect many of the distinct ways in which different sorts of
women experience gender oppression and the various kinds of social
change that seem necessary to eliminate such oppression. Like
Sandra Harding (1986a), Jane Flax (1990), and others, I believe we
must expect and welcome a certain degree of ambivalence and disagreement within feminist theorizing. Contemporary feminism cannot be reduced to a single, comprehensive, totalizing theory. I shall
try, then, to use the minimal number of theoretical commitments in
my analysis, in the hope that feminists and bioethicists of many different persuasions may find value in this study.

Critical to my analysis are the understandings that women are oppressed, that this oppression is pervasive in all aspects of social life,
and that political action (that is, collective action on a broad scale) is
necessary to understand and eliminate that oppression from our
world. Although oppression is experienced on a personal level and
some of us can make personal accommodations to lessen its impact
on our own lives, there are no personal solutions to the elimination
of oppression. Only a large-scale social transformation will rid society
of the oppression that subordinates women to men; moreover, this

transformation is demanded by an understanding of explicitly ethical and political values. Politics here is understood as the small "p" variety, running far deeper than anything we find in formal electoral politics. It involves changing the nature of power structures in the world, moving from structures that grant some people power over others to alternative social arrangements, which foster universal access to personal power. [26]

The feminist changes that are needed to eliminate sexist oppression in the world are deep and thoroughgoing; many probably cannot even be imagined right now, situated as we are within patriarchal culture. Feminists are occupied in deconstructing the habits of sexism by recognizing, criticizing, and dismantling the innumerable practices that constitute patriarchy. Much of the feminist agenda is, for now, defined negatively: we want a world free from sexual assault, battery, and pornography, where women and children are not forced into the humiliations and dangers of poverty, where women have control over their own reproductive lives, and where women are themselves nurtured and no longer solely responsible for nurturing others. Such a world will be very different from this one; if we are to bring it into existence, then we will have to make substantial changes in our major institutions, power structures, and habits of thought. If women achieve power equal to that of men and if nonhierarchical relationships become the norm—that is, if feminist values become accepted throughout society—then the world will be so changed as to be barely recognizable from where we now stand. [27]

Hence I believe that all feminist thought is ultimately revolutionary, although its strategies do not invoke the usual means of political revolution. Armed rebellion cannot achieve feminist ideals; nor can propaganda or coercion. Rather, a revolution in thought and behavior is called for, and that will continue to occur in a piecemeal fashion as women address the oppressive conditions of their own circumstances and the institutions that are responsible for these conditions. This book offers suggestions about what that transformation might require in the vast area of health care and proposes moral constraints that should be considered if we are to achieve a health care system compatible with feminist aims.

In addition to the themes already mentioned, I want to stress my commitment to the initial perception of feminist consciousness, which is not usually ascribed to any particular feminist school:

namely, that the personal is political, that is, that the particular ways in which women (and men) experience sexism is worthy of political analysis. Furthermore, just as the personal is political, the political is personal; feminism is also a way of life. To become a feminist is to change the way one lives in the world, and this process is usually experienced as exciting, terrifying, exhilarating, confusing, challenging, depressing, frustrating, and joyous. The only thing it does not seem to be is reversible. Once we learn to see how things really are, they are not easily hidden from us again.

2

Ethics, "Feminine" Ethics, and Feminist Ethics

Philosophical Ethics

The philosophical study of ethics (or moral theory)[1] is concerned with value questions about human conduct. It addresses the meanings of and standards of use for such terms as "ought," "right" and "wrong," "good" and "bad," "obligation" and "responsibility," "justice" and "injustice," and "praise" and "blame," as they are applied to persons, actions, character traits, and social practices and arrangements. Ethics also explores the legitimacy of using such categories at all. In the field of ethics theorists question whether there are such things as moral facts and examine the type of knowledge that is claimed when ethical assertions are made. They seek to specify the appropriate grounds of justification for moral judgments.

Although the technical questions associated with the theoretical study of ethics tend to be addressed principally by philosophers, practical ethical questions are part of everyone's experience. Ethical reflection seems to be part of conscious living; it is the familiar experience of finding oneself driven to wonder what should be done or what should have been done during difficult moments. What characterizes the specifically philosophical investigation of ethics is the search for a systematic approach to evaluate the standards of justification adopted.

Philosophers are not the only specialists interested in questions about acceptable and prohibited forms of behavior, but they define their role in ethics differently from the way others who pursue related aspects of these questions define their tasks. For example, most philosophers do not present moral rules as commandments from a higher authority, as religious leaders often do. Unlike legislators and those engaged in the interpretation and enforcement of the law, philosophers neither prescribe nor impose sanctions for failure to comply with their recommended rules. Furthermore, ethical theorists differ from social scientists, whose task is to observe various cultural arrangements and deduce the moral assumptions that may be reflected by those practices. Rather than describing what rules already exist or enforcing rules set out by those in positions of power, philosophers are interested in determining which rules ideally should be followed and what justifications are adequate to support such proposals.

Those engaged in the philosophical work of ethics seek to understand the underlying value scheme that determines the moral evaluation of practices. Most moral theorists assume that particular features (termed "right-making" qualities) characterize morally acceptable practices, whereas other features ("wrong-making" ones) belong to behaviors that should be prohibited. One of the principal tasks of moral theory is to clarify the basis for making sound moral claims, by determining and explaining the appropriate sorts of considerations that we can invoke to make justifiable value judgments.

This book is in the tradition of philosophical moral theory, because like other moral theorists, I am interested in understanding the basis of adequate moral choice. More specifically, this book fits within the evolving tradition of "applied ethics," because it explores the implications of a set of theoretical claims in specific contexts of behaviors. I make proposals about the kinds of considerations that should be part of normal moral evaluations. I adopt an approach I characterize as feminist ethics, a form of ethics that considers oppression generally (and, particularly, the oppression of women) to be a principal matter of moral concern, which should be addressed in moral evaluations.

In Parts Two and Three I show how feminist ethics reveals that some practices are more likely to be morally right than others and why some seem not to be morally tolerable at all. In this chapter, I explain the theoretical underpinning of my analysis. In Chapter 4, I describe the contextual features that I think are central to the specific area of ethics and health care.

Traditional Ethics

Several different traditions are followed by the philosophers who currently work in ethics. Because I mean to distinguish my own position of feminist ethics from the major competitors in traditional, mainstream (malestream)[2] ethics, I shall briefly review the positions adopted by most philosophers working in the field of nonfeminist ethics and try to explain why I reject these alternatives. To explain my departure from the leading traditions, I focus on the elements that I find problematic within each theory. Because my orientation is feminist ethics, I only explore nonfeminist theories to the extent necessary to explain my understanding of the relevant contrasts with my own approach.

Most modern, Western theorists pursue one of three distinct approaches, which are known by philosophers as deontological ethics, consequentialism, and social contract theory.[3] Deontologists believe that ethics is a matter of determining which actions are required or prohibited as a matter of moral duty. These actions are right (or wrong) because they are required (or proscribed) by a moral law or set of rules that is binding on persons, independent of their specific interests. Immanuel Kant is the most influential of the deontologists, and although his most important work in ethics was published more than two hundred years ago (*Groundwork of the Metaphysic of Morals* [1785]), his general approach is still widely followed today.

Kant proposed that the right-making characteristic of an action is defined by the logical nature of the principle it embodies. He believed that moral duties are identified by rational, free persons through the purely abstract process of reason. Kant argued that the moral law must be above personal considerations, that is, independent of the feelings of those involved in particular applications. The moral evaluation he called for explicitly disallows consideration of the specific circumstances of the agent or of other parties affected. Rather, moral conclusions must be reached through reasoning that has been abstracted from the circumstances of application, whereby agents decide if the maxims under which they would act could be willed to be universally binding. (For example, the maxim to tell the truth can be willed to be universal without contradiction, but the maxim to lie to take advantage of others' good faith cannot.) Kant was well aware that the specific consequences of performing an action prescribed by such a principle might be undesirable in a particular circumstance, but he believed that morality consists in following the moral law and not in pursuing the consequences we prefer.

Deontological ethics in the form advocated by Kant can be characterized as implying that some actions are morally required, regardless of their consequences or their effects on "human weal and woe." More recent deontological theories, such as that offered by W. D. Ross (1930; 1939), are more sensitive to consequences but still deny them decisive relevance in many circumstances. (For Ross, the final measure of the degree of relevance is to be determined by the rational intuition of "the plain man" [sic].)

Deontological theories pay scant attention to the specific details of individuals' moral experiences and relationships. They admit that special obligations arise from specific relationships—for example, to friends and family—but little discussion is devoted to exploring the range or force of such duties. Almost all the theoretical work is concentrated on exploring the nature of general, rather than specific, obligations. As Cheshire Calhoun (1988) argues, such neglect creates two ideological views about the moral life that amount to an inherent gender bias: most moral theorists imply (1) that it is self-evident that special obligations are less important than the general, impersonal duties that theorists chiefly emphasize, and (2) that general, rather than special, obligations are experienced most frequently in the moral lives of persons. The moral lives of women are often taken up with the details of special obligations, yet these concerns are discounted.

Deontological theories also pose a problem in cases where duties conflict. Kant seemed not to acknowledge this possibility at all, but Ross was well aware of it and recommended resolving the conflict through appeal to rational intuition. Suppose, however, that what is at stake in the resolution of such a conflict are the interests of the oppressor and the oppressed. Whose rational intuitions should count in these cases? Ross's referral to the generic "plain man" fails to address satisfactorily the power issue that may be at the root of this problem.

These versions of deontological ethics do not express any interest in accommodating feminist concerns about the effects of oppressive practices on subordinate groups as part of their moral evaluations of such practices. Indeed, it is difficult to see how such accommodation could be made within the confines of the deontological theories now available; neither Kant nor Ross provides grounds for directing our attention to the specific experiences and interests of members of oppressed groups. Hence feminists cannot find space within the leading proposals of deontological ethics to address the specific harms of the patterns of dominance they seek to change.

Moreover, feminists must object to the formulation of Kant's ethics, because like many other moral theorists, Kant assumed that only men would fully qualify as moral agents. He believed that women—together with children and idiots—were unable (or unwilling) to engage in a process that requires them to ignore personal sentiments in their moral decision-making. Because of this "deficiency," he considered women inferior moral agents, unfit for public life. Rather than accept Kant's view of women as deficient moral agents, feminists generally judge his determination to discount the role of sentiment to be a mark of inadequacy in the theory itself. With many other critics, feminists reject the notion of a moral theory that is wholly detached from concern about consequences.

Consequentialists have an entirely different vision of morality from Kant's: they believe that the moral worth of an action is measured in terms of the worth of the consequences of the action. Consequentialists determine a measure against which states of affairs can be evaluated and hold that an action is right if it maximizes what is desirable in its outcome, in comparison with the results of all alternatives. The most familiar form of consequentialism is utilitarianism, in which consequences are evaluated in terms of the aggregate effects of an action on the welfare or happiness of persons (or sentient beings). Like other consequentialists, utilitarians deny that rules should be followed if they result in less desirable outcomes, even if those rules appear rational in the abstract.[4] Unlike Kantians, consequentialists believe that the particular feelings and attitudes both of agents and of those affected by the actions in question should be considered when determining the moral value of actions; in this sense, their analysis focuses on concrete experiences.

Those who promote consequentialism in its traditional formulations still operate on an abstract plane, however, because ultimately, rightness of an action is calculated by appeal to the total amount of happiness and suffering created by an act, without regard to whose happiness or suffering is at issue. For example, if a utilitarian can produce the greatest amount of happiness by performing an action that will benefit her enemies rather than her children, she is obligated to do that. Although the individual agent would find it preferable to benefit her loved ones rather than her enemies, and although her own pain at the outcome is an element to be considered in the calculation, the theory says that what is important is the total amount of happiness that will be produced by the act. There is no assurance that this requirement will allow her to act on behalf of those she loves, rather than on behalf of those she fears or loathes. As Bernard Williams has argued, this requirement alienates the agent "in a real sense from his [sic] actions and the source of his action in his own convictions. . . . It is thus, in the most literal sense, an attack on his integrity" (Williams 1973, 116–17). Moreover, utilitarianism is not directly concerned with merit or fairness in the provision of happiness. What is important about persons is their status as bearers of utility; an individual's relationship to the agent contemplating action and all other qualities that are specifically associated with the individual are of indirect relevance only.

Like Kantianism, then, consequentialism has usually been understood to demand a level of impartiality on the part of agents, which many people find psychologically unacceptable and morally repugnant. The details of the emotional lives and the relationships of the particular persons affected are rendered irrelevant from the moral point of view, except insofar as these details contribute to overall measures of happiness or suffering. All persons are essentially interchangeable for the purposes of both moral theories. Specifically, no special role is directly assigned to a person's status in dominance/subordination relationships. In both Kantian deontology and consequentialism moral agents are asked to distance themselves from their personal experience and concerns. Kant directs agents to think in terms of universal laws, without regard to the circumstances from which actions arise; consequentialists direct them to weigh their own interests equally with those of everyone else, and on most accounts there is no moral evaluation of the worth of the interests themselves. Both theories deny giving special weight to the details of individuals' actual positions in dominance hierarchies. This abstract neutrality is objectionable from the perspective of feminist ethics, which demands explicit focus on the social and political contexts of individuals in its moral deliberations.

Contractarianism, or social contract theory, is the third form of moral theory widely embraced in contemporary Anglo-American philosophy. It combines elements of both Kantian theory and consequentialism; moreover, it shares with feminism a commitment to placing the discussion of moral judgments within an explicitly social context (although for contractarians, this context is likely to be an artificial one). Nevertheless, most contractarians differ from feminists in their assumptions about human nature. Most believe persons are inherently independent and self-interested, and they see the task of morality as that of ensuring cooperation among essentially competitive individuals. They appeal to the notion of a hypothetical agreement—what they commonly call "the social contract"—which would be the logical outcome of reasoned negotiation that would be conducted among separate, self-interested beings. The contract is the means by which these hypothetical selves acknowledge the mutual advantage of restraining aggressive (non-moral) behavior against one another; without this agreement, their relationships presumably would be characterized by aggression and coercion (a life that is "solitary, poor, nasty, brutish, and short," as Thomas Hobbes so vividly put it). Because most contractarians assume that other people pose a serious threat to one's self-interest, morality is presented as the rational option by which to limit the dangers of social life.[5]

Like Kant, most contractarians propose that only the abstract features common to all persons can have moral significance in determining the terms of the contract; hence they usually limit their assumptions about human beings to the characteristics that are assumed to define moral agency, those of rationality, autonomy, and self-interest. They share with consequentialists the belief that the role of morality is to help facilitate humanly desired ends. The ideal moral community that contractarians invite us to imagine is described as being composed of equal, rational, autonomous, independent persons. Generally, social contract theorists do not address the moral status of persons who do not meet these ideal standards, nor do they investigate the nature of the moral relationships that exist among persons of unequal power. Attention to the particular details of the lives of the contractors (for example, family life, status in the hierarchical pecking order, specific skills and talents, or disabilities) is generally thought to compromise, rather than enhance, the legitimacy of the contract.[6] But these kinds of details are important. Contracts made under the "veil of ignorance" tend to perpetuate, rather than correct, the structures that maintain oppressive practices. Even though some versions of contractarian theory (for example, Gauthier 1986) allow contractors to acknowledge details about themselves, they do not develop the means necessary to prevent existing power relations from determining what is just. By refusing to distinguish between various differences among people, most contractarians proceed as if traits such as gender and race can be treated as being on a par with eye color; they fail to identify the mechanisms that must be put in place in a currently oppressive society to achieve the equality they presume. Therefore, most feminists find none of the existing social contract theories adequate to address their political concerns.[7]

Because all three moral theories are extraordinarily abstract, most people who appeal to them to inform actual moral decision-making have found the theories woefully inadequate for the practical tasks of moral life. (See Chapter 4 for a discussion of the limitations many bioethicists have found in such theories.) Moral behavior arises in the context of particular lives that are embedded in particular sorts of relationships. Therefore, ethics should attend to the nature of the relationships that hold among those who are involved in situations requiring moral deliberation. As we have seen, none of the leading formulations of traditional theories allows sufficient room for such considerations.

"Feminine" Ethics

Many women have found the approaches discussed above (as well as most of the other proposals for ethics that have been presented throughout the history of Western thought) to be alienating and unsatisfactory, leading, in Kathryn Morgan's (1987) apt phrase, to "moral madness." They have identified a number of objections to traditional ethical theory as it is usually conceived. Their concerns can be categorized into two distinct groups. The first set, which I label "feminine" ethics, consists of observations of how the traditional approaches to ethics fail to fit the moral experiences and intuitions of women. It includes suggestions for how ethics must be modified if it is to be of value to women. The other set of concerns, addressed in the next section, is what I consider to be feminist ethics proper; it applies a specifically political perspective and offers suggestions for how ethics must be revised if it is to get at the patterns of dominance and oppression as they affect women. It is feminist, rather than feminine, ethics that shapes the analysis of this book, but it is helpful to begin with a description of feminine ethics.

Among the many reasons women have identified for developing new approaches to ethics, perhaps the most obvious comes from the experience of being caught up short by the antiwoman bias that pervades so much of the existing theoretical work in ethics. Even the most cursory feminist review of the work of the leading moral theorists reveals that the existing proposals of philosophic ethics do not constitute the objective, impartial theories that they are claimed to be; rather, most theories reflect and support explicitly gender-biased and often blatantly misogynist values.

Perhaps this should come as no surprise, because the leading moral theorists have historically described their audience as being exclusively male. Aristotle's theory of virtues, especially as it was developed in the *Nicomachean Ethics* and the *Politics*, made clear that there was a different set of virtues for (free) women from the one developed for (free) men; whereas men's virtues were those required for freedom and political life, women's virtues consisted in obedience and silence.[8] Only the male virtues were treated as being of philosophic interest or genuine moral worth. This misogynist vision did not end with Aristotle, for his influence has continued for centuries: it was especially important in the development of the thought of the church fathers, who accepted his division of moral worth and made it a centerpiece of their theology, shaping Western values through the ages.

Most of the influential moral theorists in the history of Western thought, including not only Kant and Aristotle but also Thomas Aquinas, Jean-Jacques Rousseau, G.W.F. Hegel, Friedrich Nietzsche, and Jean-Paul Sartre, saw women as having a significantly different character from men, one they considered morally inferior because it was too focused on the particular and inattentive to the level of generality that moral thought was said to require.[9] They took it as obvious that men were associated with reason (the essential feature of morality) and women were associated with inclination (a barrier to moral thought). Women's deficiency in this regard was taken as justification for excluding women from active roles in political life and for limiting their power and influence in the home. Moreover, many moral theorists believed that subordination was the natural condition of women and perceived in them a willingness to accept their status passively. Rousseau put it most bluntly: women were suited by nature "to please and to be subjected to man. . . . Woman is made to put up even with injustice from him. You will never reduce young boys to the same condition, their inner feelings rise in revolt against injustice; nature has not fitted them to put up with it" (quoted in Canovan 1987, 86–87).

Modern readers may be inclined to dismiss such views as quaintly anachronistic, a reflection of earlier times but no longer inherent in moral theory, but this would be a mistake. Most contemporary work in ethics and social and political philosophy is not so blatantly offensive, but it does, nevertheless, usually ignore or exclude the perspective of women. For example, in his influential *A Theory of Justice* John Rawls (1971) assumed that he could develop a theory of just social arrangements without attending to the special perspective of women; therefore, he proposed having the "heads" of households represent the interests of the whole family, without acknowledging the tendency of patriarchy to grant men authority to disregard and regularly violate the interests of other family members. Rawls also failed to account for the development of any sexual division of labor.[10] Two important responses to Rawls that share his contractarian orientation, Robert Nozick's *Anarchy, State and Utopia* (1974) and David Gauthier's *Morals by Agreement* (1986), demonstrate even more dramatically how the tendency to presume philosophy can be done in a gender-neutral fashion perpetuates male privilege.[11] Although blatant misogyny has finally become rare in ethical theory, the specific experiences and interests of women are still wholly excluded from the conceptual framework of philosophical ethics. Women are assumed to fall under the generic rubric of "the agent," but the moral concerns that are examined are always those most salient from the male perspective.

Furthermore, insofar as moral theorists and moral authorities offer women any moral guidance at all, such guidance is often contradictory, demeaning, and restrictive. Kathryn Morgan has expressed this dilemma vividly by documenting the complex ways in which the implications for women of traditional moral theory lead to "moral madness" (Morgan 1987). Morgan found that traditional moral theories follow one or more of four basic patterns: (1) they deny that women are capable of full moral reasoning; (2) they draw a distinction between public and private moral thought, restrict women to the domain of the private, and then deny that the private domain really constitutes moral thought; (3) they force women into a series of perverse moral double binds; and (4) they make invisible the domains wherein women's moral decision-making is concentrated.

Such views about the nature of moral agents in general and women in particular have not been restricted to the ivory-tower debates of philosophers; they are part of our cultural heritage and shape our daily lives. Sigmund Freud (1925), for instance, also considered women incapable of justice because of their commitment to the personal and their unwillingness to evaluate ethical claims in abstraction. Lawrence Kohlberg (1981), in seeking to develop cross-cultural data on the development of moral reasoning in human subjects, deliberately excluded women from his sample groups on the assumption that their inclusion would contaminate the data. In other words, he anticipated that women would follow different patterns in the development of their moral-reasoning skills and therefore excluded them from consideration when setting up a scale intended to measure the moral development of all agents. The evidence is that Kohlberg was right in this expectation; when the tests he developed on the basis of male norms for moral development are applied, men tend to score higher than women (Gilligan 1982). In other words, according to Kohlberg's criteria of what constitutes moral reasoning, the statistical evidence shows women to be deficient in their moral development relative to men.[12]

For years, feminists fought against men's claim that women pursue morality differently from men. They sought to establish an equality of moral ability between men and women; this equality was deemed necessary if women were to achieve equal political rights with men. Hence many important reformist thinkers and activists, including prominent figures of the Anglo-American feminist movement, argued that women have, at least in principle, the same moral capacities as men. Others, however, including leading feminists of the European community, accepted the claim that there is a gender difference in male and female moral thinking; they sought to have the feminine approach to moral thought recognized as a legitimate and important element, which needs to be added to discussions in the public sphere (Offen 1988). These theorists argued that rather than disqualifying women from public life, women's distinctive moral perspective makes it urgent that they be included in public debates so that their voices can be heard. Recently, many feminists on both sides of the Atlantic have embraced this notion of women's different approach to moral reasoning.

Carol Gilligan has provided us with an important empirical study that seems to identify a gender difference in moral thinking (Gilligan 1982). She found that when women are presented with moral conflicts, they tend to focus on details about the relationships that hold between the individuals concerned, and they seek out innovative solutions that protect the interests of all participants; that is, they strive to find options that avoid bringing harm to anyone. Men, in contrast, tend to try to identify the appropriate rules that govern the sort of situation described; they select the course of action most compatible with the dominant rule, even if someone's interests may be sacrificed to considerations of justice. Gilligan named the former an ethic of responsibility or care and the latter an ethic of justice. The empirical gender correlations are not perfect, because women sometimes opt for a justice solution and men sometimes choose in accordance with an ethic of care; but statistically, she found that girls and women are likely to choose responses that are sensitive to considerations of responsibility, whereas boys and men are likely to reflect considerations of justice in their analysis. On Gilligan's view, the ideal for all moral agents would be an ethics that includes elements of both approaches.

Thus it appears that Gilligan supports the assumption, common to Kant, Freud, and others, that women focus on the particular, expressing their concern for the feelings and special relationships of the persons involved in moral dilemmas, but unlike Kant and his followers (and also unlike her mentor, Kohlberg), she does not disallow such responses from the realm of the moral. Instead, she expands the definition of moral considerations, so that traditionally feminine thinking is recognized as morally relevant, rather than deficient. Gilligan thereby includes women's characteristic moral experiences and approach to moral decision-making in the field of legitimate moral thinking.

Not all women share Gilligan's analysis of how best to accommodate women's moral reasoning in the development of theoretical ethics. Jean Grimshaw (1986) and various other critics, both feminist and nonfeminist, have objected to Gilligan's insistence on two distinct ethics and have suggested that the considerations of care can be accommodated under the ethics of justice. As Calhoun (1988) argues, however, the point is not whether care can be subsumed under an ethic of justice; rather, what is significant is that the proponents of traditional ethics have chosen not to address issues of care. The cumulative effect of generations of male-defined theorizing amounts to gender bias and a denial of the ethical significance of women's perspective and concerns.

Interestingly, Gilligan also found that most men reflect a fear of intimacy: they identify separation as the desirable norm and view interactions as anomalous and threatening. It appears, then, that men have constructed ethics in their own psychological image. The ethical theories in the tradition of mainstream philosophy seem to have been principally designed to protect the rights of independent beings in the "disturbing" circumstances of human interaction.[13]

Ethical models based on the image of ahistorical, self-sufficient, atom-like individuals are simply not credible to most women. Because women are usually charged with the responsibility of caring for children, the elderly, and the ill as well as the responsibility of physically and emotionally nurturing men both at work and at home, most women experience the world as a complex web of interdependent relationships, where responsible caring for others is implicit in their moral lives. The abstract reasoning of morality that centers on the rights of independent agents is inadequate for the moral reality in which they live. Most women find that a different model for ethics is necessary; the traditional ones are not persuasive.

Nel Noddings (1984) has taken Gilligan's move a step further; she, too, accepts that caring is morally significant, but she goes so far as to argue that it is the only legitimate moral consideration. In *Caring* she argues that everyone (men and women alike) ought to pursue a feminine ethic of caring and abandon the insensitive demands of the abstract moral rules of justice. She focuses on "how to meet the other morally" and defines the proper locus of ethical thought as the quality of relationships, rather than a quality of judgments or acts. An agent's moral obligation, in Noddings's view, is to meet others as "one-caring" and to maintain conditions that permit caring to flourish. These others, for their part, have a responsibility to exhibit reciprocity or, at least, to acknowledge the caring. Ethical behavior, for Noddings, involves putting oneself at the service of others, seeing the world from their perspective, and acting "as though in my own behalf, but in behalf of the other" (Noddings 1984, 33).

Other women engaged in moral theory have spoken of the ethics associated with the characteristically feminine activity of mothering. Most notably, Sara Ruddick has proposed that maternal thinking, the moral perspective appropriate to the demands of mothering, is a distinctive way of knowing and caring that has implications for such important social issues as pacifism and antimilitarism (Ruddick 1984a; 1984b). She believes that women are particularly skilled at such thinking, whether or not they are mothers, because they have been raised to be mothers.

Virginia Held (1987a; 1987b) shares Ruddick's concern with the ethics of mothering and urges us to explore the relationships between mothering persons and their children as an alternative model for moral thought (in contrast to the contractarian model of anonymous, isolated individuals). Held objects to the emphasis in mainstream ethics on relationships among rational, self-interested, independent beings; she suggests that "instead of importing into the household principles derived from the marketplace, perhaps we should export to the wider society the relations suitable for mothering persons and children" (Held 1987a, 122). Like several other female theorists, she proposes developing an ethics rooted in characteristically female activities to replace the traditional approaches that seem tied to men's stereotypical development and interests.

Another important motivation for development of feminine ethics is recognition of the explicit maleness of the model pursued by those engaged in traditional ethics. As Annette Baier (1985b) has observed, the objective of most men who work in traditional ethics is the development of a comprehensive theory, but most female theorists do not seem interested in building an abstract, encompassing system. Baier challenges the suitability of a comprehensive, abstract model that rests on a few fundamental building blocks as a basis for theoretical ethics. Moreover, she calls into question the value of a moral theory that is defined in terms of abstract, universal principles, which are divorced from actual moral experience. In *Postures of the Mind* (Baier 1985a) she advises theorists to abandon the search for a rationalistic, universal system, chosen from purely theoretical concerns, and to concentrate instead on the search for a more accurate understanding of moral experience.[14]

Held (1984) echoes some of these sentiments; like Baier, she objects to the pursuit of a single, abstract, principle-driven moral theory as the end of philosophical ethics. She advises that we reject the reductionist scientific model, wherein one unified theory is sought to encompass all moral experience; in its place she envisions—and she goes a long way toward developing—a pluralistic set of theories that are jointly needed to cover the diverse range of moral experiences. Baier argues and Held demonstrates, then, that many women want something different from moral theory than what is sought by most male theorists. They argue that for an ethics to be of value to women, it must differ in structure as well as in content from the model that is usually envisioned within traditional moral theorizing.

It seems, then, that the traditional approaches to ethics are not adequate for addressing all of women's moral intuitions or concerns. Obviously, those that are explicitly antiwoman cannot be accepted as useful guides for women's moral deliberations. Those that are simply silent on the question of women's moral experiences are also problematic, because they are based on a model of moral experience that reflects a psychology chiefly associated with men; its conception seems naive and inadequate from the perspective of most women's experiences. Hence many women have begun to spell out the elements of moral reasoning that must be included in any moral theory that might be useful to them. The general consensus of female theorists is that such theories should involve models of human interaction that parallel the rich complexity of actual human relationships and should recognize the moral significance of the actual ties that bind people in their various relationships.

Feminist Ethics

Feminist ethics is different from feminine ethics. It derives from the explicitly political perspective of feminism, wherein the oppression of women is seen to be morally and politically unacceptable. Hence it involves more than recognition of women's actual experiences and moral practices; it incorporates a critique of the specific practices that constitute their oppression. Nevertheless, it is not altogether separate from what I have termed "feminine ethics."

In my view, feminist ethics must recognize the moral perspective of women; insofar as that includes the perspective described as an ethics of care, we should expand our moral agenda accordingly. Feminists have reason, however, to be cautious about the place of caring in their approach to ethics; it is necessary to be wary of the implications of gender traits within a sexist culture. Because gender differences are central to the structures that support dominance relations, it is likely that women's proficiency at caring is somehow related to women's subordinate status.

Within dominance relations, those who are assigned the subordinate position, that is, those with less power, have special reason to be sensitive to the emotional pulse of others, to see things in relational terms, and to be pleasing and compliant. Thus the nurturing and caring at which women excel are, among other things, the survival skills of an oppressed group that lives in close contact with its oppressors. This could help explain the evidence cited by Sandra Harding (1987), which shows that the orientation and associated worldview that are ascribed to women in Gilligan's study of American women are similar to the orientation and worldview held by contemporary Africans and Afro-Americans of both genders. The dichotomy of values that Gilligan identifies between men and women is paralleled by a dichotomy between Europeans and formerly colonized peoples. Whatever positive value these common traits may hold, the virtues to which women have been shown to aspire seem to be virtues of subordination. Further, the African data reveal that the perspective that Gilligan associates with men is actually held only by some men, specifically those of European descent.

Just as the gender associations that Gilligan identified have developed in a particular historical context, the attitudes that Ruddick (1984a) described as maternal thinking reflect the usual experience of mothering in Western, middle-class life, where a socially and economically defined nuclear family is assumed to be the norm. We should be wary of assuming gender-based dichotomies of moral thought too readily, whatever their empirical origin; such dualisms perpetuate assumptions of deep difference between men and women and limit our abilities to think creatively about genuinely gender-neutral ethical and power structures.

Another danger inherent in proposals for feminine ethics is that caring about the welfare of others often leads women to direct all their energies toward meeting the needs of others; it may even lead them to protect the men who oppress them. Hence feminists caution against valorizing the traits that help perpetuate women's subordinate status. Therefore, Barbara Houston warns that "women's distinctive morality is self-defeating, or highly dubious, when exercised in our relations with men, with those more powerful than ourselves, or when exercised in conditions in which the social constructions are likely to deform our caring or disguise it as a form of consent to the status quo" (Houston 1987, 252); or, as Catharine MacKinnon dryly phrased it, "Women value care because men have valued us according to the care we give them, and we could probably use some" (MacKinnon 1987, 39).

Within the existing patterns of sexism, there is a clear danger that women will understand the prescriptions of feminine ethics to be directing them to pursue the virtues of caring, while men continue to focus on abstractions that protect their rights and autonomy. Although Gilligan sees the two perspectives of moral reasoning as complementary, not competitive, and believes that both elements must be incorporated into any adequate moral view, it is easy to read her evidence as entrenching the gender differences she uncovers. In a society where the feminine is devalued and equated with inferiority, it is not easy to perceive men embracing a moral approach described as feminine. Because the world is still filled with vulnerable, dependent persons who need care, if men do not assume the responsibilities of caring, then the burden for doing so remains on women.

Nonetheless, despite its politically suspect origins, caring is often a morally admirable way of relating to others. Feminists join with feminine ethicists in rejecting the picture that malestream ethicists offer of a world organized around purely self-interested agents—a world many women judge to be an emotionally and morally barren place that we would all do well to avoid. Feminists perceive that the caring that women do is morally valuable, but most feminists believe that women need to distinguish between circumstances in which care is appropriately offered and those in which it is better withheld. Therefore, an important task of feminist ethics is to establish moral criteria by which we can determine when caring should be offered and when it should be withheld. Feminist analyses of power structures suggest that specific instances of moral caring should be evaluated in the context of the social and political relations that each instance supports or challenges (Houston and Diller 1987). In feminist ethics, evaluating the moral worth of specific acts and patterns of caring involves making political judgments.

Feminist ethics also takes from feminine ethics its recognition that personal feelings, such as empathy, loyalty, or guilt, can play an ethically significant role in moral deliberations. I think, however, that the proponents of abstraction are right to insist that there are limits to the place of caring in ethics. We should guard against allowing preferences, especially those tied to feelings of personal animosity, from being granted full range in ethical matters. For example, it would not be appropriate to decide to withdraw life support from a patient because she has been aggressive, complaining, and uncooperative, and hence her caregivers do not like her. Although there is something morally abhorrent about the obligation to make moral decisions without regard for the effects on loved ones, there is also great danger in believing we are only responsible for the interests of those for whom we feel affection. Morality must include respect for sentiments, but it cannot give full authority to particular sentiments without considering both their source and their effects.[15] Because feminism arises from moral objections to oppression, it must maintain a commitment to the pursuit of social justice; that commitment is not always compatible with preferences derived from existing relationships and attitudes. Hence we must recognize that feminist ethics involves a commitment to considerations of justice, as well as to those of caring.[16]

Feminist ethics takes its inspiration for other important features from what I have characterized as feminine ethics. It can agree with Gilligan (1982) that the morally relevant features of any decision-making situation include the agents' responsibilities to specific persons, including themselves. It also shares with feminine ethics a recognition of the significance of rooting ethical discussion in specific contexts and thus rejecting traditional ethical theory's commitment to purely abstract reasoning. Like feminine ethics, feminist ethics directs us to consider the details of experience when evaluating practices. For example, when one is asked to decide about a morally uncertain policy such as euthanasia, it is important to remember the terror and pain of any of our own friends and relatives who were denied that option and also the constraints we may have observed in specific individuals' ability to make such decisions once their illnesses took over their lives. We cannot adequately develop moral attitudes toward a controversial practice such as euthanasia if we restrict our reasoning to abstract rules about the duty to respect life or about the importance of autonomy.

In addition, feminist ethics shares with feminine ethics a rejection of the paradigm of moral subjects as autonomous, rational, independent, and virtually indistinguishable from one another; it seems clear that an ontology that considers only isolated, fully developed beings is not adequate for ethics (Whitbeck 1984). We must reconceive the concept of the individual, which has been taken as the central concept of ethical theory in Western thought. People have historical roots; they develop within specific human contexts, and they are persons, to a significant degree, by virtue of their relations to others like themselves (Baier 1985a). We value persons as unique individuals whose lives are of concern to us, and in that respect, the individual person is still an important element of ethical thought. We cannot speak of the individual as the central unit of analysis, however, without considering that persons only exist in complex, social relationships. Unless we recognize that a person's desires, needs, and beliefs are formed only within human society, we may mistakenly imagine ourselves and our interests to be independent from others and their interests.

Individual persons learn moral values, judgments, and behaviors within human communities that teach them how to interpret the events and sensations that they experience. People do not approach a social contract with no moral history, as most contractarians would have it; nor do they privately deliberate about moral laws as purely rational beings, as Kant presumes. Further, they can only follow the utilitarian injunction to value the happiness of others if they experience themselves as members of a community where people are mutually caring about one another's well-being. Because persons do not exist in abstraction, apart from their social circumstances, moral directives to disregard the details of personal life under some imaginary "veil of ignorance" are pernicious for ethical and political analysis. These injunctions trivialize many of the most important moral facts.

From a feminist perspective, one can see clearly the significance of the social situation of persons to moral deliberations. In place of the isolated, independent, rational agent of traditional moral theory, feminist ethics appeals to a more realistic and politically accurate notion of a self as socially constructed and complex, defined in the context of relationships with others. Moral analysis needs to examine persons and their behavior in the context of political relations and experiences, but this dimension has been missing so far from most ethical debates.

In this regard, feminism seems closely allied with communitarianism, another recent response to the abstract, liberal vision of contractarian theories.[17] Communitarian theory shares with feminism a critique of the abstract nature of the individual agent, which is so central to most moral theory. It objects to how the individual is privileged over the needs and interests of the community in the essentially liberal conception of social contract theories, and it recognizes the need to develop and support bonds of community. For these reasons, feminist proposals are sometimes read as being simply different formulations of the communitarian position. This conclusion is mistaken, however, because communitarian theories are essentially conservative. They are committed to protecting and preserving community values, without evaluating their status in the hierarchies of oppression. They privilege the status quo, whereas feminist ethicists deliberately challenge it. Hence it is important to distinguish feminist ethics from this other critique of traditional liberal theories.[18]

Most important, feminist ethics is characterized by its commitment to the feminist agenda of eliminating the subordination of women— and of other oppressed persons—in all of its manifestations. The principal insight of feminist ethics is that oppression, however it is practiced, is morally wrong. Therefore, moral considerations demand that we uncover and examine the moral injustice of actual oppression in its many guises. When pressed, other sorts of moral theorists will acknowledge that oppressive practices are wrong, but such general declarations are morally inadequate in the face of insidious, systematic oppression. If we want moral change and not mere moral platitudes, then the particular practices that constitute oppression of one group by another must be identified and subjected to explicit moral condemnation; feminists demand the elimination of each oppressive practice.

Given the extent of sexism and other oppressive systems, such as racism, homophobia, and discrimination against the disabled, it is necessary to examine the particular effects of practices on the various oppressed groups. We cannot uncover and dismantle sexist (or racist) prejudices by proceeding with a gender-neutral (or race-neutral) account, because within a sexist (racist) society, such an account is more likely to mask bias than remove it. Marilyn Frye advises that if we want to understand the specific barriers that jointly constitute oppression, we must look at each barrier and ask certain questions about it: "Who constructs it and maintains it? Whose interests are served by its existence? Is it part of a structure which tends to confine, reduce and immobilize some group?" (Frye 1983, 14). In pursuing feminist ethics, we must continually raise the question, What does it mean for women? When, for example, feminists consider medical research, confidentiality, or the new reproductive technologies, they need to ask not only most of the standard moral questions but also the general questions of how the issue under consideration relates to the oppression of women and what the implications of a proposed policy would be for the political status of women. Unless such questions are explicitly asked, the role of practices in the oppression of women (or others) is unlikely to be apparent, and offensive practices may well be morally defended. According to feminist ethics, other moral questions and judgments come into play only if we can assure ourselves that the act or practice in question is not itself one of a set of interlocking practices that maintains oppressive structures.

In practice, the constraints imposed by feminist ethics mean that, for instance, we cannot discuss abortion purely in terms of the rights of fetuses, without noticing that fetuses are universally housed in women's bodies. We cannot discuss the acceptability of institutionalizing patients for mental illness without noting that women are far more likely to be diagnosed as mentally ill than are men. Any morally adequate discussion of such practices must come to terms with the fact that the resulting social policy will have profound implications on the lives of women. Feminist ethics demands that the effects of any decision on women's lives be a feature of moral discussion and decision-making.

In its appeal to contextual features, feminist ethics resists the model of traditional ethics, wherein the principal task is to define a totalizing or universal theory that prescribes rules for all possible worlds. Feminist ethics focuses instead on the need to develop a moral analysis that fits the actual world in which we live, without worrying about the implications of these considerations in some radically different set of circumstances. That is not to say that feminist ethics involves no concern with principles. It encompasses theories that are committed to concerns about social justice, because it demands criticism of the various patterns of dominance, oppression, and exploitation of one group of persons by another. Concern about justice, however, cannot be adequately defined in the abstract. To speak meaningfully about justice, it is necessary to examine the actual forces that undermine it, as well as those that support it.

Feminism is not, however, solely interested in issues of oppression.

It is also concerned with the possibilities of women's agency, despite their oppression. Therefore, Sarah Hoagland (1988) characterizes her ethical study as one of agency, an exploration of new value within a group committed to opposing oppression. Feminists perceive that women have created many diverse means of survival and resistance in the face of appalling brutality and hostility. They do not believe that the oppression of women is inevitable; their political action is founded on a belief that women can end oppression. Feminist ethics includes exploration of actions that represent the escape from and overturning of the forces of oppression.

This exploration involves searching for ways of empowering those who are now subordinate, through the creation of different relationships and new, nonoppressive social structures. Without such analysis, women would be left with the morally unsatisfactory prospect of insisting on equal access to the existing positions of power and dominance. An ethics built on a rejection of oppressive structures cannot settle for reformist measures that promise equal opportunities to positions in the hierarchy but must offer new perspectives on social and political possibilities.

Feminist ethics is not an ethics whose conclusions are appropriate only to feminists. The subordination of one group of persons by another is morally wrong, as well as politically unjust, and all adequate moral theories ought to make that plain. Hence those engaged in ethical theorizing and policy formation should always ask about the connections between the subject at hand and patterns of oppression, especially, but not solely, those associated with sexism. Consideration of the feminist implications of any recommendation, whether on the level of moral theory, medical practice, or specific action, belongs in all ethical discussion. There are probably issues where the question will make no real difference to the outcome, because the effects of the practice on women are not distinct; for example, the ethical wrong of destroying the ozone layer for the sake of economic profit can probably be adequately explored without addressing the issues of women's subordination. There will be many surprising cases, however, where the issue is highly relevant, although hidden until raised, and this is true of far more cases than the work currently done by most nonfeminist moral theorists indicates. To correct the gender bias that, until recently, has been central to ethical theorizing, it is necessary to make gender an explicit element of ethics (Calhoun 1988).

I label this approach "feminist ethics" and not simply "ethics," because only feminists (male and female) have really concerned themselves with the details of oppression. The leading moral theorists in the mainstream tradition have not only failed to object to the oppression of women; they have often actively contributed to its perpetuation. They legitimized the subjection of women by insisting on women's moral, rational, and epistemological inferiority. Hence the ethical systems they proposed are not only inadequate but also morally wrong, because they promote behavior and relationships that are morally reprehensible. In a world where women are systematically oppressed, an adequate ethics must address that oppression. Feminist ethics, in making explicit the moral offense of sexism and illuminating some of its many forms, is the only approach to ethics that lives up to this obligation.

In keeping with the insights of Annette Baier (1985b) and Virginia Held (1984) and many other commentators, both male and female,[19] I do not envision feminist ethics to be a comprehensive, universal, single-principle theory that can be expected to resolve every moral question with which it is confronted. It is a theoretical perspective that must be combined with other considerations to address the multitude of moral dilemmas that confront human beings. What feminist ethics claims is that oppression is a pervasive and insidious moral wrong and that moral evaluation of practices must be sensitive to questions of oppression, no matter what other moral considerations are also of interest. Such analysis requires an understanding not only of the nature of oppression in general but also of the nature of specific forms of oppression.

I believe that anyone with a genuine interest in ethics should be interested in the connections between specific practices and the patterns of dominance in society. I recognize that not all ethicists will be persuaded to become thoroughgoing feminists, in the sense of adopting a version of feminism as a worldview and a way of life; not every ethicist will wish to become involved in political activism. Nevertheless, I think all ethicists can and should include discussions of sexism in their analyses of particular practices, as well as discussions of racism, anti-Semitism, heterosexualism, and so on. Although very little of the literature in ethics addresses the issue of sexism or any other form of systematic oppression, surely the responsibility to do so in one's moral evaluations is implicit. Feminist ethics has assumed leadership in pursuing such analysis.

3

Feminism and Moral Relativism

Feminism and Metaethics

In Chapter 2, I argued that ethicists have much to learn from feminists and that they should incorporate feminist analysis into their approaches to theory and their evaluation of practices. In this chapter I explain why I believe that feminists should engage in the theoretical work of ethics, and I set out more clearly some of the norms that I believe are central to the practice of feminist ethics.

It is necessary to explore this question, because many feminists have expressed profound distrust of theoretical ethics. Ethical theory, as it has generally been pursued, appears to be antifeminist, male, and elitist. Its practitioners have displayed little interest in the practical work of correcting imbalances of power, despite the moral harms that such imbalances create; rather, as we saw in Chapter 2, the normative conclusions reached by traditional theorists generally support the mechanisms of oppression: for example, by promoting subservience among women. Ethics is often invoked to rationalize conservative responses to movements for social change.[1] Therefore, many feminists have been led to rebel against the powerful, moralizing injunctions that have historically issued from such theorizing.

Many mainstream ethicists are occupied with metaethics, that is, theorizing about the nature of ethics. Much of the work of metaethics is conducted at a high level of abstraction, in technical language that is exclusionary and elitist. These theorists often claim that there are no practical, normative conclusions to be drawn from their work, because they are investigating the nature of ethics, not actual moral judgments. Such disclaimers only serve, however, to further alienate many feminists; few feminists have patience for intellectual puzzles that genuinely have no practical relevance.

Furthermore, the debates that occupy people engaged in meta-ethics often presuppose a dichotomous structure of reasoning: (for example, questions of whether moral statements have truth values or whether we can actually know moral truths are usually approached as yielding yes or no answers). Several feminists have argued against the acceptance of dualistic thinking. They have seen that the mechanisms of oppression rest on the polarization of differences between oppressors and those oppressed; such polarization makes an implicit appeal to the fundamental dualisms of good/bad and superior/inferior. As Joyce Trebilcot argues, "The dualistic pair is the unit of hierarchy—that is, a hierarchy consists of overlapping dualistic pairs" (Trebilcot 1986, 358). Moreover, dichotomous thinking narrows our imagination by restricting the range of thought on a particular issue.

Nevertheless, some metaethical debates are important to feminist thought. Some of the same issues that are addressed by ethical theorists resonate through feminist writing. For example, the subject of relativism and its relation to authoritarianism in ethics raises questions of particular importance and challenge for feminists. In the ethical literature, theorists argue about whether ethical judgments can be applied universally (that is, whether they apply across different cultural contexts and historical periods), or whether moral norms are (merely) relative to the actual social context in which they arise. This question is important for feminists because, as we shall see, absolutist principles are often oppressive, but relativist ones seem to undermine the strength of moral arguments against oppression. It is important for feminists to address such concerns in ways that maintain their commitment to the ideals of democratic empowerment and resistance to oppressive structures.

Feminist Ambivalence about Relativism

Despite some feminists' reluctance to enter into metaethical debates, current feminist thought reveals its own tension and ambivalence on the subject of relativism, which overlap some of the strands of the traditional moral relativism debate.

On the one hand, feminists are inclined to criticize oppressive practices in terms that appear absolutist. When they condemn the practices that together create the systematic patterns of gender discrimination that constitute oppression, they argue that such oppressive practices are wrong, no matter what the prevailing social view may be. Feminists judge the sexual dominance of women by men; the celebration of dominance and the eroticization of violence in pornography; the sexual use of children by adults; and the epidemic practices of rape, sexual harassment, and battering of women as wrong, despite the ambivalent acceptance of these practices within the community at large. Similarly, other forms of oppression, including racism, classism, heterosexism, sizeism, ageism, and able-bodiedism, are considered wrong, even though they are well entrenched in our society.

On the other hand, most versions of moral relativism imply that moral judgments must be made relative to the existing moral standards of a community. This measure is problematic with respect to sexist practices, because these practices tend to be widespread and widely accepted within the societies in which they are found. Although a few such practices have a long history of social disapproval (incest, for instance, has always been formally frowned upon in Western society, in spite of the efforts of some sexual "reformers"), many of the customs that jointly make up the institutions of male dominance are practiced widely; few serious efforts are made to prohibit them. Some aspects of gender oppression, such as the sexual division of labor, have at times been accepted and defended almost universally throughout society. Within our own society, there is certainly no social consensus about the moral wrongness of restrictions placed on women's reproductive freedom, and tolerance for pornography is endemic, extending so far as to include members of the feminist community. As I acknowledged in Chapter 1, many of the very women who are oppressed by sexist practices still believe in the legitimacy of those practices and do not perceive them as wrong.

Feminist objections to sexist practices are not meant to be interpreted merely as subjective, emotive expressions of attitude, which can be freely translated into "I disapprove of these actions." Feminists claim that these practices are objectively wrong. Moreover, they claim that these practices are wrong even when they are widely accepted within the community (as many of them are); therefore, many standard versions of relativism do not seem adequate to feminist goals of ridding society of its deeply entrenched patterns of oppression.

Gilbert Harman, for example, argues that "the judgment that it is wrong of someone to do something makes sense only in relation to an agreement or understanding" (Harman 1982, 189–90). Like most other relativists, Harman denies that there is any basis for moral criticism without such an agreement.

Given the long history of patriarchy, we cannot expect to find evidence of any prior agreement or understanding that is violated by these practices. In fact, most of the recognized moral leaders of society—the moral theorists, political and religious authorities, and jurists—throughout the history of Western thought have explicitly argued in favor of aspects of the sex/gender system. Feminists insist that the practices of male domination are nevertheless morally wrong. If we restrict the scope of moral judgments to violations of a given society's actual moral agreements, as is proposed by moral relativists such as Harman, then we cannot engage a feminist moral criticism of these practices. Therefore, it is important to find a basis for moral criticism of those very agreements.

When we, as Westerners, look at practices that seem connected with patriarchy in completely foreign societies, many feminists seek grounds for moral objection there, too, despite widespread agreement within those societies about the legitimacy of the practice; standard forms of moral relativism, however, seem to deny this possibility. Consider, for example, the genital mutilation that is ritually practiced in many countries of Africa and the Middle East, and in parts of Indonesia, Malaysia, Australia, Brazil, El Salvador, Pakistan, and the Soviet Union (Morgan 1984).

The least invasive form of clitoridectomy involves the removal of the prepuce and sometimes the tip of the clitoris; it may also involve removal of the entire organ and adjacent parts of the labia minora. Infibulation is the removal of the entire clitoris, the labia majora, and the labia minora, followed by the joining of the scraped sides of the vulva across the vagina, secured with thorns or thread; a small opening is maintained by inserting a sliver of wood for passage of urine and menstrual blood. The woman who has undergone infibulation must be cut open to permit intercourse and cut further to permit childbirth, and it is common for her to be closed up again after delivery. In some countries genital mutilation is performed within days after a child's birth; in others it is done when the child is four to six years old or when a girl nears puberty. It is seldom performed by formally trained health care professionals; usually, the task falls to midwives or older women in a community, and it is commonly performed under unsanitary conditions. Not surprisingly, such surgery often results in death from shock, hemorrhage, or infection, and numerous physical, psychological, and sexual complications are found among survivors.[2]

The justifications offered for this brutal practice include appeals to custom, religion, family honor, cleanliness, esthetics, initiation, assurance of virginity, promotion of social and political cohesion, enhancement of fertility, improvement of male sexual pleasure, and prevention of female promiscuity (Koso-Thomas 1987). Although genital mutilation is most often practiced by followers of Islam and defended on religious grounds, it is not required by the Koran, the authoritative text of Islam; moreover, the practice has been associated with other religions (Morgan 1984). Given the associated risk of infection, it is clear that genital mutilation is not an appropriate means of promoting cleanliness. The most plausible ground for its continued acceptance is the control it offers over women's sexual behavior (the general rationale for its occasional use in the West).[3] It is estimated that more than 84 million women now living have undergone some form of genital mutilation (Seager and Olson 1986).

Genital mutilation is widely accepted in the societies in which it is practiced today. In a 1983 survey in northern Sudan, 82 percent of women and 87.7 percent of men approved of the practice (Morgan 1984). Forms of moral relativism such as Harman's, cannot establish the moral wrongness of genital mutilation if it is generally supported within the communities that practice it. Thus most traditional formulations of relativism are not compatible with (my) feminist moral sensibilities.

Nevertheless, feminists are wary of moral absolutism. There are a number of reasons for their resistance, not all of them metaethical. On a pragmatic level, absolutism seems to promote an acceptance of authoritarianism in ethics. Theorists often find it a short step from the belief that there is a single, true morality to the belief that they have identified that true morality—or, at least, have come closer to it than others have. Within a culture like ours, which is structured on dominance relations and which relies on experts for scientific, legal, medical, esthetic, sexual, interpersonal, and religious judgments, some individuals are inclined to appoint themselves as moral authorities and to be accepted as having special competence in the moral arena. Although there is no logical necessity that metaethical moral absolutism leads to establishment of practical moral authoritarianism, the latter is more easily established in a climate created by the former. Moreover, in a society that teaches that men are morally superior to women and promotes doctrines of racial supremacy and survival of the fittest—one that accepts, in other words, that might makes right—the position of moral authority is generally claimed by members of the dominant group.

Indeed, an absolutist morality has served as part of the structure of oppression. It has legitimized the cultural and religious dominance of both colonialism and patriarchy. Under the banner of moral absolutism, rebellion or challenge to hierarchical patterns is met with strong moral criticism, often accompanied by force. Women are particularly susceptible to moral criticism, having been taught the strong link between femininity and moral approval. Negative moral judgments are effective tools for maintaining the social order, especially when they are offered with the arrogance of absolute certainty. In practice, then, absolutism is a dangerous position to endorse within a society structured by dominance relations.

The absolutism implied by traditional ethics leads Sarah Hoagland (1988) and other feminist theorists to reject the whole enterprise associated with traditional ethics. Hoagland perceives traditional ethics as founded explicitly on the values of dominance and subordination, because it focuses on social control and undermines individual moral agency. Representatives of the dominant group assume the authority of interpreting morality; they direct individuals, especially those in subordinate positions, to comply with the prevailing social values as they define them. The discipline of ethics legitimizes oppression by redefining it as social organization.

Logically, there is a large gap between the claim that some truth exists and the claim that someone knows that truth. Nevertheless, in actual human experience those who believe that there is such a thing as moral truth are likely to believe that they have access to it, especially when the rest of their experience encourages them to believe in their own superior abilities and when there is no conclusive refutation of their moral claims. Many social scientists have endorsed versions of relativism precisely out of their sense that the alternative promotes cultural dominance. They may be making a philosophical error in drawing that conclusion, but I do not think that they are making an empirical one.

Feminists and social scientists are not alone in their attention to psychological connections between asolutism and authoritarianism. Several nonfeminist philosophers have worried about the possible normative implications of the relativism–absolutism controversy. They too have explored whether belief in relativism entails a commitment to moral reform or a greater tolerance of the moral beliefs of others, or both. Some, such as Bernard Williams (1982) and Geoffrey Harrison (1982), explicitly reject any normative support of tolerance based on relativism. Others, however, see a clear connection: Harman, for instance, supports moral relativism principally on logical grounds, but he also observes that absolutism sometimes leads to a fairly conservative morality, noting that this "is not surprising given the privileged position assigned to our initial moral beliefs" (Harman 1985, 31). David Wong (1984) also recognizes the two as linked; he argues that a belief in relativism restricts the degree of intervention one can properly take with behavior motivated by a different moral code. On his view, an important advantage of relativism over absolutism is that the former, when combined with standard, normative views, demands tolerance of the moral values of others.

Feminist writing reveals other grounds for support of some form of relativism. Most current feminist theory is very sensitive to the difference that one's perspective makes to the experience of reality, so that few authors think that any meaningful sense can be made of the concept of a single, true reality. Feminist thought has developed from the analysis and interpretation of the experiences of particular women, and this methodology has led to a self-conscious recognition of the diversity among women. Most feminists have learned that the "same" event (for example, the birth of a child, the death of a fetus, or permanent sterilization) can be experienced in different ways.

Most feminists recognize that one's understanding of the world and the conceptual scheme by which it is approached are socially constructed; they are not simple "givens." What individuals usually perceive as reality is what the dominant forces of society have taught them to see, at least until their consciousness is "raised" through political analysis; the perspectives generated by alternative political views offer other ways of perceiving reality.

Marilyn Frye traces the etymology of the term "real" to its association with royalty, or supreme power: "Reality is that which pertains to the one in power, is that over which he has power, is his domain, his estate, is proper to him" (Frye 1983, 155). Sarah Hoagland observes that "language is a tool of oppression, for we remain trapped in oppression when we perceive only what the oppressors perceive, when we are restricted to their values and categories" (Hoagland 1988, 14). Sandra Harding, echoing the views of postmodern feminists, claims that "there are as many interrelated and smoothly connected realities as there are kinds of oppositional consciousness. By giving up the goal of 'one true story,' we embrace instead the permanent partiality of feminist inquiry" (Harding 1986b, 194). Jane Flax proposes: "Perhaps reality can have 'a' structure only from the falsely universalizing perspective of the master. That is, only to the extent that one person or group can dominate the whole, can 'reality' appear to be governed by one set of rules or be constituted by one privileged set of social relations" (Flax 1990, 49). Postmodern thinkers urge feminists to abandon the search for a single, grand theory that encompasses all experience and interpretation, arguing that such a quest is futile (Nicholson 1990). The presumption that there is such a theory leads to domination by those with the power to enforce their view.

Thus much contemporary feminist thought proposes that there are many different realities; it would follow, then, that there cannot be a single true morality or any single way of interpreting the application even of a relativist morality. We must be careful, however, not to conclude that this implies that no sort of moral objectivity is available, that any set of values and perceptions is as valid as any other. In the face of such diversity feminists and other sorts of moral relativists need some way to distinguish between respect for difference and universal tolerance of all perspectives. Most feminists believe, for instance, that rape really is wrong; it is not just another mode of interaction. Hence moral theory must retain the authority to assert such judgments.

In stressing the importance of listening respectfully to the different voices in which women express their experience of oppression, some feminists come precariously close to surrendering all grounds of judgment. Most are wary of imposing their own values on the interpretations of other victims of oppression. Joyce Trebilcot offers an extreme version of feminist relativism, in which she rejects the "conceptual/intellectual hegemony" in order to respect differences among women.

She adopts three principles for herself in contexts of "wimmin's space":

> *First principle*: I speak only for myself.
> *Second principle*: I do not try to get other wimmin to accept my beliefs in place of their own.
> *Third principle*: There is no "given" (Trebilcot 1988, 1).

Trebilcot does acknowledge, however, that these principles are not appropriate guides for behavior in situations that are predominantly patriarchal. This suggests that the application of relativism is itself relative to the absence of patriarchy. Hers is not necessarily a fully relativist position. In a similar vein, Hoagland (1988) develops a theory of lesbian ethics for relationships within the lesbian community; her objective is to promote individual agency, rather than to define constraining rules. Hoagland offers ethical recommendations for relationships within that community, where new forms of value are being created by the workings of the community—for example, that moral agents should promote the moral agency of one another and should resist appeal to the constraints of traditional ethical norms, such as accountability. She allows, however, for the likelihood that different moral considerations and different standards may apply in interactions with members of the larger society; at this time, she acknowledges, it is not possible to assume a shared commitment to empowerment and to the pursuit of new values outside of the lesbian community.

Feminist Moral Relativism

Questions about the role of relativism in ethics parallel questions that feminists have pursued in epistemology (the theory of knowledge). When exploring the issue of epistemological relativism, Lisa Heldke seeks to avoid the relativism/foundationalism dichotomy, because "the assumption that our epistemological options are limited to two is unwarranted. . . . Foundationalism and relativism hobble efforts to inquire into, and theorize about, our experiences" (Heldke 1988, 16). Heldke proposes that we consider cooking as a model of inquiry, to see how we could reconceive epistemology as neither wholly absolutist nor completely relativist. Other feminists have noted that when debates are centered on choosing within a dichotomy, they are often directed away from the important questions.

Therefore, Anne Seller refuses to choose between realism and relativism in epistemology, because she believes that neither alone is adequate and that the distinction that should be addressed concerns the nature of the context (community) in which beliefs are acquired (Seller 1988).

Such insights are useful for the relativism debate in ethics. Although feminists need to explore whether all or any moral knowledge is relative to a given society, many seek to avoid restricting their analysis to two opposing options; the proposals of feminist epistemology offer direction toward (at least) a third option that we can pursue in the domain of moral theory and practice.

We can, I think, find the clue to feminist moral relativism in the limits proposed by Trebilcot and Hoagland. In evaluating relativism we need to know what context we are talking about and what sort of moral problem is meant to be considered. We need to know not only what community standards or agreements are in place for moral matters but also how these standards were reached, whose interests they serve, and what the procedures are for discussion and change. I think that the relativists are right that we do not have access to anything more foundational than community standards in ethics, but we cannot treat all communities as the same; we should not grant blanket legitimacy to all moral standards that are accepted in a community. Power relations shape the moral values adopted by a community, although these relations are, in turn, justified by the moral standards of the community. Within a community, moral values are interconnected with political structures. Hence it is important to evaluate moral relativism in its political context, so that we can pay attention to the role of existing dominance relations in the moral standards that a community endorses.

In her discussion of relativism in epistemology, Seller (1988) concludes that, ultimately, our only epistemological standards are those of community. She stresses, however, the importance of democratic structures within the community if its proposals are to be trusted. Similarly, in ethics we need to be assured of a community worthy of trust if we are to accept its moral standards as adequate. The difficulty with existing moral standards is that most have been developed in communities that feminists see as more worthy of antitrust (to use Annette Baier's term) than of trust. Hence we need some deeper measure than mere community agreement for moral truth.

Nonfeminist moral relativism, then, starts in the wrong place. It takes communities as given, and says that what is moral is whatever we find accepted as moral within a particular community. Instead, we must first make some evaluative judgments about the community itself and about the basis of the moral agreements that operate within it; that is, we must make some nonrelative judgments about moral methodology that are prior to our evaluations of particular practices within any actual community. How a community reaches moral decisions and the actual reasons for particular decisions are relevant to moral evaluation.

In making this claim, I do not appeal to some absolute moral reality or to a foundational source for ethics; rather I acknowledge the inseparable political nature of moral decision-making within a community. If we are to link moral judgments with community standards, as most relativists propose, then we must be able to evaluate the history of those standards. This requirement should be understood as a methodological, rather than a substantive, demand.

In ethics, as in epistemology, "the ultimate test of the realist's views is their acceptance by a community" (Seller 1988, 175). Community acceptance does not make either moral or scientific views true, but it is the best test available for judging the reliability of a knowledge claim. Seller notes that facts, values, and decisions are often agreed upon together, not in chronological order. Therefore, to choose among different ways of interpreting "reality" and evaluating behavior, she proposes that we engage in conversation within a group we can trust. By questioning and checking within such a group, we engage in a process of intersubjectively evaluating our personal feelings; such techniques are necessary if we are to make decisions about the world we experience. Rejecting the methodology of solipsism, Seller argues that conversation is necessary for knowledge: "As an isolated individual, I often do not know what my experiences are." (Seller 1988, 180).

Seller addresses relativism in epistemology, but we can address ethics the same way. We cannot understand morality through pure reason, with each rational agent legislating for herself simply by reflecting on the logic of the moral law (as Immanuel Kant proposed). Individuals gain understanding about ethics through discussion within a community; we cannot work out moral principles apart from the context of their application. But if we are to be able to explore moral matters and reach decisions upon which we can agree, then that discussion should be conducted democratically; it should reflect genuine sharing and listening among participants. Therefore, communities should meet appropriate standards of moral conversation before we accept their moral conclusions as adequate. "Community" in this sense is not just any gathering of people in some sort of sociopolitical structure but a group with shared concern for one another and governed by democratic structures.

To be confident about the moral worth of a community's standards, then, we need to evaluate moral decision-making within the community itself and be assured that it is not achieved through oppressive forces. Practices whose acceptance derives from the use of oppressive power should remain subject to moral criticism. The process of reaching moral agreements should be democratic and contain safeguards against using moral arguments for the further exploitation of those already oppressed.

The moral criteria we use to evaluate how a community develops and reviews its moral standards involve attention to process, to see whether there is genuine agreement or simply compliance enforced by threat. They require us to consider how the moral views of a community actually evolved and whether they are open to revision. Anne Seller characterizes knowledge as more of a process than an achievement, and we can extend this argument to moral knowledge. What is important with morality is how a community sets standards, how the members of the community feel about the standards, and how they reevaluate their standards in the face of changing circumstances. There is unlikely to be a single, true moral code that all communities would agree upon or even that a given community would find eternal; hence absolutism in ethics seems implausible if not incomprehensible. This does not imply, however, that community standards of morality are all there is, because a community may have reached its standards through coercion, exploitation, ignorance, deception, or even indifference. Such standards can have no legitimate moral standing. It is important to be especially sensitive to community acceptance of practices that exploit and entrench power differentials among the groups that make up the society in question.

Although there may be a place for moral expertise in a community's deliberations (as there is for other forms of epistemological expertise), where input is sought from those who are particularly skillful at keeping track of existing moral standards, moral authoritarianism is unacceptable where democratic processes are necessary for reaching moral decisions. Unless the process of moral deliberation has been conducted in a morally acceptable fashion, we should not feel bound by the outcome of that process. Other considerations, principally those about the unjust use of power in promoting agreement, are also relevant to proper evaluation.

Lisa Heldke (1988) argued that there is no single, correct way for a community's epistemological norms to be determined; there is, she says, more than one way to make an omelet. The same might be said for a community's moral norms. Nevertheless, just as there are many possible techniques whose outcome cannot be considered an acceptable omelet (substituting peaches for eggs, placing the beaten eggs in the freezer rather than the frying pan, sending the children out to make mudpies, and so forth), there are also many wrong ways to go about setting moral standards within a society. Criteria are needed to limit the range of acceptable moral standards within a society. From a feminist perspective, the criteria must address whether or not oppressive circumstances limit input from segments of the population. They must also take into account whether the compliance of the oppressed has been coerced or reflects genuine support.[4]

The Advantage of Feminist Moral Relativism

The feminist restriction on relativism is important, because it allows us to make forceful moral arguments about the practices that feminists judge to be wrong and dangerous but which other forms of relativism seem unable to criticize. I find David Wong's (1984) treatment of relativism one of the most sensible and useful to be found in the nonfeminist literature. He claims that one of the virtues of relativism is that "the inability to justify one's actions to the people one affects is relevant to the rightness of one's actions" (Wong 1984, 8). When he attempts to explain the application of the principle, however, he appeals to its place in the abortion debate, and feminists can readily see the problems of settling for a nonfeminist form of relativism.

Wong's discussion is rooted in his belief that moral relativism is normatively connected with tolerance of other moral views. He argues that a Kantian "justification principle" can be derived from both Kantian and utilitarian ethics; it states that "one should not interfere with the [permissible] ends of others unless one can justify the interference to be acceptable to them were they fully rational and informed of all relevant circumstances"[5] (Wong 1984, 181). He defines moral relativism as the view that two persons can have conflicting moralities that are equally true and equally justified. When a belief in relativism is combined with the justification principle, we have grounds for tolerance of the behavior of others, even when that behavior conflicts with our own moral views. If we cannot justify our moral beliefs to others, that is, if we cannot lead them to see that their behavior is wrong, Wong says we should not then interfere with their actions.

Wong applies this principle of tolerance to the abortion debate where, he notes, sensible people disagree strongly about the moral acceptability of abortion, but neither side has been able to provide reasons the other sees as justification for a change in its own beliefs. Because both positions are defensible on the basis of well-established moral systems, he concludes, "there is a good case for saying that these positions are equally justifiable" (Wong 1984, 190). It follows that if conservatives and liberals regarding the issue of abortion hold the justification principle, then both may pursue ongoing debate and engage in campaigns to convert more people to their positions, but both should refrain from more serious intervention in the choices of their opponents. The justification principle directs conservatives to refrain from seeking legal sanctions against abortion and also directs liberals to refrain from demanding public funding for abortions. Wong argues that each side should be more tolerant of the moral convictions of the other and should seek means of social coexistence that limit the moral violence done to the other group's beliefs.

On my view of feminist moral relativism, the test of the views of the proponents of each position on abortion should not be simply their connection with a "well-established moral system." Rather, the moral justafiability of either side must be determined on the basis of the nature of its particular moral system; it is necessary to consider how the system evolved, whose interests are served by it, and, most importantly, whose interests are sacrificed to it. In the context of abortion, conservatives trace their arguments to their concern with the human life of the fetus, but as I shall argue in Chapter 5, their arguments can also be linked to a continuing history of patriarchal control over women's reproductive and sexual lives. The interest that most conservatives take in protecting human life is focused exclusively on protecting life while it is housed in the body of a woman. No similar vigor is extended to supporting the lives of the millions of children in the world who are dying from starvation or abuse. Most antiabortionists do not campaign for adequate housing, child care, and educational opportunities—the sorts of services necessary to make childbirth affordable for many of the women choosing abortion. Indeed, many antiabortionists are actively engaged in a struggle to limit such supports.

Furthermore, women themselves are not included in some of the most influential of these discussions.[6] The strongest force in the antiabortion movement is the Catholic church, a characteristically undemocratic institution where moral policy-making is determined by celibate, male clerics who have climbed through increasingly insulating hierarchical structures. In almost every nation the legal status and accessibility of abortion is determined by legislatures whose membership is overwhelmingly male. Further, Wong's justification principle ignores the power dimensions embedded within the moral systems that are appealed to in the actual abortion debate. Like other forms of moral relativism, his favors conservative acceptance of established traditions, even when they can be shown to arise from oppressive structures.

Feminist moral relativism would require that these historical features of the abortion debate be considered when deciding how to respond to the controversy. We should consider how each side arrived at its position before we agree that one side should be given the maximum scope for pursuit of its moral convictions. Because conservatives have not adequately taken into account the effects of their policy on the oppressed status of women, liberals should not be obliged to refrain from intervening in their actions. Given the arguments in favor of including abortion in the services covered in countries where medicine is socialized, it is not acceptable to deny women the use of state resources when they seek abortions, just because abortion offends the moral values of conservatives. Until conservatives are prepared to develop a moral policy on abortion in conjunction with all the women who are most directly affected by that policy, their own position does not constitute a moral position that we are obliged to protect. Nor is it only conservatives who have failed to pursue democratic processes in the development of their moral views; as I shall explain in Chapter 5, most liberals also need to consult more effectively with women when developing the details of their own position if it is to have full moral force.

Further, when we examine practices that are part of cultures different from our own, Wong's ethical relativism, like that of the cultural relativist, would probably again deny us grounds for moral criticism. Nevertheless, the widely practiced genital mutilation of women can be deemed morally abhorrent. Most Western feminists are uncertain of how to address this subject because of their sensitivity to the dangers and history of arrogant Western moralizing in the Third World. Few feminist books or journals even mention the practice, largely out of fear of offending members of the communities that engage in the practice.[7] As Mary Daly demonstrated (1978), however, genital mutilation is related to other forms of patriarchy and demands feminist moral criticism. Moreover, feminists within the societies that perpetuate the practice seek international support in changing traditional patterns that are oppressive to women.[8]

Obviously, practices occur within specific cultures, and therefore they must be evaluated with attention to their contexts. Ethical judgments about foreign, as well as local, practices are important foundations for generating cooperative action for change; feminists should not be constrained by national borders and boundaries from commenting on the variety of ways in which women are kept in subordinate positions around the world. Male dominance of women is an international practice that is expressed in different ways in distinct contexts. It is necessary to judge it across political and cultural boundaries. Because ethics so often lends itself to judging what is different as inferior, however, it is essential that we be consciously wary of the temptation to offer comprehensive moral condemnation of foreign cultures, without adequately understanding their complexities or appreciating their strengths. Therefore, it is important to recognize that feminist moral relativism provides a basis only for challenging oppressive practices in other cultures, not all local customs.

The approach to moral relativism that I propose allows us to judge our own moral license for condemning certain practices of societies different from our own. Genital mutilation is linked to interests associated with male dominance—assurances of sexual fidelity, tight vaginas for male pleasure, protection against women's demands for sexual satisfaction, and cruelty to women.[9] Unless there is evidence that women would agree to this practice if they were free of patriarchal coercion, we cannot treat it as an acceptable local custom, even if the majority of citizens in areas where it is customarily practiced now approves of it.[10]

That being said, Western feminists are still confronted with the problem of how to respond to the moral outrage they experience when considering this practice. Dangers are involved in imposing external moral judgments on an already oppressed community. Western feminists need to be careful that they are not simply engaged in the familiar exercise of imposing Western global power and values on other communities. Such action would itself constitute oppression in the form of Western imperialism and would not be countenanced by the criteria that define feminist moral relativism.

Feminist moral relativism implies that Western feminists are morally entitled to offer support as it is requested by feminists within the societies where an oppressive practice continues, even though the majority of the population, including many women, in the society in question may express support for the practice. Feminists from other societies can help relieve women in those countries of some of the coercive forces that may generate their compliance with this cruel practice, using their moral conclusions as the basis for support of minority voices in different cultures. In so doing, however, they need to maintain their concern for democratic processes of moral decision-making and to engage in such processes themselves with the women who are directly involved in the practice at issue. Therefore, feminists external to the culture in question should not impose their own solutions without the support of some women who are part of that culture, lest they be guilty of engaging in the sort of dominating processes they have identified as morally objectionable. (Moreover, as a pragmatic concern, externally defined strategies are unlikely to be effective, because attacks on local customs that are pursued without understanding the dynamics of the cultures concerned are likely to be resented and resisted. Insensitive criticisms made from outside the culture may very well worsen the situation of women within the society addressed.)[11]

A moral relativism that reviews the process of moral decision-making, as well as the outcome, would not be as tolerant as Wong or other nonfeminist relativists have been of people who sincerely cling to moral views that contribute to women's continued oppression, either in our own society or in others. A feminist moral relativism demands that we consider who controls moral decision-making within a community and what effect that control has on the least privileged members of that community. Both at home and abroad, it gives us grounds to criticize the practices that a majority believes acceptable if those practices are a result of oppressive power differentials. It will not, however, always tell us precisely what is the morally right thing to do, because there is no single set of moral truths we can decipher. Feminist moral relativism remains absolutist on the question of the moral wrong of oppression but is relativist on other moral matters; in this way, it is better able to incorporate feminist moral sensibilities.

4

Toward a Feminist Ethics of Health Care

The Role of Context

Biomedical ethics, like feminist ethics, is a new, rapidly developing area of philosophic specialization. It, too, is committed to developing analyses that can offer meaningful guidance in the morally troubling situations of real life, and it shares with feminist ethics a sense of frustration with the level of abstraction and generality that characterizes most traditional philosophic work on ethics. Writers in both fields are critical of the limitations that are created when we restrict ethical analysis to the level of general principles; both perceive a need to focus on the contextual details of actual situations that morally concerned persons find problematic. The use of context is quite different in the two fields, however, and in this chapter I shall examine this difference, so that we can see what is needed to develop a feminist ethics of health care. Looking at the gaps in nonfeminist bioethics, we can see that a contextually based moral theory must maintain a level of generality that supports an analysis of gender-based power relations in its evaluations.

In Chapter 2, I reviewed some ways in which feminists have been influenced by Carol Gilligan's (1982) claim that women are more likely than men to understand morality as consisting of caring for others and men are more likely than women to understand morality as a system of abstract, universal rules. Although intrigued by the empirical evidence of an existing gender difference in moral reasoning, many feminists remain uneasy about the normative significance of this gendered description of ethics and are unwilling to endorse an unqualified commitment to caring as a moral ideal.

In interpreting her research data, Gilligan also identifies a methodological difference in women's and men's distinctive patterns of moral reasoning. She finds that girls and women tend to evaluate ethical dilemmas in a contextualized, narrative way, looking at the particular details of a problem situation when making ethical decisions; in contrast, boys and men seem inclined to apply a general, abstract principle to the situation without paying specific attention to the unique circumstances of the case. Several feminists have found this difference in method to be a promising basis for building feminist ethics. Although still cautious of the implications of gender-specific patterns of moral reasoning, most feminists endorse including context as a central element in moral reasoning.

There is general agreement among feminists that theorists should resist the assumption that ethics can be boiled down to a set of abstract, universal rules, which can be specified apart from their context of use. Virginia Held, for example, suggests that feminist moral theory should emphasize "the domain of particular others in relations with one another" and warns that we must understand this task as one of focusing on "particular flesh and blood others for whom we have actual feelings in our insides and in our skin," not on "all others" (Held 1987b, 117–18). Seyla Benhabib urges us to include attention to the "concrete" other in our moral analysis, arguing that the focus of traditional moral theory on the abstract, "generalized" other is inadequate to our moral aims (Benhabib 1987). Marilyn Friedman stresses that contextualized thinking is important for adequate moral reasoning, noting that "contextual detail matters overridingly to matters of justice as well as to matters of care and relationships," because "a rich sense of contextual detail awakens one to the limitations in moral thinking that arise from the *minimalist* moral principles with which we are familiar" (Friedman 1987, 203).

Among proponents of feminist ethics, there is widespread criticism of the masculinist tendency of mainstream ethical theory to demand a very high degree of abstraction and to deny the relevance of concrete considerations. The pursuit of universal, rather than contextual, ethics seems to restrict the very scope and analysis of ethics: broad principles are difficult to instantiate in the complexities of daily life, because they often obscure some of the most telling features of a situation. I believe, however, feminist ethicists must be more precise about the term "context." As we shall see, although mainstream med-

ical ethics also expresses a commitment to contextual ethics, it is by
no means a form of feminist ethics. In reviewing the differences between feminist ethics and medical ethics, the importance of clarifying
the contextual details relevant to a distinctively feminist ethical analysis will become apparent.

The Pursuit of Context in Bioethics

In the "early days" of philosophical medical ethics
(that is, the 1970s), many theorists attempted to derive answers to
moral dilemmas from the general frameworks offered by the standard
moral theories, especially utilitarianism and Kantian deontology. It
became apparent quite early on, however, that the simple appeal to
theory and principle often did not offer satisfying analyses of the sorts
of dilemmas that arise in medical ethics; concrete practical advice
could not be readily inferred from abstract theories. Over the past two
decades it has become progressively clearer to many bioethicists that
the texture and the details of specific cases are important elements of
moral decision-making about such perennial issues as confidentiality,
truth-telling, and euthanasia. Many authors now believe that universal principles governing all cases where these problematic issues arise
cannot be found.

For example, in his basically deontological book on the subject H.
Tristram Englehardt, Jr., claims: "The obligation to do to others their
good is a fundamental one. However, the obligation as such is abstract. Only in concrete contexts can one determine the extent of the
obligation, and how to rank the various goods that can be at stake"
(Englehardt 1986, 92). Ronald Christie and Barry Hoffmaster are
more explicit about their rejection of a theory-based medical ethics.
They argue that "general moral theory does not illuminate specific
cases and therefore is not helpful. . . . The principles of moral philosophy are simply too abstract and too formal to contribute to the
resolution of concrete cases" (Christie and Hoffmaster 1986, xv). Arthur Caplan (1980) rejects the notion that moral theories can simply
be wheeled on stage and applied where needed without careful attention to the details of a particular case.

Albert Jonsen and Stephen Toulmin developed a comprehensive
critique of attempts to practice bioethics in a theory-governed form.
In The Abuse of Casuistry (1988) they describe their involvement in a

major bioethical project, the (U.S.) National Commission for the Protection of Human Subjects of Biomedical and Behavioral Research. The commission was charged with reviewing the regulations governing research with human subjects and was asked to consider a wide scope of ethical issues that arise in connection with human-subject research. Although the commission was made up of people of diverse personal backgrounds and different ethical orientations, the group was able to achieve a remarkable degree of moral consensus on specific issues. Jonsen and Toulmin observed that consensus was possible to the degree that commission members proceeded in a case-by-case manner and refrained from trying to ground their specific judgments in general, foundational principles.

Jonsen and Toulmin characterize as "moral geometry" traditional approaches to moral problem-solving that rely on appeals to a scientific, deductive model of ethics. They argue that this sort of deductive model is not adequate for most scientific reasoning, and it is wholly inappropriate for most forms of moral reasoning. In its place they recommend a more informal model of moral reasoning, known as casuistry, which is built around the "recognition of significant particulars" and "informed prudence" (Jonsen and Toulmin 1988, 19). In defense of this alternative, they argue that "casuistry redresses the excessive emphasis placed on universal rules and invariant principles by moral philosophers. . . . Instead we shall take seriously certain features of moral discourse that recent moral philosophers have too little appreciated: the concrete circumstances of actual cases, and the specific maxims that people invoke in facing actual moral dilemmas" (Jonsen and Toulmin 1988, 13). They, too, find that the specific concerns of medical ethics cannot be properly addressed from within "a morality built from general rules and universal principles alone" but require attention to "the subtle individual differences [that obtain] among otherwise similar circumstances" (Jonsen and Toulmin 1988, 341).

Other evidence of the widespread recognition among bioethicists of the need to attend to contextual details in moral deliberations can be seen by looking at their publications. Case studies are a central element in influential journals, in many textbooks, and in individual articles within the field; often the analysis of such cases is offered with no reference to general theories at all.

We can see, then, that the trend in medical ethics has been to examine moral issues in context and to avoid dependence on general, abstract rules and rights. As in feminist ethics, in the literature of medical ethics the theme of seeking a practical, context-specific approach to ethics is widely stressed. In both fields the inadequacy of abstract moral reasoning for resolving real moral dilemmas is frequently acknowledged.

The Theory-Based Alternatives

Some philosophers who are still entrenched in mainstream moral theory have difficulty seeing the distinction being cited here, because all moral theories are context-sensitive to some degree. Kantian theory, for example, demands an interpretation of context to determine which maxim really applies in a given case. Nevertheless, Kantian theory assumes that the maxims, once identified, will be universal, and it demands that an agent's position on a practice such as suicide, truth-telling, or confidentiality should be consistent across the full spectrum of relevant cases. It does not direct moral agents to make their ethical assessments in terms of particular details of the lives of the individuals affected.

Utilitarianism is often espoused precisely as an antidote to such a rigid ethics. It seems extremely sensitive to contextual features in that it recommends that we calculate relevant utilities for all possible options in a given set of circumstances. Nevertheless, it discounts features that both medical ethics and feminist ethics consider important. In particular, utilitarianism requires us to calculate the relevant utility values for all persons (or beings) who are affected by an action or practice and to proceed according to a calculation of the relevant balances.

In contrast, those engaged in feminist ethics and many who write in the area of medical ethics recognize the necessity of taking explicit account of the details of the specific relationships involved. It is common, for instance, in both fields to assign special weight to particular features such as caring and responsibility. A basic assumption of medical ethics is that health care providers are obligated to place priority on the welfare of their patients, even if greater aggregate utility could be achieved by other means. Feminist ethicists see the further necessity of distinguishing among individuals on the basis of their places within dominance and subordination structures. On feminist accounts special weight should be assigned to actions that challenge—and thereby help to undermine—oppressive practices. In such matters it seems necessary that the preferences of the oppressed be weighted more heavily than those of members of the dominant group. (Feminist objections to pornography, for instance, do not rely on comparing the harms it creates against the pleasure it produces but reflect concern about the dehumanizing effect of the message of pornography, whatever the utilities involved may turn out to be. Such concerns are not captured by traditional formulations of utilitarianism.)

In both feminist and medical ethics, then, it is important to consider factors that do not carry any special significance in utilitarianism. Both require that our analysis look at the nature of both the persons and the relationships involved, and both consider it inadequate just to calculate the sums of such values as preference satisfaction or pleasure and pain quotients. Although utilitarianism recognizes that pleasures and pains are specifically held, it considers their importance as coming from their abstract sum and not from their attachment to particular persons in particular situations. Neither Kantian nor utilitarian theory satisfies the requirement of particularity, as it is conceived in feminist and medical ethics. Similarly, for the reasons reviewed in Chapter 2, standard versions of contractarian and communitarian theories also fail to capture this contextual concern.[1]

Theorists still closely affiliated with traditional ethical theories are often inclined to fear that contextual ethics opens the door to situation ethics,[2] a practical, humanistic ethical methodology that purports to be disconnected from general theory. Although situation ethics is often quite popular with health professionals (perhaps because the absence of theory seems to make it far more "user-friendly" than proposals rooted in conceptually difficult philosophical systems), most moral theorists are disdainful of such an approach.[3] Situation ethics directs moral agents to seek "a loving and humane solution" in the face of moral dilemmas, but it refrains from suggesting how they are to identify which solution is the loving and humane one. Readers may perceive similarities with the "feminine" ethics of caring, but the latter is actually more theoretically developed, as it offers specific norms for the balancing of obligations owed to the self and to others affected by an agent's actions. Neither medical nor feminist ethicists recommend a theory-free analysis in their proposal to focus on context.

Most medical ethicists and many feminist ethicists still envision a place for principles in ethics; what they deny is that principles alone are sufficient for resolving most moral problems. My own proposals are also committed to the view that principles retain a role in ethics; my argument against oppression is a principled one, resting on a conception of justice that is defined in terms of its opposition to oppression. The principle to which I appeal, however, only makes sense when the relevant contextual details are spelled out. Oppression is not a phenomenon that can be adequately explored in the abstract; contextual details about the specific form of oppression and about other relevant features of the situation in question must be added to make sense of the moral concerns raised.

Further Areas of Similarity between Feminist and Medical Ethics

There is also substantial agreement between those who pursue feminist and medical ethics on the importance of certain kinds of contextual features. Both recognize that an ethics of actions must be supplemented by discussion of the nature of the relationships that hold between the agents performing an action and those who are affected by it. Both feminists and medical ethicists are critical of the traditional assumption—made most explicitly by contractarians but also often assumed by other sorts of theorists—that the role of ethics is to clarify the obligations that hold among individuals who are viewed as paradigmatically equal, independent, rational, and autonomous.

Feminist ethicists accept the arguments offered within the realm of "feminine" ethics, which demand that attention be paid to the interdependent, emotionally varied, unequal relationships that shape human lives. Similar claims are found in the literature of medical ethics, where it is widely recognized that the relationships that exist between physicians and their patients are far from equal (especially if the patient is very ill) and that the model of contracts negotiated by independent, rational agents does not provide a useful perspective for this sort of interaction. In particular, the disadvantaged position of the dependent patient is a major theme in the many discussions of paternalism that are found throughout the medical ethics literature. Further, many authors are sensitive to the fact that the physician–patient relationship is not a dyad that exists in some abstract, eternal realm; it is found within overlapping networks of other relationships, which bind patients and physicians to their respective family members, other health professionals, neighbors, employers, health services administrators, and so on (for example, Hardwig 1990).

In addition, we can find parallel claims in the literatures of feminist and medical ethics of the importance of evaluating behavior in terms of its effect on the quality of relationships among persons concerned. For instance, discussions in medical ethics on the importance of telling patients the truth about their condition often refer to the effect that a discovered lie would have on the physician–patient relationship; it is frequently claimed that patients who learn that their physicians have deliberately deceived them are likely to feel especially betrayed by the violation of trust in light of their feelings of vulnerability and dependency, despite the supposedly benevolent motives that might have contributed to the deceptive behavior. Feminist theorists, for their part, note that ethics should not only be concerned with actions and relationships but also focus on questions of character and the development of attitudes of trust—and antitrust—within those relationships (see Baier 1986). For example, Sarah Hoagland (1988), Marilyn Friedman (1989), and Iris Marion Young (1989) all focus on the conditions necessary for the building of (feminist) community.[4]

Moreover, as in feminist ethics, discussion in medical ethics often raises considerations of caring; this requirement is usually couched in the language of beneficence—an attitude that is generally assumed to be owed to patients. Medical dilemmas are sometimes discussed in terms that appear to rank sensitivity and caring ahead of applications of principle; compassion is frequently claimed to be more compelling than honesty or justice.[5]

There seems, then, to be agreement between the two fields on a variety of concerns regarding traditional moral theory. Authors in both disciplines argue that matters of character, responsibility, and other features that affect trust are morally significant. Both reject the oversimplifying tendency of normative theorists to reduce all moral considerations to short sets of universal principles. Given their shared commitment to focusing on context in moral problem-solving, their common understanding of the ethical significance of inequality within relationships, and the tendency of some authors in both traditions to include caring values in their analyses, it might appear that medical ethics is already well on its way to being feminist. Medical ethics, however, does not display any commitment to ending oppression; thus most of the writings of contemporary medical ethics must be judged as lacking from the perspective of feminist ethics.

Interpreting Silence as Tolerance

As I argued in Chapter 2, feminist ethics requires that any evaluation of moral considerations attend to the power relations that structure the relevant interactions. Political analyses of the unequal power of women and men, of white people and people of color, of First World and Third World people, of the rich and the poor, of the healthy and the disabled, and so forth are central to feminist ethics. To date, that sort of analysis has been almost entirely absent from the literature of mainstream medical ethics, although the institutions in which health care is provided are deeply implicated in the maintenance of structures of oppression (see Chapter 11).

The complicity of medical institutions in some aspects of the oppression of women and their outright causal role in other aspects have been well documented by feminist researchers (Ehrenreich and English 1978; Fee 1983; Corea 1985a; Todd 1989). Elizabeth Fee, for example, labels physicians "the patriarchs of the body" (Fee 1983, 8). There is abundant evidence that current medical practice, like its historical predecessors, constitutes a powerful social institution that contributes to the oppression of women. As many feminists have shown, and as I elaborate in Parts Two and Three of this book, the practice of medicine serves as an important instrument in the continuing disempowerment of women (and members of other oppressed groups) in society. It thrives on hierarchical power structures, which themselves maintain interactions characterized by their patterns of domination and subordination.

Feminist criticisms range over all aspects of modern medical practice, from its institutional structures to its insistence on authoritarian patterns of control; from its different treatment of male and female patients to its obsessive interest in women's reproductive functions; from its perpetuation of sex-role stereotypes to its role in reinforcing women's subservience in family relationships. Further, feminism helps us understand that medical researchers set their agendas with respect to women's conditions according to male-defined interests in women (for example, women's reproductive functioning); medical practitioners also authoritatively dictate patterns of mental and physical normalcy for women that serve the interests of men.

Within the mainstream health-delivery systems, women are discouraged from developing self-help approaches to health care, which would empower them to control their own health needs. Insofar as women are offered any role in their own health care, it is usually put in terms of negative injunctions: they are urged to measure their behavior according to standards few women are able to satisfy, and thus women are blamed for eating, drinking, or smoking to excess, for their failure to exercise sufficiently, and for dieting or exercising beyond "reason." Women are encouraged (or required) to be dependent on expert medical opinion and, correspondingly, to distrust their own intuitions on the welfare of their own bodies and the state of those they care for. Men maintain the positions of power and authority in medical institutions, and women, for the most part, are relegated to the support staff or are made invisible in their roles as caretakers of the ill at home. Male doctors (or female doctors trained within male value schemes) are described as the active agents who deliver babies from women who passively carry them. Physicians determine if a woman's request for abortion or contraception is legitimate, and they decide when a woman's reproductive organs are redundant and a threat to her well-being. Many doctors accept and promote advertising's view of ideal female shapes and conspire with such masculinist imaging to "help" women fit these expectations through cosmetic surgery and diet programs. With the male-dominated legislatures and legal systems, doctors decide when to spend hundreds of thousands of dollars to prolong the life of a seriously damaged, premature infant; meanwhile, funds cannot be found to protect millions of women and children from starvation.

In addition, by medicating socially induced depression and anxiety, medicine helps to perpetuate women's oppression and deflects attention from the injustice of their situation. With its authority to define what is normal and what is pathological and to coerce compliance to its norms, medicine tends to strengthen gender roles and racial stereotyping; thus it reinforces existing power inequalities (see

Chapter 9). Some practitioners and theorists offer expert advice that explains and excuses such common male practices as wife battering, incest, and male sexual aggression and thereby inhibits evaluation of these practices in moral and political terms (Stark, Flitcraft, and Frazier 1983).

Despite these comprehensive and disturbing criticisms of medical practice, the discussion in medical ethics to date has been largely myopic; for the most part, bioethicists have not commented on the political role of medicine. The institutional organization and agenda of medicine are usually accepted without question. Most debates in bioethics have focused on specific matters of concern within the existing health care system, such as truthfulness, consent, confidentiality, the limits of paternalism, the allocation of resources, incurable illness, and abortion. The effect of this narrow orientation has been to provide an overall ethical legitimization of the existing health care institutions, whereas general structures and patterns are left largely unchallenged. Apart from occasional discussions about the allocation of limited life-saving resources, it would appear from much of the current medical ethics literature that all that is needed to make medical interactions ethically acceptable is a bit of fine-tuning in specific problem areas.

A good indication of the legitimizing function of medical ethics is its gradual acceptance among those who are influential within the medical profession. Increasingly, medical practitioners recognize the value of incorporating discussions of medical ethics within their own work; most medical schools now devote at least a few hours of their precious scheduling time to exploring of the "basics" of medical ethics, and most professional licensing exams include a few ethics questions in their format. Nevertheless, the very willingness of the medical establishment to absorb bioethics into their credentials for membership raises suspicions. By such action, the profession is able to demonstrate its serious interest in moral matters, and this explicit professional concern in medical ethics encourages the public to maintain its trust in physicians' judgment. When intolerable abuses of that trust become public, damage control is usually initiated through a renewed professional commitment to moral education and enforcing ethical standards. Physicians are not required to engage in deep soul-searching or to address any significant challenges to their traditional ways of organizing health-care delivery. The scope of medical ethics has been kept narrow so that the principal focus is on specific problems of individual provider–patient interaction.

Cheryl Noble observes that applied ethics has a strong tendency to "justify" social practices by appealing to principles that are really "only highly abstract descriptions of norms already embodied in those practices" (Noble 1982, 9). In bioethics we can see at work some of the inclination to conservatism that she warns against, because often the apparatus of technical theory is invoked to defend or, at most, to modestly reform existing practices. Conferences, textbooks, and journals of medical ethics are chiefly occupied with establishing an ethical rationale for existing practices within the field of health care; vigorous criticism has been largely reserved for new practices (for example, fetal tissue transplants), traditions that violate current social norms (for example, paternalism), or politically controversial practices (for example, abortion).

Feminists must be critical of the fact that most of the authors writing in the field of medical ethics have remained silent about the patriarchal practice of medicine. Few nonfeminist bioethicists have been critical of practices and institutions that contribute to the oppression of women; fewer still have written on the role of medicine in the oppression of women and men of color or have discussed medicine's effects on the social status of disabled people.

For the most part, bioethicists have even failed to address medicine's role in the most horrifying excesses of oppression in modern Western culture, namely, the abuses perpetrated by Nazi doctors. Robert Proctor (1988) has documented the leading role played by physicians and scientists in the Holocaust. Nazi ideology rested on the theory of racial hygiene, which was developed and promoted by biomedical theorists. Many physicians and scientists were influential party members and welcomed the opportunities created by the Nazi regime to put their theories into practice; both science and medicine flourished under Hitler. Further, the connection between medicine and racism was not an isolated German phenomenon: American doctors and scientists were engaged in their own eugenic theories and practices at the time. Today many biologists and physicians promote some of the same dangerous eugenic views (and some more sophisticated, subtle variations), but for the most part, such abuses of medical power and authority have been treated as anomalous and uninteresting in the main work of medical ethics.

The deep questions about the structure of medical practice and its role in a patriarchal and racist society are largely inaccessible within the framework customarily adopted for work in bioethics; such questions are certainly not part of the standard curriculum in textbooks of medical ethics. Even though medical ethics is meant to be critical of all morally unacceptable medical practices, it has failed to oppose those that contribute to the oppression of women. By not opposing them, it has implicitly supported patriarchal policies within the medical establishment. Although writers in the field of medical ethics share some of the central insights of what I have labeled a "feminine" ethics, most do not provide a feminist analysis. Consequently, medical ethics, as it is usually practiced, does not amount to a feminist approach to ethics. We need to add to bioethics an analysis of the political role of medicine, if we are to develop something that might properly be called a "feminist ethics of health care."

Defining Context

We must be quite specific about the nature of the context that is relevant to our ethical analysis. Cheshire Calhoun writes about the importance of feminist assessments of harm as it is "*contextualized* in an interlocking system of harmful practices" (Calhoun 1989, 397) and observes that "the actual harmfulness of some forms of behavior becomes visible only when contextualized in a system of offenses" (Calhoun 1989, 397 n. 17). The context that feminists must explore is the place of the relevant behavior within that interlocking system of oppressive practices—or, in Marilyn Frye's (1983) metaphor, its role in shaping the bird cage that structures women's oppression.

Therefore, we must be cautious of the growing tendency in feminist theory to reject the very notion of a general analysis on the grounds that the experiences of women are so varied and diverse that they do not permit conclusions that would include all women. Maria Lugones and Elizabeth Spelman (1983), for instance, warn against the tendency of generalized feminist theory to demoralize some groups of women while empowering others. Sandra Harding also criticizes totalizing theories as inadequate because of their tendency to assume falsely that the experiences of specific, privileged individuals constitute what is essential and universal about human nature. She observes: "Once essential and universal man dissolves, so does his hidden companion, woman. We have, instead, myriads of women living in elaborate historical complexes of class, race, and culture" (Harding 1986a, 647).

I believe, however, that the experience of medical ethics provides evidence of the need to maintain a certain level of generality in feminist moral claims. It establishes the importance of considering the ways in which medicine supports and participates in the complex systems of practices that constitute the oppression of women. Therefore, even though individual women experience oppression differently and are treated differently within medical contexts, some important commonalities define women's experiences in society and within medicine. Medicine favors physiological understandings of the people it treats, and for the most part, women are perceived as being physiologically the same. Social differences do play a role in the sort of treatment each woman receives from the health care providers she encounters, but some generalities about women also play a critical role in her care. Feminists must look closely at those generalities, as well as at the specific assumptions that govern the ways in which practitioners approach various subgroups of women.

In Part Two I explore in greater detail some of the ways in which differing interpretations of the methodological concern for contextual specificity lead to very different analyses in the contrasting realms of medical and feminist ethics. Here I offer some brief examples of concrete differences that result from adopting an explicitly feminist understanding of contextual analysis.

One important difference is that most nonfeminist writers in bioethics choose to examine particular medical practices, such as abortion, genetic screening, embryo transfer, or surrogate mothering, in isolation from the historical and political contexts in which they are performed. In considering only the abstract features of these sorts of practices, most bioethicists—at least, those of the secular varieties— are led to conclude that the practice in question violates no major moral rules; hence, they argue, the only moral dilemmas posed by each practice will be ones that concern their application in specific cases. They then turn to a case-study approach, where, it is assumed, all the relevant features of a particular case can be clarified in a short description of its features. We should understand, however, that adopting a context-specific approach to case analysis for an issue such as surrogacy often shapes the outcome of analysis: it is easy to identify very strong grounds for allowing individuals to choose contractual pregnancy in specified circumstances by offering an example in which surrogacy seems to be both benign and desirable (and those who believe that surrogacy should be prohibited can readily offer an example in which it appears abhorrent).

From a feminist perspective, it is obvious that we need to clarify the role of such a practice within the broader patterns of women's subordinate status in society. Surrogacy contracts cannot be evaluated simply by seeing whether they fit within the norms of voluntary legal contracts; it is not sufficient to determine whether they are analogous to other sorts of contracts that the state and common understanding have already deemed acceptable. Unlike their mainstream colleagues, most feminists believe that before we can address the details of specific cases where this procedure is sought, it is necessary to consider the implications of the practice on existing and potential patterns of oppression. They try to determine whether an increased incidence of contractual pregnancies will pose further dangers to the already disadvantaged positions that women and children occupy. They ask about such matters as the value that society assigns to women's biological role in reproduction, the costs and benefits involved in encouraging women to engage in commercial transactions over the "products" of their reproductive labor, and how such practices might further oppress poor and disadvantaged women.[6]

For similar reasons, a feminist analysis of health services for the disabled requires us to go beyond the narrow conception of traditional bioethicists. Should nonfeminist theorists take up this subject at all, they are likely to restrict their concerns to a review of how the health care system responds to the defined needs of disabled people. Traditional medical ethics teaches us to explore such issues as justice in allocation of benefits for specific disabilities and to ensure that informed consent is solicited before treatment is initiated. As Susan Wendell (1989) has argued, however, what is really needed is a feminist theory of disability, which would reveal how disability is a socially constructed response to a biological condition. She urges us to understand the degree to which medicine has created the sorts of arrangements and constructed the types of social attitudes that lead the disabled to feel alienated from their own bodies and leave them frustrated by their socially supported sense of failure. The contextual analysis sought by feminist ethics involves examination of the phenomenology and politics that arise from being assigned a position among the disabled in a society that demands perfection of its members.

Kathryn Morgan (1991) explores the frightening realm of cosmetic surgery from a feminist perspective. As she argues, the traditional subjects of concern within medical ethics—informed consent, confidentiality, resource allocation, and so forth—do not begin to uncover the moral problems that are posed by this booming industry. Her work indicates the need for feminist analyses of the industry's context, in which women invest years of savings to gain access to dangerous and painful operations that promise to reduce their natural "flaws"— to make their bodies and their faces fit the norms that fashion editors have dictated. Such analysis must be prominent if we are to undertake an adequate moral evaluation of "voluntary" cosmetic surgery.

Further, Virginia Warren (1989) argues that feminist attention to medical ethics requires an examination of the context of engaging in ethics itself. She claims that the context and methods of the activity of ethical analysis are themselves significant to the outcomes proposed. Warren presents a picture of "Sexist Ethics," characterized by its use of the male perspective to frame moral questions and propose solutions, its habit of cloaking itself in a commitment to gender neutrality, and its selection of topics that ensure that women are always kept on the defensive by making matters of concern to them a constant subject of controversy (for example, abortion and affirmative action). In contrast to this not-so-fanciful picture, she proposes a conception of feminist medical ethics that would include the perspectives of diverse sorts of women and would shift the focus of attention from crisis issues to housekeeping issues of an ongoing nature, such as those that arise in the daily activities of health care contexts.

Feminist arguments indicate that we need to interpret quite broadly the ideal of considering ethical questions in a contextually based framework, if we are serious in our moral concerns about sexism. There is a need to define context in social and political terms and to consider actions in terms of the practices with which each is connected, attending to the effect of these larger practices on women's pursuit of greater power in a society that currently subordinates them.

Other Features of a Feminist Ethics of Health Care

There are numerous other ways in which work in feminist ethics can inform and transform work in medical ethics and in which medical ethics can provide models (both good and bad) for work in feminist ethics. For instance, the literature in both feminist and medical ethics reflects an interest in questions concerning the nature and quality of particular relationships, because both feminist and medical ethicists recognize that rights and responsibilities depend upon the roles and relationships that exist among persons of differing power and status. New models of interaction within the area of health care are needed to develop a system of care that is less hierarchically structured and less focused on matters of power and control than the current institutions. Feminist explorations of friendship (Code 1987) or mother–child (Held 1987a) relationships are worth pursuing as a basis of alternative models for these institutions.

A feminist ethics of health care will have other distinctive dimensions that mark its departure from the familiar mainstream approaches to medical ethics. For example, it demonstrates how the role of the patient is perceived as feminine. Patients are required to submit to medical authority and respond with gratitude for attention offered. Most recognize their vulnerability to medical power and learn the value of offering a cheerful disposition in the face of extraordinary suffering, because complaints are often met with hostility and impatience. Like those who are socially defined as subservient, patients often find themselves apologizing for the inconvenience of needing attention; most know their obligation to listen submissively to medical direction. Because feminism is occupied with redefining feminine roles, a feminist ethics of health care takes a natural interest in redefining the feminine aspects of the role of patient.

For this reason, a feminist ethics of health care includes reflection on the underlying medical views of the body. Medical practice involves the explorative study, manipulation, and modification of the body; because, under patriarchal ideology, the body is characteristically associated with the feminine, the female body is particularly subject to medical dominance. Its practitioners presume the license to probe the body for its secrets, as well as the authority to define its norms and deviations. As the contributors to *Body/Politics:*

Women and the Discourses of Science (Jacobus, Keller, and Shuttleworth 1990) make clear, there are significant political and moral
questions to be explored regarding the relations between medicine
and the feminine body. The discourses common to medicine and
science both reflect and support attitudes about the body that reinforce patriarchal forces.

Further, as Esther Frances (1990) proposes, a feminist ethics of
health care should evaluate the significance of challenges to allopathic medicine with respect to the oppression of women. There are
numerous critiques of the assumptions and practices of allopathic
medicine and many competing visions of alternative health care practices. Many women have found some of these alternatives attractive;
some seem to promise a more empowering, less hierarchical understanding of health than is found in mainstream allopathic medicine.
In a feminist ethics of health care these various approaches should be
explored and examined with regard to their promise for relieving
some of the harms women now experience under sexism.

Like other projects in feminist ethics, a feminist ethics of health
care is concerned with going beyond analysis of how women have
been systematically oppressed by patriarchy; it seeks to foster agency
where agency has previously been restricted by patriarchal patterns
and assumptions. The agenda of traditional bioethics has been largely
occupied with questions about the responsibilities of health professionals; the agenda of a feminist ethics of health care is significantly
farther-reaching. It is directed also at exploring the various roles that
may be open to patients and nonprofessionals in the pursuit of health
and health policy. It is not sufficient to put specific moral restrictions
on the behavior of health-care providers; we must also ensure that the
health care delivery system is modified in appropriate ways to allow
consumers to achieve their ends with respect to their own health.

A principal task of a feminist ethics of health care is to develop
conceptual models for restructuring the power associated with healing, by distributing the specialized knowledge on health matters in
ways that allow persons maximum control over their own health. It is
important to clarify how excessive dependence can be reduced, how
caring can be offered without paternalism, and how health services
can be obtained within a context worthy of trust. Feminists seek to
spread health information widely and foster self-help approaches to
health matters. Feminist values imply that medical expertise should

be viewed as a social resource, and as such, it should be held under the control of patients and their caregivers. A feminist ethics of health care suggests that the institution of medicine should be transformed from one principally occupied with crisis management to one primarily committed to fostering health empowerment. We must, then, look at the existing structures of medicine and medical interaction when attempting to understand the details of any particular medical experience.

I have spelled out some important features of what I envision as a feminist ethics of health care, but this is not an exhaustive description. This book represents an initial step in the task of developing such an ethics, but much more work remains to be done. Others will add further dimensions. The common agenda of work characterized by the label "feminist ethics of health care" will be to provide a more comprehensive and fairer approach to medical ethics than has been evident in the literature to date.

I do not expect that all questions in feminist medical ethics can be addressed solely in terms of the political implications of the practices they represent. I suspect that, just as in other areas of feminist ethics, many decisions will still be best carried out by looking to the details of the specific circumstances and the people involved. For example, questions about who has the final authority in determining what should be done in the case of critically ill children when there is disagreement between parents and physicians should be resolved by considering details of the particular cases. Parents are usually best at identifying their child's best interests; for example, in a case where doctors want to try a painful and largely unsuccessful therapy in an effort to provide at least "a chance" for a child suffering from a terminal disease, the parents may decide that the child cannot sustain more pain. There are situations, however, in which children have been subject to violent abuse or serious neglect and it is not appropriate to trust the parent(s) with the child's well-being. To resolve these sorts of controversies, we need to look at the details of the particular relationships that exist among the child, its parents, and the physicians and other health professionals involved.

Even here, however, political questions may need to be asked. In addition to examining the relationships that shape parental and medical decision-making, we need to recognize that, in most cases, the burden of caring for severely disabled children falls on women. Seldom are adequate support services made available to them. There-fore, our analysis should include exploration of the types of support that can be expected from the community should the child be saved. The ethical discussion extends to questions of the responsibilities others have for providing assistance in the special care that may be required by the child.

In other words, we must keep in mind the wisdom of Virginia Held's (1984) analysis of ethics, namely, that we ought not expect a single theory or strategy to be adequate for settling all kinds of ethical questions. Different forms of analysis are appropriate to different sorts of moral dilemmas. The important constant is that we must always decide these questions within the wider political context of consider-ing how this analysis affects (if at all) our general feminist objectives of eliminating oppression in all its forms. Which sort of analysis is appropriate to which sort of problem is a matter for a feminist ethics of health care to explore.

Two

Traditional Problems in
Health Care Ethics

5

Abortion

Although abortion has long been an important issue in bioethics, the distinctive analysis of feminist ethics is generally overlooked in the discussion. Authors and readers commonly presume a familiarity with the feminist position and equate it with other liberal defenses of women's right to choose abortion; but feminist ethics yields a different analysis of the moral questions surrounding abortion from that usually offered by liberal abortion arguments.[1] Although feminists agree with some of the conclusions of nonfeminist arguments on abortion, they often disagree with the way the issues are formulated and with the reasoning that is offered in the mainstream literature.

Feminist reasoning in support of women's right to choose abortion is significantly different from the reasoning used by nonfeminist supporters of similar positions. For instance, most feminist accounts evaluate abortion policy within a broader framework, according to its place among the social institutions that support the subordination of women. In contrast, most nonfeminist discussions of abortion consider the moral or legal permissibility of abortion in isolation; they ignore (and thereby obscure) relevant connections with other social practices, including the ongoing power struggle within sexist societies over the control of women and their reproduction. Feminist arguments take into account the actual concerns that particular women attend to in their decision-making on abortion, such as the nature of a woman's feelings about her fetus, her relationships with her partner, other children she may have, and her various obligations to herself and others. In contrast, most nonfeminist discussions evaluate abortion decisions in their most abstract form (for example, questioning what sort of being a fetus is); from this perspective, specific questions of context are deemed irrelevant. In addition, nonfeminist arguments in support of choice about abortion are generally grounded in masculinist conceptions of freedom (such as privacy, individual choice, and individuals' property rights with respect to their own bodies), which do not meet the needs, interests, and intuitions of many of the women concerned.

Feminists also differ from nonfeminists in their conception of what is morally at issue with abortion. Nonfeminists focus exclusively on the morality and legality of performing abortions, whereas feminists insist that other issues, including the accessibility and delivery of abortion services, must also be addressed. Disputes about abortion arise even at the stage of defining the issue and setting the moral parameters for discussion. Although many nonfeminist bioethicists agree with feminists about which abortion policies should be supported, they tend to accept the proposals of the antifeminists as to what is morally at issue in developing that policy.

Thus although feminists welcome the support of nonfeminists in pursuing policies that grant women control over abortion decisions, they generally envision policies for this purpose that are very different from those considered by their nonfeminist sympathizers. Feminist ethicists promote a model for addressing the provision of abortion services different from the one conceived in traditional bioethical arguments. For example, Kathleen McDonnell urges feminists to develop an explicitly "'feminist morality' of abortion. . . . At its root it would be characterized by the deep appreciations of the complexities of life, the refusal to polarize and adopt simplistic formulas" (McDonnell 1984, 52). Here I propose one conception of the shape such an analysis should take.

Women and Abortion

The most obvious difference between feminist and nonfeminist approaches to abortion lies in the relative attention each gives in its analysis to the interests and experiences of women. Feminist analysis regards the effects of unwanted pregnancies on the lives of women individually and collectively as the central element in the moral examination of abortion; it is considered self-evident that the pregnant woman is the subject of principal concern in abortion decisions. In many nonfeminist accounts, however, not only is the pregnant woman not perceived as central, she is often rendered virtually invisible. Nonfeminist theorists, whether they support or oppose women's right to choose abortion, generally focus almost all their attention on the moral status of the fetus.[2]

In pursuing a distinctively feminist ethics, it is appropriate to begin with a look at the role of abortion in women's lives. The need for abortion can be very intense; no matter how appalling and dangerous the conditions, women from widely diverse cultures and historical periods have pursued abortions. No one denies that if abortion is not made legal, safe, and accessible in our society, women will seek out illegal and life-threatening abortions to terminate pregnancies they cannot accept. Antiabortion activists seem willing to accept this cost, although liberals definitely are not; feminists, who explicitly value women, judge the inevitable loss of women's lives that results from restrictive abortion policies to be a matter of fundamental concern.

Antiabortion campaigners imagine that women often make frivolous and irresponsible decisions about abortion, but feminists recognize that women have abortions for a wide variety of compelling reasons. Some women, for instance, find themselves seriously ill and incapacitated throughout pregnancy; they cannot continue in their jobs and may face insurmountable difficulties in fulfilling their responsibilities at home. Many employers and schools will not tolerate pregnancy in their employees or students, and not every woman is able to put her job, career, or studies on hold. Women of limited means may be unable to take adequate care of children they have already borne, and they may know that another mouth to feed will reduce their ability to provide for their existing children. Women who suffer from chronic disease, who believe themselves too young or too old to have children, or who are unable to maintain lasting relationships may recognize that they will not be able to care properly for a child when they face the decision. Some who are homeless, addicted to drugs, or diagnosed as carrying the AIDS virus may be unwilling to allow a child to enter the world with the handicaps that would result from the mother's condition. If the fetus is a result of rape or incest, then the psychological pain of carrying it may be unbearable, and the woman may recognize that her attitude to the child after birth will be tinged with bitterness. Some women learn that the fetuses that they carry have serious chromosomal anomalies and consider it best to prevent them from being born with a condition that is bound to cause them to suffer. Others, knowing the fathers to be brutal and violent, may be unwilling to subject a child to the beatings or incestuous attacks they anticipate; some may have no other realistic way to remove the child (or themselves) from the relationship.[3]

Finally, a woman may simply believe that bearing a child is incompatible with her life plans at the time. Continuing a pregnancy may have devastating repercussions throughout a woman's life. If the woman is young, then a pregnancy will likely reduce her chances of pursuing an education and hence limit her career and life opportunities: "The earlier a woman has a baby, it seems, the more likely she is to drop out of school; the less education she gets, the more likely she is to remain poorly paid, peripheral to the labor market, or unemployed, and the more children she will have" (Petchesky 1985, 150). In many circumstances, having a child will exacerbate the social and economic forces already stacked against a woman by virtue of her sex (and her race, class, age, sexual orientation, disabilities, and so forth). Access to abortion is necessary for many women if they are to escape the oppressive conditions of poverty.[4]

Whatever the specific reasons are for abortion, most feminists believe that the women concerned are in the best position to judge whether abortion is the appropriate response to a pregnancy. Because usually only the woman choosing abortion is properly situated to weigh all the relevant factors, most feminists resist attempts to offer general, abstract rules for determining when abortion is morally justified.[5] Women's personal deliberations about abortion involve contextually defined considerations that reflect their commitments to the needs and interests of everyone concerned, including themselves, the fetuses they carry, other members of their household, and so forth. Because no single formula is available for balancing these complex factors through all possible cases, it is vital that feminists insist on protecting each woman's right to come to her own conclusions and resist the attempts of other philosophers and moralists to set the agenda for these considerations. Feminists stress that women must be acknowledged as full moral agents, responsible for making moral decisions about their own pregnancies. Women may sometimes make mistakes in their moral judgments, but no one else can be assumed to have the authority to evaluate and overrule their judgments.[6]

Even without patriarchy, bearing a child would be a very important event in a woman's life, because it involves significant physical, emotional, social, and (usually) economic changes for her. The ability to exert control over the incidence, timing, and frequency of childbearing is often tied to a woman's ability to control most other things she values. Because we live in a patriarchal society, it is especially important to ensure that women have the authority to control their own reproduction.[7] Despite the diversity of opinion found among feminists on most other matters, most feminists agree that women must gain full control over their own reproductive lives if they are to free themselves from male dominance.[8]

Moreover, women's freedom to choose abortion is linked to their ability to control their own sexuality. Women's subordinate status often prevents them from refusing men sexual access to their bodies. If women cannot end the unwanted pregnancies that result from male sexual dominance, then their sexual vulnerability to particular men may increase, because caring for an(other) infant involves greater financial needs and reduced economic opportunities for women.[9] As a result, pregnancy often forces women to become dependent on particular men. Because a woman's dependence on a man is assumed to entail her continued sexual loyalty to him, restriction of abortion serves to commit women to remaining sexually accessible to particular men and thus helps to perpetuate the cycle of oppression.

In contrast to most nonfeminist accounts, feminist analyses of abortion direct attention to how women get pregnant. Those who reject abortion seem to believe that women can avoid unwanted pregnancies "simply" by avoiding sexual intercourse. These views show little appreciation for the power of sexual politics in a culture that oppresses women. Existing patterns of sexual dominance mean that women often have little control over their sexual lives. They may be subject to rape by their husbands, boyfriends, colleagues, employers, customers, fathers, brothers, uncles, and dates, as well as by strangers. Often the sexual coercion is not even recognized as such by the participants but is the price of continued "good will"—popularity, economic survival, peace, or simple acceptance. Many women have found themselves in circumstances where they do not feel free to refuse a man's demands for intercourse, either because he is holding a gun to her head or because he threatens to be emotionally hurt if she refuses (or both). Women are socialized to be compliant and accommodating, sensitive to the feelings of others, and frightened of physical power; men are socialized to take advantage of every opportunity to engage in sexual intercourse and to use sex to express dominance and power. Under such circumstances, it is difficult to argue that women could simply "choose" to avoid heterosexual activity if they wish to avoid pregnancy. Catharine MacKinnon neatly sums it up: "The logic by which women are supposed to consent to sex [is]: preclude the alternatives, then call the remaining option 'her choice'" (MacKinnon 1989, 192).

Furthermore, women cannot rely on birth control to avoid pregnancy. No form of contraception that is fully safe and reliable is available, other than sterilization; because women may wish only to avoid pregnancy temporarily, not permanently, sterilization is not always an acceptable choice. The pill and the IUD are the most effective contraceptive means offered, but both involve significant health hazards to women and are quite dangerous for some.[10] No woman should spend the thirty to forty years of her reproductive life on either form of birth control. Further, both have been associated with subsequent problems of involuntary infertility, so they are far from optimal for women who seek to control the timing of their pregnancies.

The safest form of birth control involves the use of barrier methods (condoms or diaphragms) in combination with spermicidal foams or jelly. But these methods also pose difficulties for women. They are sometimes socially awkward to use. Young women are discouraged from preparing for sexual activity that might never happen and are offered instead romantic models of spontaneous passion; few films or novels interrupt scenes of seduction for a partner to fetch contraceptives. Many women find their male partners unwilling to use barrier methods of contraception, and they often find themselves in no position to insist. Further, cost is a limiting factor for many women. Condoms and spermicides are expensive and are not covered under most health care plans.[11] Only one contraceptive option offers women safe and fully effective birth control: barrier methods with the back-up option of abortion.[12]

From a feminist perspective, the central moral feature of pregnancy is that it takes place in women's bodies and has profound effects on women's lives. Gender-neutral accounts of pregnancy are not available; pregnancy is explicitly a condition associated with the female body.[13] Because only women experience a need for abortion, policies about abortion affect women uniquely. Therefore, it is important to consider how proposed policies on abortion fit into general patterns of oppression for women. Unlike nonfeminist accounts, feminist ethics demands that the effects of abortion policies on the oppression of women be of principal consideration in our ethical evaluations.

The Fetus

In contrast to feminist ethics, most nonfeminist analysts believe that the moral acceptability of abortion turns entirely on the question of the moral status of the fetus. Even those who support women's right to choose abortion tend to accept the premise of the antiabortion proponents that abortion can be tolerated only if we can first prove that the fetus lacks full personhood.[14] Opponents of abortion demand that we define the status of the fetus either as a being that is valued in the same way as other humans and hence is entitled not to be killed or as a being that lacks in all value. Rather than challenging the logic of this formulation, many defenders of abortion have concentrated on showing that the fetus is indeed without significant value (Tooley 1972, Warren 1973); others, such as L. W. Sumner (1981), offer a more subtle account that reflects the gradual development of fetuses and distinguishes between early fetal stages, where the relevant criterion for personhood is absent, and later stages, where it is present. Thus the debate often rages between abortion opponents, who describe the fetus as an "innocent," vulnerable, morally important, separate being whose life is threatened and who must be protected at all costs, and abortion supporters, who try to establish that fetuses are deficient in some critical respect and hence are outside the scope of the moral community. In both cases, however, the nature of the fetus as an independent being is said to determine the moral status of abortion.

The woman on whom the fetus depends for survival is considered as secondary (if she is considered at all) in these debates. The actual experiences and responsibilities of real women are not perceived as morally relevant to the debate, unless these women too, can be proved innocent by establishing that their pregnancies are a result of rape or incest.[15] In some contexts, women's role in gestation is literally reduced to that of "fetal containers"; the individual women disappear or are perceived simply as mechanical life-support systems.[16]

The current rhetoric against abortion stresses that the genetic makeup of the fetus is determined at conception and the genetic code is incontestably human. Lest there be any doubt about the humanity of the fetus, we are assailed with photographs of fetuses at various stages of development that demonstrate the early appearance of recognizably human characteristics, such as eyes, fingers, and toes. Modern ultrasound technology is used to obtain "baby's first picture" and stimulate bonding between pregnant women and their fetuses (Petchesky 1987). That the fetus in its early stages is microscopic, virtually indistinguishable to the untrained eye from fetuses of other species, and lacking in the capacities that make human life meaningful and valuable is not deemed relevant by the self-appointed defenders of the fetus. The antiabortion campaign is directed at evoking sympathetic attitudes toward a tiny, helpless being whose life is threatened by its own mother; the fetus is characterized as a being entangled in an adversarial relationship with the (presumably irresponsible) woman who carries it (Overall 1987). People are encouraged to identify with the "unborn child," not with the woman whose life is also at issue.

In the nonfeminist literature, both defenders and opponents of women's right to choose abortion agree that the difference between a late-term fetus and a newborn infant is "merely geographical" and cannot be considered morally significant. Daniel Callahan (1986), for instance, maintains a pro-choice stand but professes increasing uneasiness about this position in light of new medical and scientific developments that increase our knowledge of embryology and hasten the date of potential viability for fetuses; he insists that defenders of women's right to choose must come to terms with the question of the fetus and the effects of science on the fetus's prospects apart from the woman who carries it. Arguments that focus on the similarities between infants and fetuses, however, generally fail to acknowledge that a fetus inhabits a woman's body and is wholly dependent on her unique contribution to its maintenance, whereas a newborn is physically independent, although still in need of a lot of care.[17] One can only view the distinction between being in or out of a woman's womb as morally irrelevant if one discounts the perspective of the pregnant woman; feminists seem to be alone in recognizing the woman's perspective as morally important to the distinction.[18]

In antiabortion arguments, fetuses are identified as individuals; in our culture, which views the (abstract) individual as sacred, fetuses qua individuals are to be honored and preserved. Extraordinary claims are made to establish the individuality and moral agency of fetuses. At the same time, the women who carry these fetal individuals are viewed as passive hosts whose only significant role is to refrain from aborting or harming their fetuses. Because it is widely believed that a woman does not actually have to do anything to protect the life of her fetus, pregnancy is often considered (abstractly) to be a tolerable burden to protect the life of an individual so like us.[19]

Medicine has played its part in supporting these attitudes. Fetal medicine is a rapidly expanding specialty, and it is commonplace in professional medical journals to find references to pregnant women as "the maternal environment." Fetal surgeons now have at their disposal a repertoire of sophisticated technology that can save the lives of dangerously ill fetuses; in light of the excitement of such heroic successes, it is perhaps understandable that women have disappeared from their view. These specialists see the fetuses as their patients, not the women who nurture the fetuses. As the "active" agents in saving fetal lives (unlike the pregnant women, whose role is seen as purely passive), doctors perceive themselves as developing independent relationships with the fetuses they treat. Barbara Katz Rothman observes: "The medical model of pregnancy, as an essentially parasitic and vaguely pathological relationship, encourages the physician to view the fetus and mother as two separate patients, and to see pregnancy as inherently a conflict of interests between the two" (Rothman 1986, 25).

Perhaps even more distressing than the tendency to ignore the woman's agency altogether and view her as a passive participant in the medically controlled events of pregnancy and childbirth is the growing practice of viewing women as genuine threats to the well-being of the fetus. Increasingly, women are described as irresponsible or hostile toward their fetuses, and the relationship between them is characterized as adversarial. Concern for the well-being of the fetus is taken as license for doctors to intervene to ensure that women comply with medical "advice." Courts are called upon to enforce the doctors' orders when moral pressure alone proves inadequate, and women are being coerced into undergoing unwanted cesarean deliveries and technologically monitored hospital births (Annas 1982; Rodgers 1989; Nelson and Milliken 1990). Some states have begun to imprison women for endangering their fetuses through drug abuse and other socially unacceptable behaviors (Annas 1986). Mary Anne Warren reports that a bill was recently introduced in an Australian state that makes women liable to criminal prosecution "if they are found to have smoked during pregnancy, eaten unhealthful foods, or taken any other action which can be shown to have adversely affected the development of the fetus" (Warren 1989, 60).

In other words, some physicians have joined antiabortion campaigners in fostering a cultural acceptance of the view that fetuses are distinct individuals who are physically, ontologically, and socially separate from the women whose bodies they inhabit and that they have their own distinct interests. In this picture, pregnant women are either ignored altogether or are viewed as deficient in some crucial respect, and hence they can be subject to coercion for the sake of their fetuses. In the former case, the interests of the women concerned are assumed to be identical with those of the fetus; in the latter, the women's interests are irrelevant, because they are perceived as immoral, unimportant, or unnatural. Focus on the fetus as an independent entity has led to presumptions that deny pregnant women their roles as active, independent, moral agents with a primary interest in what becomes of the fetuses they carry. The moral question of the fetus's status is quickly translated into a license to interfere with women's reproductive freedom.

A Feminist View of the Fetus

Because the public debate has been set up as a competition between the rights of women and those of fetuses, feminists have often felt pushed to reject claims of fetal value, in order to protect women's needs. As Kathryn Addelson (1987) has argued, however, viewing abortion in this way "rips it out of the context of women's lives." Other accounts of fetal value are more plausible and less oppressive to women.

On a feminist account fetal development is examined in the context in which it occurs, within women's bodies, rather than in the isolation of imagined abstraction. Fetuses develop in specific pregnancies that occur in the lives of particular women. They are not individuals housed in generic female wombs or full persons at risk only because they are small and subject to the whims of women. Their very existence is relationally defined, reflecting their development within particular women's bodies; that relationship gives those women reason to be concerned about them. Many feminists argue against a perspective that regards the fetus as an independent being and suggest that a more accurate and valuable understanding of pregnancy would involve regarding the pregnant woman "as a biological and social unit" (Rothman 1986, 25).

On this view, fetuses are morally significant, but their status is relational rather than absolute. Unlike other human beings, fetuses do not have any independent existence; their existence is uniquely tied to the support of a specific other. Most nonfeminist accounts have ignored the relational dimension of fetal development and have presumed that the moral status of fetuses could be resolved solely in terms of abstract, metaphysical criteria of personhood as applied to the fetus alone (Tooley 1972; Warren 1973). Throughout much of the nonfeminist literature, commentators argue that some set of properties (such as genetic heritage, moral agency, self-consciousness, language use, or self-determination) will entitle all who possess it to be granted the moral status of persons. They seek some feature by which we can neatly divide the world into moral persons (who are to be valued and protected) and others (who are not entitled to the same group privileges).

This vision, however, misinterprets what is involved in personhood and what is especially valued about persons. Personhood is a social category, not an isolated state. Persons are members of a community, and they should be valued in their concrete, discrete, and different states as specific individuals, not merely as conceptually undifferentiated entities. To be a morally significant category, personhood must involve personality as well as biological integrity.[20] It is not sufficient to consider persons simply as Kantian atoms of rationality, because persons are embodied, conscious beings with particular social histories. Annette Baier has developed a concept of persons as "second persons," which helps explain the sort of social dimension that seems fundamental to any moral notion of personhood:

> A person, perhaps, is best seen as one who was long enough dependent upon other persons to acquire the essential arts of personhood. Persons essentially are *second* persons, who grow up with other persons. . . .
> The fact that a person has a life *history*, and that a people collectively have a history depends upon the humbler fact that each person has a childhood in which a cultural heritage is transmitted, ready for adolescent rejection and adult discriminating selection and contribution. Persons come after and before other persons (Baier 1985: 84–5).

Persons, in other words, are members of a social community that shapes and values them, and personhood is a relational concept that must be defined in terms of interactions and relationships with others.[21]

Because humans are fundamentally relational beings, it is important to remember that fetuses are characteristically limited in the "relationships" in which they can "participate"; within those relationships, they can make only the most restricted "contributions."[22] After birth human beings are capable of a much wider range of roles in relationships with a broad variety of partners; that very diversity of possibility and experience leads us to focus on the abstraction of the individual as a constant through all these different relationships. Until birth, however, no such variety is possible, so the fetus must be understood as part of a complex entity that includes the woman who currently sustains the fetus and who will, most likely, be principally responsible for it for many years to come.

A fetus is a unique sort of human entity, then, for it cannot form relationships freely with others, and others cannot readily form relationships with it. A fetus has a primary and particularly intimate sort of "relationship" with the woman in whose womb it develops; connections with any other persons are necessarily indirect and must be mediated through the pregnant woman. The relationship that exists between a woman and her fetus is clearly asymmetrical, because she is the only party to it who is capable of even considering whether the interaction should continue; further, the fetus is wholly dependent on the woman who sustains it, whereas she is quite capable of surviving without it.

Most feminist views of what is valuable about persons reflect the social nature of individual existence. No human, especially no fetus, can exist apart from relationships; efforts to speak of the fetus itself, as if it were not inseparable from the woman in whom it develops, are distorting and dishonest. Fetuses have a unique physical status—within and dependent on particular women. That gives them also a unique social status. However much some might prefer it to be otherwise, no one other than the pregnant woman in question can do anything to support or harm a fetus without doing something to the woman who nurtures it. Because of this inexorable biological reality, the responsibility and privilege of determining a fetus's specific social status and value must rest with the woman carrying it.

Many pregnancies occur to women who place a very high value on the lives of the particular fetuses they carry and choose to see their pregnancies through to term, despite the possible risks and costs involved; it would be wrong of anyone to force such a woman to terminate her pregnancy. Other women, or some of these same women at other times, value other things more highly (for example, their freedom, their health, or previous responsibilities that conflict with those generated by the pregnancies), and so they choose not to continue their pregnancies. The value that women ascribe to individual fetuses varies dramatically from case to case and may well change over the course of any particular pregnancy. The fact that fetal lives can neither be sustained nor destroyed without affecting the women who support them implies that whatever value others may attach to fetuses generally or to specific fetuses individually should not be allowed to outweigh the ranking that is assigned to them by the pregnant women themselves.

No absolute value attaches to fetuses apart from their relational status, which is determined in the context of their particular development. This is not the same, however, as saying that they have no value at all or that they have merely instrumental value, as some liberals suggest. The value that women place on their own fetuses is the sort of value that attaches to an emerging human relationship.

Nevertheless, fetuses are not persons, because they have not developed sufficiently in their capacity for social relationships to be persons in any morally significant sense (that is, they are not yet second persons). In this way they differ from newborns, who immediately begin to develop into persons by virtue of their place as subjects in human relationships; newborns are capable of some forms of communication and response. The moral status of fetuses is determined by the nature of their primary relationship and the value that is created there. Therefore, feminist accounts of abortion emphasize the importance of protecting women's rights to continue or to terminate pregnancies as each sees fit.

The Politics of Abortion

Feminist accounts explore the connections between particular social policies and the general patterns of power relationships in our society. With respect to abortion in this framework, Mary Daly observes that "one hundred percent of the bishops who oppose the repeal of antiabortion laws are men and one hundred percent of the people who have abortions are women. . . . To be comprehended accurately, they [arguments against abortion] must be seen within the context of sexually hierarchical society" (Daly 1973, 106).

Antiabortion activists appeal to arguments about the unconditional value of human life. When we examine their rhetoric more closely, however, we find other ways of interpreting their agenda. In addition to their campaign to criminalize abortion, most abortion opponents condemn all forms of sexual relations outside of heterosexual marriage, and they tend to support patriarchal patterns of dominance within such marriages. Many are distressed that liberal abortion policies support permissive sexuality by allowing women to "get away with" sex outside of marriage. They perceive that ready access to abortion supports women's independence from men.[23]

Although nonfeminist participants in the abortion debates often discount the significance of its broader political dimensions, both feminists and antifeminists consider them crucial. The intensity of the antiabortion movement correlates closely with the increasing strength of feminism in achieving greater equality for women. The original American campaign against abortion can be traced to the middle of the nineteenth century, that is, to the time of the first significant feminist movement in the United States (Luker 1984). Today abortion is widely perceived as supportive of increased freedom and power for women. The campaign against abortion intensified in the 1970s, which was a period of renewed interest in feminism. As Rosalind Petchesky observes, the campaign rested on some powerful symbols: "To feminists and antifeminists alike, it came to represent the image of the 'emancipated woman' in her contemporary identity, focused on her education and work more than on marriage or childbearing; sexually active outside marriage and outside the disciplinary boundaries of the parental family; independently supporting herself and her children; and consciously espousing feminist ideas" (Petchesky 1984, 241). Clearly, much more than the lives of fetuses is at stake in the power struggle over abortion.

When we place abortion in the larger political context, we see that most of the groups active in the struggle to prohibit abortion also support other conservative measures to maintain the forms of dominance that characterize patriarchy (and often class and racial oppression as well). The movement against abortion is led by the Catholic church and other conservative religious institutions, which explicitly endorse not only fetal rights but also male dominance in the home and the church. Most opponents of abortion also oppose virtually all forms of birth control and all forms of sexuality other than monogamous, reproductive sex; usually, they also resist having women assume positions of authority in the dominant public institutions (Luker 1984). Typically, antiabortion activists support conservative economic measures that protect the interests of the privileged classes of society and ignore the needs of the oppressed and disadvantaged (Petchesky 1985). Although they stress their commitment to preserving life, many systematically work to dismantle key social programs that provide life necessities to the underclass. Moreover, some current campaigns against abortion retain elements of the racism that dominated the North American abortion literature in the early years of the twentieth century, wherein abortion was opposed on the grounds that it amounted to racial suicide on the part of whites.[24]

In the eyes of its principal opponents, then, abortion is not an isolated practice; their opposition to abortion is central to a set of social values that runs counter to feminism's objectives. Hence antiabortion activists generally do not offer alternatives to abortion that support feminist interests in overturning the patterns of oppression that confront women. Most deny that there are any legitimate grounds for abortion, short of the need to save a woman's life—and some are not even persuaded by this criterion (Nicholson 1977). They believe that any pregnancy can and should be endured. If the mother is unable or unwilling to care for the child after birth, then they assume that adoption can be easily arranged.

It is doubtful, however, that adoptions are possible for every child whose mother cannot care for it. The world abounds with homeless orphans; even in the industrialized West, where there is a waiting list for adoption of healthy (white) babies, suitable homes cannot always be found for troubled adolescents; inner-city, AIDS babies, or many of the multiply handicapped children whose parents may have tried to care for them but whose marriages broke under the strain.

Furthermore, even if an infant were born healthy and could be readily adopted, we must recognize that surrendering one's child for adoption is an extremely difficult act for most women. The bond that commonly forms between women and their fetuses over the full term of pregnancy is intimate and often intense; many women find that it is not easily broken after birth. Psychologically, for many women adoption is a far more difficult response to unwanted pregnancies than abortion. Therefore, it is misleading to describe pregnancy as merely a nine-month commitment; for most women, seeing a pregnancy through to term involves a lifetime of responsibility and involvement with the resulting child and, in the overwhelming majority of cases, disproportionate burden on the woman through the child-rearing years. An ethics that cares about women would recognize that abortion is often the only acceptable recourse for them.

Expanding the Agenda

The injunction of feminist ethics to consider abortion in the context of other issues of power and oppression means that we need to look beyond the standard questions of its moral and legal acceptability. This implies, for instance, that we need to explore the moral imperatives of ensuring that abortion services are actually available to all women who seek them. Although medically approved abortions are technically recognized as legal (at least for the moment) in both Canada and the United States, many women who need abortions cannot obtain them; accessibility is still associated with wealth and privilege in many regions.[25] In Canada vast geographical areas offer no abortion services at all, so unless the women of those regions can afford to travel to urban clinics, they have no meaningful right to abortion. In the United States, where there is no universal health insurance, federal legislation (under the Hyde amendment) explicitly denies the use of public money for abortions. Full ethical discussion of abortion reveals the necessity of removing the economic, age, and racial barriers that currently restrict access to medically acceptable abortion services.[26]

The moral issues extend yet further. Feminism demands respect for women's choices; even if the legal and financial barriers could be surpassed, this condition may remain unmet. The focus of many political campaigns for abortion rights has been to make abortion a matter of medical, not personal, choice, suggesting that doctors (but not necessarily women) can be trusted to choose responsibly. Feminists must insist on respect for women's moral agency. Therefore, feminism requires that abortion services be provided in an atmosphere that is supportive of the choices that women make. This could be achieved by offering abortions in centers that deal with all matters of reproductive health in an open, patient-centered manner, where respectful counseling on all aspects of reproductive health is available.[27]

Furthermore, the moral issues surrounding abortion include questions of how women are treated when they seek abortions. All too frequently hospital-based abortions are provided by practitioners who are uneasy about their role and treat the women involved with hostility and resentment.[28] Health care workers involved in providing abortions must recognize that abortion is a legitimate option that should be carried out with respect and concern for the physical, psychological, and emotional well-being of the patient. In addition, we need to turn our moral attention to the effects of antiabortion protests on women. Increasingly, many antiabortion activists have personalized their attacks and focused their energies on harassing the women who enter and leave abortion clinics, thereby requiring them to pass a gauntlet of hostile protesters to obtain abortions. Such arrangements are not conducive to positive health care, so these protests, too, must be subject to moral criticism within the ethics of health care.

Feminist ethics promotes the value of reproductive freedom, which is defined as the condition under which women are able to make truly voluntary choices about their reproductive lives. Women must have control over their reproduction if patriarchal dominance over women is to be brought to an end. In addition to reliable and caring abortion services, then, women also need access to safe and effective birth control, which would provide them with other means of avoiding pregnancy.[29]

Moreover, we must raise questions about the politics of sexual domination in this context. Many men support women's right to abortion because they perceive that if women believe that they can engage in intercourse without having to accept an unwanted pregnancy, they will become more sexually available. Some of the women who oppose abortion resist it for this very reason; they do not want to support a practice that increases women's sexual vulnerability. Feminists need to develop an analysis of reproductive freedom that includes sexual freedom as it is defined by women, not men. Such an analysis would, for example, include women's right to refuse sex. Because this right can only be assured if women have power equal to men's and are not subject to domination because of their sex, women's freedom from oppression is itself an element of reproductive freedom.

Finally, it is important to stress that feminist accounts do not deny that fetuses have value. They ask that fetuses be recognized as existing within women's pregnancies and not as separate, isolated entities. Feminists positively value fetuses that are wanted by the women who carry them; they vigorously oppose practices that force women to have abortions they do not want. No women should be subjected to coerced abortion or sterilization. Women must be assured of adequate financial and support services for the care of their children, so that they are not forced to abort fetuses that they would otherwise choose to carry. Further, voluntarily pregnant women should have access to suitable pre- and postnatal care and nutrition, lest wanted fetuses be unnecessarily harmed or lost.

Feminists perceive that far more could be done to protect and care for fetuses if the state directed its resources toward supporting women who choose to continue their pregnancies, rather than draining those resources to police the women who try to terminate undesired pregnancies. Unlike their conservative counterparts, feminists recognize that caring for the women who maintain the lives of fetuses is not only a more legitimate policy than is regulating them but also probably more effective at ensuring the health and well-being of more fetuses and, ultimately, of more infants.

In sum, then, feminist ethics demands that moral discussions of abortion reflect a broader agenda than is usually found in the arguments put forth by bioethicists. Only by reflecting on the meaning of ethical pronouncements on actual women's lives and the connections that exist between judgments on abortion and the conditions of domination and subordination can we come to an adequate understanding of the moral status of abortion in a particular society.

6

New Reproductive Technologies

New technologies in human reproduction have provoked wide-ranging arguments about their desirability and moral justifiability. Authors in the fields of both bioethics and feminist ethics have been active participants in public policy debates on the implementation of these technologies and related practices. Once again, there are striking differences in the focus of the arguments as they are presented by feminist ethicists and by their counterparts among nonfeminist medical ethicists: feminist writers see reproductive practices as having very broad social implications, but most nonfeminist commentators have adopted a comparatively narrow perspective on the topic. In this chapter I shall show why I believe it is necessary to incorporate an explicitly feminist analysis into ethical evaluations of the various reproductive technologies.

Although public attention focuses on a few sophisticated and dramatic innovations in the area of reproductive control, the category of reproductive technologies is broad and has a long and interesting history. It includes the full range of means that have been employed or pursued to gain control over human reproduction from conception through to birth. We can consider this label to include the various measures and devices that are used to monitor and sometimes intervene in pregnancy and birth, such as ultrasound, electronic fetal monitors, and surgical deliveries. It also encompasses the means that are pursued to prevent or terminate unwanted pregnancies (contraception and abortion).

Most commonly, the label of "new reproductive technologies" is applied to a variety of techniques that are employed to facilitate conception or to control the quality of fetuses that are produced, including such increasingly common practices as artificial insemination, ova and embryo donation, in vitro fertilization (IVF), gamete intra-fallopian transfer (GIFT), embryo freezing, prenatal screening, and sex preselection. Included among the technologies now emerging or still on the horizon are embryo flushing for genetic inspection or transfer to another woman's womb, genetic surgery, cloning, and ec-togenesis (fetal development wholly in an artificial womb). Other practices, such as racial eugenic planning or contractual pregnancy (so-called surrogate mothering), are sometimes also raised in this con-text; although they need not involve any specific use of new technol-ogy, they pose some of the same social and political issues that arise in conjunction with some of the techniques of reproductive technol-ogy. Almost all of the reproductive technologies are carried out on women or on the fetuses they carry.

Private versus Public Interests

Complex cultural attitudes toward both technology and reproduction shape the meanings and values that the various reproductive technologies carry in our society. In evaluating a partic-ular technology in this area, it is important to consider its place within the vast network of measures that have been designed to con-trol human reproduction. The degree and extent of possible human manipulation of reproduction is rapidly expanding, but it is useful to remember that the desire to control reproduction is a long-standing one in human history. Therefore, it is especially significant that the new forms of reproductive technology promise a much greater scope for the direction and management of reproduction than has ever been possible before.

Although both technological and reproductive choices are usually placed in the sphere of private decision-making, feminist methodol-ogy directs us to evaluate practices within the broader scheme of op-pressive social structures. Therefore, the ethical evaluation of repro-ductive technologies requires us to ask questions about their social, political, and economic effects, in addition to questions about their place in the lives of those individuals who seek to use them. After all, reproductive practices carry profound social as well as private impli-cations.

The pursuit of technological intervention in reproduction is part of a larger general pattern in our society in which a search for technological solutions is often the first response to the recognition of human problems—a commitment that Barbara Wright has dubbed "technophilia" (Wright 1989, 13). Kathryn Ratcliff (1989) observes that medicine is a discipline particularly oriented toward the use of technology (what she calls "technological favoritism"), because medical education, public policy, and the profit motive combine to ensure that technological innovation is seen as the measure of medical progress. In a technophilic society such as ours, specific problems generate technological solutions, which are then marketed wherever they may be put to use. Decisions about implementation are usually left in the hands of those individuals who are directly involved, even though the use of a new technology often involves consequences that extend far beyond its immediate intended effects.

Elisabeth Beck-Gernsheim (1989) argues that a common pattern of evolution seems to govern the use of new forms of medical technology. They usually begin as innocent contributions to specific health problems, but they often end up with a nearly universal, coercive application to the population (for example, electronic fetal monitors and ultrasound). There is already evidence that some clinicians envisage such an extension for some of the more sophisticated forms of reproductive technologies, such as prenatal screening and IVF (Klein 1989). Thus many (perhaps even most) women—not just those who choose to make use of the new reproductive technologies—eventually may find themselves directly affected by the development and implementation of some of these technologies. Private decision-making cannot be sufficient for evaluating a new reproductive technology if its introduction is likely to produce political, social, and economic changes beyond its effects on specific users.

Within the sphere of technologies involving human reproduction, it is particularly important to explore the possibility that they will bring about profound cultural change. Because effective forms of reproductive technology increase the possibilities for human intervention in reproduction, they create opportunities for greater power in the hands of whoever controls that technology. Throughout history, those who have been in positions of power and authority have sought to exercise their power over the sexual and reproductive lives of the less powerful: for example, among the powers that Plato reserved for the philosopher-kings of the republic was the authority to arrange the

reproductive pairings for all classes, and in the American South slave-
holders bred their slaves as they did their livestock. Through this
century, legislators and religious leaders have tried to restrict sexual
activity to married partners by such means as declaring sex outside of
marriage to be illicit, labeling as "whores" the women who participated in extramarital sex (and making such labels sting by devaluing
the humanity of prostitutes), and classifying any offspring produced
through such unauthorized unions as illegitimate. Until quite recently, the male-dominated medical, religious, and legal communities conspired to keep contraceptive knowledge from women.[1] Even
in this century, when contraceptive information is more widely available than ever before, economic factors serve to restrict the poor from
access to the means of personal control over conception.[2] In much of
the developing world, contraception is governed by policies of population control where control and choice belong to the state, not to the
women concerned (Duggan 1986; LaCheen 1986; Yanoshik and
Norsigan 1989).

Although the new reproductive technologies can provide individuals with greater power to determine their own procreative choices,[3]
actual control may belong to others. It is, therefore, extremely important that in evaluating each practice we be clear about where that
control will actually reside. Each reproductive technology presents its
own risks and benefits and demands its own evaluation with regard to
its place within the general scheme of technologically controlled reproduction; some technologies will prove to be socially desirable,
whereas others will not.

In the struggle to decide on public policy regarding the various
innovations in reproductive technology, authors in the medical ethics
and feminist traditions have differed dramatically in their conceptions
of how the discussion should be constituted. I shall take a detailed
look at the debate surrounding one form of reproductive technology,
IVF, to show the contrast between feminist and nonfeminist approaches to bioethics and to give some indication of the importance
of evaluating these technologies from the perspective of feminist
ethics. Because it is the most widely discussed of the new reproductive technologies, IVF offers a particularly clear example of the difference in emphasis found in the approaches of feminist and nonfeminist bioethicists.

IVF in Bioethics Literature   IVF

IVF is the technology responsible for what the media likes to call "test-tube babies." It attempts to circumvent, rather than cure, a variety of barriers to conception, primarily those of blocked fallopian tubes and low sperm counts. Several stages make up the complex technology of IVF: artificial hormones are administered to stimulate the ovaries to release eggs; the released ova are removed from the woman's body (usually by a surgical procedure known as laparoscopy, although newer, less dangerous techniques of vaginal access are being pursued); semen is collected from the woman's partner (or, more rarely, from an anonymous donor) through masturbation, and the sperm is "washed"; the ova and sperm are then combined to promote fertilization. If all has gone according to plan, then some number of the newly fertilized eggs are transferred directly into the woman's womb, with the hope that one will implant itself in the uterus and pregnancy will continue normally from this point on.[4] This procedure requires that a variety of hormones be administered to the woman (often leading to dramatic emotional and physical changes), that her blood and urine be monitored daily at three-hour intervals, and that the extremely uncomfortable procedure of ultrasound be used to determine when ovulation occurs. In some programs the woman is required to remain immobile for forty-eight hours after the fertilized eggs are introduced to her womb (including up to twenty-four hours in the head-down position). The procedure may fail at any point and, in the majority of cases, it does. Most women undergo multiple attempts and may be dropped from the program at any time. Although many practitioners of IVF have tried to obscure the information, IVF is, at best, successful in 10 to 15 percent of the cases selected as suitable.[5]

The issues that bioethicists have judged important in evaluating IVF and other methods of laboratory controlled conception (such as artificial insemination) vary with the philosophic traditions of the authors. Those who adopt a theological perspective tend to object to all forms of reproductive technology, on the grounds that they are not "natural" and undermine God's plan for the family. Paul Ramsey, for instance, is concerned about the artificiality of IVF and other sorts of reproductive technology with which it is potentially associated:

"There is as yet no discernable evidence that we are recovering a sense for man [sic] as a natural object . . . toward whom a . . . form of "natural piety" is appropriate. . . . Parenthood is certainly one of those "courses of action" natural to man, which cannot without violation be disassembled and put together again" (Ramsey 1972, 220).

Leon Kass argues a similar line in "'Making Babies' Revisited" (Kass 1979). He worries that our conception of humanness will not survive the technological permutations before us and that we will treat these artificially conceived embryos more as objects than as subjects; he also fears that we will be unable to track traditional human categories of parenthood and lineage and that this loss will cause us to lose track of important aspects of our identity.

Philosophers in the secular tradition prefer a more scientific approach; they treat these sorts of concerns as sheer superstition. They carefully explain to their theological colleagues that there is no clear sense of what is "natural," and no sense that demands special moral status. All medical activity, and perhaps all human activity, can be seen in some sense as being "interference with nature," but that is hardly grounds for avoiding such action. "Humanness," too, they point out, is a concept that admits many interpretations; generally, it does not provide satisfactory grounds for moral distinctions of the sorts that Ramsey and Kass propose.

Where some theologians object that "fertilization achieved outside the bodies of the couple remains by this very fact deprived of the meanings of the values which are expressed in the language of the body and in the union of human persons" (Ratzinger and Bovone 1987, 28), secular philosophers quickly dismiss objections against reproduction that occurs without sexuality in a properly sanctified marriage. For instance, Michael Bayles argues that "even if reproduction should occur only within a context of marital love, the point of that requirement is the nurturance of offspring. Such nurturance does not depend on the sexual act itself. The argument confuses the biological act with the familial context" (Bayles 1984, 15).

IVF is a complex technology involving research on superovulation, "harvesting" of ova, fertilization, and embryo implants. It is readily adaptable to technology that requires the transfer of ova and embryos, and hence their donation or sale, as well as to programs for the "rental of womb space"; it also contributes to an increasing ability to foster fetal growth outside of the womb and, potentially, to the development of artificial wombs covering the whole period of gestation. IVF is sometimes combined with artificial insemination and is frequently used to produce "surplus" fertilized eggs, whose moral status is in doubt. Theological ethicists worry that these activities and further reproductive developments that we can now anticipate (for example, human cloning) violate God's plan for human reproduction. They worry about the cultural shift that occurs when we view reproduction as a scientific enterprise, rather than as the "miracle of love" that religious proponents prefer: "[a child] cannot be desired or conceived as the product of an intervention of medical or biological techniques; that would be equivalent to reducing him [*sic*] to an object of scientific technology" (Ratzinger and Bovone 1987, 28). Moreover, they are concerned that we cannot anticipate the ultimate outcome of this rapidly expanding technology; they fear that it leaves us balancing precariously on a slippery slope, in danger of sliding down into yet more troubling practices.

The where-will-it-all-end hand-wringing that comes with this sort of religious futurology is rejected by most secular philosophers; they urge us to realize that few slopes are as slippery as the pessimists would have us believe. In their experience, scientists are moral people and quite capable of evaluating each new form of technology on its own merits. Hence, they argue, IVF must be judged by its own consequences and not the possible result of some future technology with which it may be linked. Samuel Gorovitz is typical of the secular philosophers: "It is not enough to show that disaster awaits if the process is not controlled. A man walking East in Omaha will drown in the Atlantic—if he does not stop. The argument must also rest on the evidence about the likelihood that judgement and control will be exercised responsibly. . . . Collectively we have significant capacity to exercise judgment and control. . . . Our record has been rather good in regard to medical treatment and research" (Gorovitz 1982, 168).

The question of the moral status of the fertilized eggs is another area of controversy for some critics. Superovulation is chemically induced to produce multiple eggs for collection, because the process of collecting eggs is so difficult and the odds against conception on any given attempt are very slim. Therefore, several eggs are usually fertilized at once. A number of these fertilized eggs will be introduced to the womb with the hope that at least one will implant and gestation will begin, but there are frequently some "extras" produced. Moral problems arise as to what should be done with these surplus eggs. They can be frozen for future use; alternatively, they can be donated to other women who cannot produce viable or genetically acceptable eggs, used as research material, or simply discarded. Many clinics are ambivalent about the moral status of these developing embryos, and some choose to deal with the problem by putting them all into the woman's womb or by limiting the numbers of available eggs that are collected. The former option poses the devastating threat of four or more eggs "successfully" implanting and a woman being put into the position of carrying a litter—something her body is not constructed to do.[6] The latter option risks not collecting sufficient eggs to guarantee successful fertilization of some.

Those who take a hard line against abortion and argue that the embryo is a person from the moment of conception object to all these procedures, because each places the fertilized egg at risk and treats it merely as an object; hence, they argue, there is no morally acceptable means of conducting IVF. Nonreligious theorists offer the standard responses to this argument: personhood involves moral, not biological, categories, so a being neither sentient nor conscious is not a person in any meaningful sense. For example, Gorovitz argues: "Surely the concept of person involves in some fundamental way the capacity for sentience, or an awareness of sensations at the very least" (Gorovitz 1982, 173). Bayles says: "For fetuses to have moral status they must be capable of good or bad in their lives. . . . What happens to them must make a difference to them. Consequently some form of awareness is necessary for moral status" (Bayles 1984, 66). Fertilized eggs (which are now called "pre-embryos" by clinicians who are eager to establish their ontological status as distinct from that of embryos and fetuses) do not meet such criteria of consciousness.

Many bioethicists have agreed here, as they have in the abortion debate, that the principal moral question of IVF concerns the moral status and rights of the (pre-)embryo. Once they resolve that question, they can, like H. Tristram Englehardt, Jr., conclude that because fetuses and their precursors are not persons and because reproductive processes occurring outside a human body pose no special moral problems, "there will be no sustainable moral arguments in principle . . . against in vitro fertilization" (Englehardt 1986, 237). He argues that "in vitro fertilization and techniques that will allow us to study and control human reproduction are morally neutral instruments for the realization of profoundly important human goals, which are bound up with the realization of the good of others: children for infertile parents and greater health for the children that will be born" (Englehardt 1986, 241).

Nonfeminist moral theorists do express worries about the safety of the process, by which they tend to mean the safety to fetuses with regard to this technique; although there is evidence of a higher incidence of birth complications and defects among IVF-produced fetuses, most bioethicists conclude that the practice is safe enough.[7] There is no mention in their discussions of the dangerous side effects that IVF poses for women. The bioethics literature has not considered the chemical similarities between clomid, an artificial hormone that is commonly used to increase women's rate of ovulation, and DES, a drug that has belatedly been implicated as carcinogenic for the offspring of women who were prescribed it decades before.[8] The uncertainties surrounding superovulation and use of ultrasound and the dangers associated with administering a general anesthetic for egg collection and embryo transfer have not been deemed worthy of attention in the nonfeminist bioethics literature. Women who do succeed in achieving and sustaining pregnancies through this method experience a very high rate of surgical births, but those risks also are generally ignored.[9] Furthermore, most ethical discussions do not explore the significant emotional costs for women that are associated with this therapy. To date, only feminists have raised these issues.

Having disposed of the religious objections, most bioethicists in the secular tradition conclude that the focus of discussion should be on the values of patient autonomy and individual rights. Most judge IVF to be simply a private matter, to be decided upon by the couple concerned in consultation with a medical specialist. The desire to have and raise children is a common one; it is generally thought of as a paradigm case of a purely private subject. Because, for most people, conception is automatically a matter of private choice (or accident), bioethicists generally argue that "it would be unfair to make infertile couples pass up the joys of rearing infants or suffer the burdens of rearing handicapped children" (Bayles 1984, 32). Concern for the desires or needs of individuals is the most widely accepted argument in favor of the use of this technology.

What is left, then, in most of the nonfeminist discussions of IVF, is usually some hand-waving about costs. For instance, Gorovitz says:

"There is the question of the distribution of costs, a question that has heightened impact if we consider the use of public funds to pay for medical treatment" (Gorovitz 1982, 177). IVF is an extremely expensive (and profitable) procedure, costing several thousand dollars per attempt. Because it is often not covered by public or private health plans, it is financially inaccessible for most infertile couples.[10] Discussion in the nonfeminist forum generally ends here, in the mystery of how to balance soaring medical costs, with the added comment that IVF poses no new ethical problems.

The Feminist Perspective

A widening of perspective to include all the effects of IVF and other reproductive technologies on the women involved is called for in bioethical evaluations. In theory, mainstream approaches to bioethics could accommodate such concerns, should the philosophers involved think to look for them, and it is significant that, for the most part, they do not appear to have perceived them.

Like their nonfeminist counterparts in bioethics, most feminists are concerned to promote personal freedom. Feminists have a long history of supporting the protection of personal reproductive control in the areas of abortion and contraception. As I argued in Chapter 5, women's ability to avoid unwanted pregnancies is both personally and politically important. There is a distinction to be drawn between voluntary and involuntary childlessness, however, for where the former is desired, involuntary childlessness can be devastating in specific lives. From the point of view of those whose infertility is involuntary, IVF is likely to be positively valued, because it holds the promise of increasing their own reproductive freedom. Any public policy that restricts access to this technology will be experienced by those in search of relief for their childless condition as a serious interference with their personal reproductive freedom.

Indeed, most arguments in support of IVF are based on appeals to the rights of the individual to choose such technology. Feminists urge us to look carefully at these autonomy-based arguments, however, because as IVF is usually practiced, it does not altogether satisfy the motivation of fostering personal freedom. Like many other forms of reproductive technology, IVF is controlled by medical specialists and not by the women who seek it. It is not made available to every woman who is medically suitable but only to those who have been judged worthy by the designated medical practitioners. In almost every clinic a woman is considered eligible for this procedure only if she is involved in a stable (preferably married) relationship with a male partner. A couple must satisfy the specialists in charge that they have appropriate resources to support any children produced by this arrangement (in addition to the funds required to purchase the treatment in the first place), and they must demonstrate that they genuinely "deserve" this support. In other words, IVF is usually unavailable to single women, lesbian women, or women who are not securely placed in the middle class or beyond. Furthermore, women who are themselves affected by genetic handicaps are likely to be turned down by medical authorities who feel responsible for protecting future generations against the passing on of genetic defects (even if the condition at issue is one that the woman herself has come to terms with). IVF is also refused to those who have been judged as deficient according to the professionals' norms of good mothering.

The supposed freedom of choice, then, is provided only to selected women who have been screened according to the personal values of the experts administering the technology. Because most clinics deny service to single women, IVF may be accurately described as a technique that is available to men who are judged worthy, even though it is carried out on the bodies of their wives. Not only is this a far cry from individually controlled reproductive freedom, the selection criteria serve as one more instrument to establish the superior power and privilege of favored groups in society.

Feminist ethics directs us to examine the practice of IVF within the broader context of medical involvement in women's reproductive lives. There is a clear pattern of ever-increasing medical control over the various aspects of women's reproductive lives. Menstruation, pregnancy, delivery, lactation, childbearing, abortion, and menopause have already been subjected to medical control. In both Canada and the United States medical societies have removed midwives from their traditional place of influence and thereby have eliminated woman-centered control of reproduction. Medically supervised pregnancies and hospital births are demanded of everyone; women who fail to comply may be subject to criminal prosecution for endangering the health of the fetus. In most hospital settings it is doctors, not the women in labor, who determine the level of technology to be invoked in monitoring a woman's labor: doctors decide when to use cesarean sections and are even prepared to get court orders to perform them if the pregnant woman does not "consent."

Among its other effects, this increasingly interventionist, medicalized approach to reproduction alienates women from their own reproductive experiences. In seizing control of the various aspects of reproduction, physicians have tended to treat women as passive bodies to be subjected to medical manipulations. They focus their professional attention on the technology, rather than on the woman present, being more concerned with the product than the process of reproduction. As we saw in Chapter 5, the fetus-child is often viewed as the dominant subject of obstetric care; women may be assigned a merely passive role. With IVF, women's role is to permit their bodies to be subjected to forms of medical manipulation that they hope will "give" them the baby they desire. Here especially, women are portrayed as the passive containers for a medical miracle; their responsibility is to be compliant and accepting of the physician's active intervention. Doctors are represented as the real producers of the children created.

Viewed in the context of medicine's historical pursuit of control over women's reproductive lives and the role of the medical community in the general oppression of women, the issue of professional gatekeeping and monitoring in IVF is a matter of deep concern. IVF and most other new forms of reproductive technology constitute further areas for medical intervention in women's reproductive lives. They allow still greater decision-making power to be concentrated in the hands of medical specialists.

Some formal indication of "informed consent" is generally sought from clients, but many of the forms of reproductive technology have a poor track record in meeting the ethical demands of consent. Some of these technologies are offered to women as if they were established therapies, although they are still in a highly experimental stage; often the techniques are transferred directly from agricultural experience in animal husbandry, without the benefit of careful clinical trials performed on primates.[11] Other technologies, such as the use of ultrasound and electronic fetal monitors, represent new applications of military research, which have also been used extensively on women's bodies without adequate safety studies (Oakley 1987; Petchesky 1987; Kunisch 1989). Women's experiences with thalidomide, DES, the

Dalkon Shield, as well as the widespread use of fetal X rays until the mid-1970s and the belated warnings of the hazards of chemical contraceptives, provide ample reason for women to distrust reproductive technologies that have not yet been thoroughly tested for safety, but most bioethicists have been willing to rely on medical assurances about risks.

In many clinics relevant information is deliberately withheld from clients, which calls into question the informed nature of patients' choices and the degree of control that women actually exercise when receiving this technology. Many of the clinics that offer IVF are notoriously poor at keeping records and seldom offer full information on their low success rates to potential clients.[12] They encourage the media to present pictures of smiling parents with babies, which distract from the fact that the technology requires disruptive and dangerous hormone therapy, intrusive monitoring of the woman's blood and urine, surgery, a period of immobility, and a high likelihood of failure. Women are persuaded that only the application of complex technology can meet their needs, and therefore they feel compelled to rely on medical authority for their well-being. Doctors have been willing to take extraordinary risks with women's health in the hope of helping them to become mothers. Clearly, there is cause for concern about forms of technology that involve increased medical control over women's reproduction.

Putting IVF in Context

Feminist ethics expands the scope of ethical discussions of IVF and the other forms of new reproductive technologies in other respects. Although feminists share with their nonfeminist counterparts in bioethics an interest in matters of personal freedom, safety, fairness, and the overall contributions to human happiness and suffering that such technology may produce, they also identify many other important moral issues, which must be investigated. In evaluating the new reproductive technologies, a principal concern of feminist ethics is to see how each innovation fits into existing patterns of oppression. Technology is not neutral, so it is important to consider who controls it, who benefits from it, and how each activity is likely to affect women's subordinate status in society.

There are infertile couples with a strong desire to produce a child, and IVF does benefit many of them while it holds out hope to the rest. It is worth keeping in mind, however, that patients are not the only ones who benefit from this technology; IVF also serves the interests (commercial, professional, scholarly, and patriarchal) of the medical specialists who create and manipulate it. As the birth rates drop in the West and the traditional market for obstetric services shrinks, new reproductive technologies fill a potential void in the demand for specialist services. There is the prospect of significant prestige and profit at stake in the development of successful technologies. Michelle Stanworth observes: "Reproductive technologies often enhance the status of medical professionals and increase the funds they can command, by underpinning claims to specialized knowledge and by providing the basis for an extension of service. Such technologies may, in addition, help a profession in its attempts to dominate other competitors for control in an area of work. . . . Perhaps, most significantly, new technologies help to establish that gynecologists and obstetricians 'know more' about pregnancy and about women's bodies than women do themselves" (Stanworth 1987, 13). Renate Klein is blunter; she claims that "it is *not* the concerns of people with fertility problems that matter most. Much higher priority is given to the concerns of those who invent, practise and promote the new technologies" (Klein 1989, 247).

Moreover, it is important to investigate why so many couples feel compelled to seek technological solutions to involuntary childlessness. Why do people place such emphasis on the desire to produce their "own" child? With respect to this question, theorists in the mainstream tradition of bioethics seem to shift to previously rejected ground and suggest that this is a natural or, at least, a proper desire. Englehardt, for example, says, "The use of technology in the fashioning of children is integral to the goal of rendering the world congenial to persons" (Englehardt 1986, 239). Bayles more cautiously observes that "a desire to beget for its own sake . . . is probably irrational"; nonetheless, he immediately concludes: "These techniques for fulfilling that desire have been found ethically permissible" (Bayles 1984, 31). Robert Edwards and David Sharpe confidently state that "the desire to have children must be among the most basic of human instincts, and denying it can lead to considerable psychological and social difficulties" (Edwards and Sharpe 1971, 87). They do not seem interested in probing the desire to procreate or the expectations placed on people to develop such desires.

Generally, practitioners and critics alike accept without question the assumption that involuntary childlessness leads to "desperation," but as Naomi Pfeffer (1987) argues, this perspective is a caricature of the complex feelings that are actually experienced by infertile people. Infertility is not simply a biological state; it is a socially defined and interpreted category that is addressed through many distinct strategies, including not only the pursuit of medical solutions but also such nonmedical options as acceptance, denial, changing partners, and adoption. Attention to the specific concerns voiced by childless people reveals a complex range of responses that does not readily fit into a single social category of "desperation," but the characterization of need implied by that label rationalizes radical medical intervention as a supportive response (Pfeffer 1987). This way of conceptualizing the problem promotes a sense of urgency that denies scope for the investigation of other options. Infertile clients are regarded as desperate by the professionals they consult, and they learn to comply with the stereotyped expectations applied to them, so that they may ensure their place in oversubscribed infertility programs. They seek to establish their "normalcy" and worthiness of treatment by being eager and compliant, thereby verifying the professionals' stereotypical expectations.

These observations are not meant to deny that involuntary childlessness is a cause of great unhappiness for many people. Many individuals and couples suffer from their inability to procreate when they choose to do so; many are indeed eager to pursue whatever techniques might be offered to relieve this condition. Their motivations cannot be dismissed as irrational or misguided or judged unethical. As long as the technology that offers relief from their condition is available, it is appropriate for individuals to seek access to it.

Feminist ethics asks us to look at the social arrangements and cultural values that underlie people's drive to assume the risks that are posed by IVF and its variants. In our culture involuntary childlessness is made all the more painful by the fact that many adults have no opportunity for emotional attachment to children outside their own home. Children are valued as privatized commodities that reflect the virility and heredity of their parents. Because adults are often inhibited from having warm, stable interactions with the children of others, those who wish to know children well may find that they must have their own.

Moreover, many women are persuaded that their most important purpose in life is to bear and raise children; they are told repeatedly that their lives are incomplete, that they are lacking in fulfillment if they do not have children. Furthermore, many women do face a hollow existence without children. Far too often children remain their one hope for real intimacy and for the sense of accomplishment that comes from doing work one judges to be valuable. Children are sometimes the only means women have to secure their ties to their husbands, in a culture that makes a husband a financial and social necessity for many women.

Children also serve important symbolic functions. They are, for instance, part of the glue that holds together the institution of heterosexuality (see Chapter 10). It is significant to feminists that many of the new reproductive technologies unquestioningly accept the pronatalist and heterosexist values of our society and the sexual division of labor on which they rest. Rather than challenge the assumptions that women's destiny is best expressed in the time-honored roles of wife and mother, these technologies legitimize those assumptions and help to entrench them even more deeply by demonstrating the lengths to which women will go to achieve this status.

Furthermore, IVF is entangled within the racist and classist value system that underlies the powerful eugenic forces in our culture. For many people, one significant attraction of IVF is that it is a means of allowing for specifically biological parenthood. Although some couples who pursue IVF would be willing to accept adoption if waiting lists were shorter, many others are not interested in raising children who are not genetically related to them. As Christine Overall (1987) argues, such decisions can rest on a variety of considerations, such as the sense of continuity with previous generations of the family, the desire to experience pregnancy and childbirth, or the prospective father's unwillingness to contribute to the support of a child produced by another man's sperm; some motives, although not all, raise serious obstacles to feminist ideals of greater social equality and the elimination of oppression.[13] Whatever the actual motivation, the practice of IVF itself serves to accept and support the sorts of individualistic values that say it is fine to invest vast resources into reproducing a child of one's own genes, despite the unmet needs of millions of existing children.

Feminist analysis requires us to examine how the various forms of reproductive technology reinforce the social prejudices that constitute the oppressive structures of our society. Doctors use their own values, which reflect their privileged position in society, to determine who qualifies for artificial insemination and IVF on the one hand and sterilization on the other hand. Different criteria are invoked to foster reproduction among the preferred groups and to repress reproduction among the disadvantaged. Laurie Nsiah-Jefferson and Elaine J. Hall observe: "Population control groups have historically tended to define the problem of infertility as the absence of white babies for married couples who are able to pay for them" (Nsiah-Jefferson and Hall 1989, 111). They note that although the black community in the United States suffers significantly higher rates of infertility than the white community, infertility treatment programs are overwhelmingly directed at the latter group. The technologies of ova and embryo donation and genetic screening allow the medical specialists in charge to decide which genes are worth perpetuating. Embryo transfer, for example, allows the possibility of "pure surrogate mothering," where a couple from the dominant class can engage an economically disadvantaged member of a subordinate class to gestate their fetus for them, sparing the genetic parents the dangers and inconvenience of pregnancy but assuring them of a child of the "right" genetic makeup at the end. Sex-selection technology allows the social preference for males to be translated into coming generations of increased numbers of males and, potentially, increased influence of male values.

In Chapter 5 I noted that feminist ethics invokes a concept of reproductive freedom under which women should be free to say no or yes to reproduction. This concept cannot be understood in terms of traditional conceptions of individual autonomy, however, for the latter tends to leave out analysis of the factors of oppression. Freedom cannot always be determined in isolated cases but requires attention to a person's whole life situation. The reproductive freedom that feminists appeal to in abortion arguments is the freedom for women to choose their status as childbearers, which is especially important in the face of the social, economic, and political significance that are associated with reproduction for women.

Reproductive freedom for women requires that they have control over their sexuality, protection against coerced sterilization (or iatrogenic sterilization caused by prescribed contraceptives), and access to the social and economic support necessary to care for any children each may choose to bear. It requires that women be free to define their roles in society according to their concerns and needs as women. Feminism helps us understand that reproductive freedom involves being free from the economic, racist, and sexist oppression that prevents choices in other aspects of life. This freedom cannot be captured by focusing on single choices, in isolation from other factors.

In contrast, most nonfeminist bioethicists (outside of the theological tradition) treat reproductive freedom as if it were the consumer freedom to purchase technology. Often such choices are, by their very nature, available only to relatively few couples of the privileged classes (who are situated in traditionally approved relationships). Rather than increasing women's general freedom from oppression, this narrow concept of freedom of choice may help entrench more deeply the patriarchal notion of woman's role as childbearer. Under current social conditions, not all such choices can be seen to foster autonomy for women collectively.

From the point of view of feminist ethics, the central question is whether IVF and other forms of reproductive technology threaten to reinforce the lack of autonomy that most women now experience in our culture—even though these technologies appear to increase particular aspects of freedom for some women. Although the new reproductive technologies are advertised as increasing women's autonomy, feminists mistrust them as long as they remain intertwined with key social forces that are oppressive to women in general and, especially, to women who are multiply oppressed. By accepting the presupposition that (particular) women ought to bear children, even if they must risk their lives to do so, IVF implicitly reinforces many of the sexist, classist, and often racist assumptions of our culture. It helps to support the existing power structures, because it provides reproductive assistance to the affluent and accepts the view that it is more important for the privileged to produce children of their own genetic type than to adopt a child of a different background. On our revised understanding of freedom, the contribution of this technology to the general autonomy of women collectively seems largely negative.

Therefore, it seems appropriate to resurrect the old slippery-slope arguments against IVF. Women's existing lack of control in reproductive matters begins the debate on a pretty steep incline. Technology with the potential to remove further control of reproduction from women makes the slope very slippery indeed. IVF is a technology that will always include the active involvement of designated specialists; it will never be simply a private matter for the couple or women concerned. Although offered under the guise of increasing some individuals' reproductive freedom, IVF threatens to result in a significant decrease in freedom for women as a class.

Feminist analysis guides us in rethinking the values that drive the search for new forms of reproductive technologies. It urges us to question the appropriateness of encouraging people to spend huge sums on creating certain sorts of children through IVF and other forms of reproductive technology, while so many other children starve to death each year. IVF, like other forms of new reproductive technology, seems to strengthen, rather than weaken, the social attitudes that underlie the politics of dominance and supremacy in our world.

More positively, feminist ethics looks elsewhere for solutions to the problems of infertility. It seeks to make changes in the prevailing social arrangements that can lead to a reduction of the sense of need for this sort of solution. On the medical front, research and treatment should be stepped up to reduce the rates of sexually transmitted disease and other causes of pelvic inflammatory disease, which often result in tubal blockage; a significant percentage of female infertility is preventable, and feminist concern with reproductive freedom entails the view that involuntary sterilization should be prevented. Feminists can also support the need to direct more attention to the causes of and possible cures for male infertility. Research into eliminating the environmental and social factors (for example, malnutrition) that contribute to infertility is clearly vital. In addition, we should pursue techniques that will permit safe, reversible sterilization in both women and men, providing better fertility control options than are now available.

On the social front, we must continue the pressure to change the statuses of women and children in our society from those of breeder and possession respectively: hence we must develop a vision of society as a community where women and children are valued members. We must challenge the notion that having one's wife produce a child with his own genes is sufficient cause for the wives of men with low sperm counts to undergo the physical and emotional assault that IVF and genetic technology involves.

In contrast to their nonfeminist bioethicist colleagues, feminists

attend closely to the often devastating consequences of various reproductive technologies on the particular women who undergo them.
Nonfeminist bioethicists have chosen to skip over the significance of
the hazards to which women are exposed by this technology; they
assume that the generic informed consent requirements that they
have spelled out for all medical procedures will provide adequate protection against excessive threats to individual patients. Feminists,
however, painstakingly monitor the cumulative effects of these new
technologies.[14] Such effects are not mere details, unconnected with
the theoretical moral question of the acceptability of reproductive
technologies (as most traditional ethicists would have it). The data
demonstrate the willingness of the medical profession to risk the lives
and well-being of women to try to ensure that all women can fulfill
their biological role in reproduction. Such information leads feminists to look more deeply for explanations for the phenomenon of
fertility treatments as the new growth industry in medicine.

Traditional ethics and nonfeminist bioethics would have us evaluate individual cases without also looking at the implications of the
practices as reviewed from a wide perspective. Examination of IVF as
one form of new reproductive technology demonstrates the inadequacy of that approach for the moral evaluation of some medical
practices. Feminist ethics provides the necessary wide perspective, because its different methodology is sensitive to both the personal and
the social dimensions of issues.

7

Paternalism

A perennial topic in nonfeminist bioethics revolves around the locus of control over decision-making in the arena of health care. This issue takes many forms: it arises under the headings of disclosure, truth-telling, confidentiality, informed consent, the nature of the patient–physician relationship, and refusal of treatment; each of these subjects addresses some of the various complications that occur whenever there is a danger that patient and physician may disagree about the best treatment option to pursue. Medical tradition has been to grant physicians license to treat as they see fit, and physicians have long considered themselves authorized to proceed with whatever medical care they judge appropriate; patient consent has usually been treated as, at most, a formality. But pressure has been growing to limit physicians' power to act unilaterally, according to their best medical judgment, without allowing patients the opportunity to participate in the deliberations.

In the bioethics literature this classic power struggle between patients and their physicians is defined as a moral conflict between the patient's right to autonomy and the physician's responsibility for paternalism. The contest has been characterized as a clash between the basic moral principles of autonomy and beneficence. Feminists have reason to resist both horns of this dilemma.

In traditional philosophic conceptions autonomy is viewed as the instrument of agency for individuals who are perceived as separate, independent, and "fully rational."[1] Nevertheless, actual people are not independent, and their decision-making does not always meet the norms that define rationality. They do not, for example, always act in accordance with their own best interests.

Feminists have further difficulty with the idea of autonomy. Most have viewed the ideal of personhood, implicit in much of the autonomy literature, as both unrealistic and pernicious; they have called into question the value of independent autonomy that is promoted on this model. Sarah Hoagland, for example, argues that the standard conceptions of autonomy imply self-control, demanding that an agent limit her own actions; the limits envisioned invoke "anything from self-subordination to self-isolation" (Hoagland 1988, 144). She sees autonomy as a concept that has been built to establish self-rule within a conceptual framework that is structured around the terms of dominance relations; this connection makes it an unacceptable basis for feminist ethics.

The alternative concept in the bioethics debate is paternalism, but it, too, raises the suspicions of feminist ethicists. In medical contexts the term "paternalism" refers to the widespread practice in which physicians make decisions on behalf of their patients, without the full understanding or consent of the patient. To qualify as paternalism, the basis of the decision must be the patient's well-being; thus it is distinguished from actions the doctor might take out of self-interest. Because paternalism aims for the patient's good, it is recognized as well-intended action, but its actual achievement in bringing about the best consequences is in doubt, because it is the physician's— rather than the patient's—perception of the patient's good that is decisive. Because it bypasses patients' normal authority over themselves, paternalism is generally challenged as an infringement on patient autonomy. It is usually thought to be justified only in those circumstances where patients are incapable of making decisions in their own best interests; under such conditions, someone who is presumably better qualified must choose for them.

Although some authors are inclined to pursue their general campaign of eliminating sexist language and to rename the practice "parentalism," I think this is one occasion for retaining gendered language, because it directs our attention to the origin of the concept. The term derives from the privileges associated with the patriarchal family, where fathers are granted the right and responsibility to use their supposedly superior knowledge and judgment to make decisions on behalf of other family members. Physicians appeal to this model in claiming that their greater knowledge and understanding of the human body (and mind) constitutes justification for making authoritarian decisions about their patients' well-being, just as fathers claimed that their inherent superiority served as justification for imposing their will on other family members. Feminism has taught us that we ought not to assume that the powerful, authoritarian father ruling the household will always act in the best interests of his wife and children (although he may well believe he does). The power implicit in the hierarchical arrangements of the patriarchal family is easily abused; rather than supporting the interests of subordinate family members, it is often distorted into rationalizations of the father's self-interest. Likewise, the power inherent in the patient–physician relationship may also be abused; it, too, must be carefully limited.

Paternalistic practice has long been the norm in medicine, and most physicians continue to believe that it is an essential element in many treatment situations. Illness (or the potential for illness) causes patients to be dependent on specialized care; sometimes illness can place patients in need of paternalism. Because physicians are well-informed on medical matters and because they are obliged by their professional code to act beneficently toward their patients, they are commonly thought to be well-qualified to make medical decisions on their patients' behalf. Patients' needs for care, however, can leave them particularly vulnerable to excessive degrees of paternalism; illness (or the threat of illness) sometimes leads to patients' loss of rightful authority, by making them too weak or too frightened to protest against unjustified interference.

Increasing numbers of patients are struggling with their doctors over control of the decisions that determine their health care. Most physicians have responded reluctantly to these demands; under the threat of court challenges, they have provided for a small degree of patient involvement, by adopting minimal standards of informed consent. Many physicians still believe that, in the final analysis, medical decision-making is their unique privilege and responsibility.[2] It is, then, not surprising that a significant portion of the literature in medical ethics is devoted to determining what circumstances justify the use of medical paternalism.

Supporters of the paternalist medical model appeal to three grounds in its defence. The first is the argument that debilitating illness or the fear of such illness compromises the reasoning abilities of patients. Second is the widely held assumption that adequate medical decision-making can only be accomplished by those who possess the technical knowledge acquired from scientific, medical school training. Third is the view that patients' belief in the power of the healer is an important element in health care, which is fostered when the healing process is mystified and health care is carried out in a confident, authoritative manner.[3] In other words, patients' informational and reasoning capacities on medical matters are said to be both inadequate to the task of proper decision-making and counterproductive to the actual healing process.

These assumptions are widely criticized in the medical ethics literature, and most bioethicists agree that medical paternalism is practiced far more than is justified. Feminists share the perspective of their bioethical counterparts that much medical paternalism is unjustified, but they also have distinct objections that are not captured by the traditional accounts. Therefore, it is important to explore each of the rationales for paternalism from the perspective of feminist ethics.

Insofar as the alternative to paternalism is characterized by masculine versions of autonomy, women may also find themselves alienated from it as an ideal. After all, patients often are at a disadvantage in medical contexts: when they are ill, they are likely to be frightened of abandonment, and they may not be confident about their own judgment; hence, they may not be eager to insist on their rights to independent judgment. Individual authority is not necessarily their preferred alternative under such circumstances.

From a feminist perspective, the structure of the debate in the traditional bioethics literature seems to offer no satisfactory option.[4] An important task of feminist ethics is to reshape the problem and offer alternative models for medical relationships that neither replace patient authority with technical expertise nor abandon patients to their "rights," where that amounts to granting them the opportunity to assert their independent authority in a hostile, frightening environment. Feminists need a richer, nondichotomous account of proper decision-making in health care to address what is commonly described as the choice between paternalism and autonomy.

The Reasoning Power of Patients

The first argument offered in support of the legitimacy of medical paternalism is that paternalism is often necessary because patients frequently suffer from diminished reasoning capacity.[5] The anxiety of patients and their hesitancy in the face of medical authority is cited as evidence of the ways in which illness reduces patients' normal reasoning skills. Feminist analysis of this concern requires attention to the gendered assumptions that are implicit in the ways medicine views patients.

For instance, it is important to remember that women enter the role of patient far more frequently than men do; they are also generally the ones responsible for bringing the young, the elderly, and the injured and disabled members of their families to the doctor, and often they are the ones to speak on their behalf. Because of women's heightened contact with the institution of medicine and because of their oppressed status in society generally, special attention should be paid to the ways in which the practice of medical paternalism contributes to women's disempowerment in both the medical and social realms.

Moreover, because patients, like women, are expected to submit gratefully to the directions of a powerful, more rational authority, the status of being a patient is often conceived as feminine in character. Feminists can hear the echoes of more general rationalizations for women's oppressed condition in defenses of paternalism that claim that patients benefit from their subordinate status in relationships with their doctors and they willingly choose to defer to physician authority. Because of the feminine nature of the role of patient, authorization of paternalism in medicine both mirrors and helps to strengthen the attitudes that support the domination of whatever is classified as female in other contexts.

Further, because traditional norms of reason play such a significant role in supporting paternalistic interventions in medicine, it is important to reflect on the evidence that feminist researchers have uncovered, which establishes that gender bias is built into those norms. Genevieve Lloyd (1984), for example, shows that the concept "reason" has itself been used as an ideological tool by those in power throughout Western history to serve their various political purposes. Her research reveals that changing normative concepts of reason have played (and continue to play) an integral role in the politics of dominance, particularly as they are applied in the context of gender. Because political power is inherent in the definition of reason, it would be a mistake to accept unqualified appeals to the quality of an individual's reasoning ability, without examining the interests that are served by the term's current interpretations. In light of the different roles that men and women play in the health care system, it is especially important to reflect on the ways in which gendered assumptions about reason have infected the norms of medical practice.

Therefore, feminists have reason to be wary of the commonplace medical assumption that the reasoning capacity of patients is somehow defective, that is, that the very condition of being patients—the physical and emotional aspects of illness—clouds their judgment and makes them unreliable decision-makers. In a sexist society where women are regularly denied the status of competent reasoners, where patients are typically women, and where physicians are mostly men, that physicians experience patients as lacking in reason does not constitute reliable evidence that patients really are incapable of the reasoning that is required to arrive at reliable decisions about their own care.

Let us turn, then, to the question of whether or not it is reasonable to assume that the judgment of patients is so clouded by their condition that they are unable to make their own decisions. There is no single answer here; a wide variety of cases must be considered, because patients consult physicians for many different reasons in many different circumstances. Conditions certainly exist under which decision-making is severely compromised by illness: for example, serious accidents, high fevers, and neurological disturbances can all detract from ideal reasoning conditions. Hence, although Eric Cassell (1976) is a strong supporter of the value of individual autonomy, he finds that illness seriously reduces autonomy and is really "a thief of autonomy." He argues that when people are sick, they are not "themselves"; their reason is impaired and so their autonomy is greatly diminished.

In many of the interactions between women and physicians, however, the contact has nothing to do with illness: the medicalization of a wide range of functions in women's normal reproductive life cycle has brought the events that characterize healthy development for women under medical control. Thus most healthy women must see physicians regularly for contraceptives or for monitoring of their pregnancies. In other cases, such as those in which women bring family members for medical care, the women who speak on behalf of the actual patients are not even ill, but they may still be dismissed as incapable of coming to the right decision. In these contexts, at least, claims about the compromised reasoning power of the ill do not de-

scribe the conditions of the women who seek medical care. Therefore, they cannot constitute relevant grounds for restricting patient
control of decision-making.

Sometimes the argument is that the fear of illness can distort patients' reasoning abilities and increase their dependence on medical
authorities, so that even though a patient is not seriously ill, she may
be unable to think clearly. If true, it is important to look more closely
at the circumstances of this fear: often the fear is generated or magni-
fied by the medical community itself. For example, Sue Fisher (1986)
has documented instances where physicians manipulated women into
having hysterectomies by alluding to the fact that "it" may return,
where "it" is the existence of abnormal (so called precancerous, but
not cancerous) cells that have been detected by Pap smear. By hoar-
ding and mystifying medical information, declaring it too complex
for consumption by ordinary citizens, physicians encourage fear and
dependency in patients. Indeed, the power of the healer is often
maintained by promoting fear, rather than strength, on the part of
patients. If it actually is the case that fear interferes with patients'
decision-making functions, then more honest and open communication by physicians could do a great deal to prevent the fear that accompanies ignorance from undermining the reasoning process of patients. Reducing fear would surely be a preferable strategy to that of
authorizing paternalistic intervention in the face of the effects fear is
said to have on reasoning abilities.

When patients are really unable to reach reasonable decisions, it
may be necessary for someone else to decide on their behalf. It is
important, then, to have a nonsexist measure of reasoning ability by
which we can determine when patients are in need of substitute decision-making. We cannot rely on the subjective judgment of practitioners for this task, for they may hold beliefs or stereotypes that assume that most women, or most minority women, are irrational or
stupid. A feminist understanding of the potential for bias in the face
of entrenched patterns of oppression is an important prerequisite for
developing an adequate measure of reasoning ability. Respect for the
patient is a necessary condition for making such judgments; genuine
respect for women, however, and particularly respect for minority or
poor women, is seldom learned in our society (and is certainly not
taught in most medical schools).

Even if the patient is deemed unable to make an appropriate decision according to such a politically sensitive test, bioethicists have shown that paternalistic intervention still would not necessarily be justified. James Childress (1982), for instance, argued that a second condition must also be satisfied: there should be a reasonable probability of significant harm coming to the patient if paternalism is not invoked. On his view, justified paternalism requires both that the patient be clearly lacking adequate reasoning ability and that the intervention will avert some clear and relevant danger. In other words, diminished reasoning capacity does not by itself constitute license for general intervention. Further, even if both conditions are satisfied, it does not follow that physicians are the best people to rely on in the event of diminished reason.

When patients are not competent to make their own decisions, someone else may have to help them; in such circumstances, their needs can best be addressed by deferring to whoever is most likely to make decisions that are compatible with each patient's overall interests and values. Physicians propose themselves for this role on the grounds that their scientific perspective makes them objective, knowledgeable surrogates. As I argue in the next section, however, a scientific perspective is no assurance of objectivity; nor is objectivity necessarily a primary consideration in seeking surrogate decision-makers. The ideal decision-maker in circumstances of justified paternalism would more likely be someone with deep concern for and understanding of the person whose interests are at stake—someone who is caring, rather than objective. Because most physicians are trained to develop an orientation to science over humanistic care, they may be particularly inappropriate for this role.

Insofar as it is true that patients' illnesses or fears result in serious deficiencies in their reasoning abilities, patients must rely on others to help make their medical decisions on their behalf. Feminists would have to agree that medical care, as it is customarily delivered, does not foster the reasoning abilities of patients. We do not have to conclude, however, that the solution to this problem is to transfer patients' normal authority to their physicians in matters regarding their own health. An alternative approach is to explore means of revising the nature of the patient–physician encounter in order to seek ways of empowering patients who are currently unable to assert their own wills.

Medicine and Science

The second argument in support of widespread paternalism in medicine appeals to the relevance of the special scientific expertise of physicians. The authoritarian medical model relies heavily on the belief that neither patients nor health care professionals other than physicians possess the appropriate skills and capacities to exercise decision-making power. In particular, patients (and their guardians) are thought to be too uneducated, too emotionally distraught, or too stupid to make adequate decisions in the face of illness. Other health professionals are thought to have only partial training, only a piece of the relevant medical knowledge, and without more complete training (or, preferably, appropriate supervision), a little knowledge is considered a dangerous thing. The argument is that physicians alone are able to make proper judgments about health care options, because they are the only ones with sufficient scientific training, the practical knowledge that derives from their specific clinical experience, and the uniquely "objective" perspective required by this scientific enterprise. Feminists have good reason, however, to distrust appeals to science as a defense of medical paternalism.

Interestingly, the scientific basis of medicine, on which arguments for medical dominance now rest, is a relatively recent phenomenon in the history of medicine. It dates to the late nineteenth century, when physicians set out to consolidate their dominance in the competitive field of health care providers. At that time, many physicians recognized the necessity of upgrading the standards that governed their profession; they agreed that doctors who practiced with no formal education or with a degree from an unknown and inadequate medical school should no longer be tolerated. In an era when scientism was gaining increasing respect and authority in Western thought, the medical community moved to establish scientific educational standards for the licensing of physicians. The influential Flexner report of 1910 cemented the move to require a firm scientific foundation for all medical school programs in America.

One effect of this process was that a great many medical schools were closed, and many candidates were eliminated from access to medical training (including most women and minority students). Although there was, as yet, little evidence of success to recommend a scientific approach to medicine, the schools that survived this period of transition accepted the ideological recommendations of the Flexner report to make their programs scientific and to develop in them a class orientation that would ensure that doctors become part of the educated elite of gentlemen. Medicine's adoption of the ideology of science was the key to its gaining exclusive control over the field of health care. The image of medicine and its practitioners was deliberately transformed to raise the prestige and authority of physicians (Shorter 1985). Modern medical education, like modern education in general, accepted the legitimacy of scientific training as foundational.

Today all medical schools stress the centrality of a technical, scientific background to their work. The physical sciences are viewed as the paradigm for all knowledge in medical training; students are taught to concentrate on the "hard" sciences at the expense of social sciences and humanities. Indeed, emphasis on science in medical education has increased through the years to the point where current medical training demands mastery of an enormous quantity of technical data and has little space left for the study of the humanities, social sciences, or interpersonal relationships. Moreover, this technical orientation has evolved to the point where specialization defines every area of medicine, so that even medically trained practitioners are considered inferior decision-makers in fields beyond their own speciality. The scientific model serves to persuade both doctors and patients that medicine is a complex field and that medical decision-making involves a level of understanding far beyond the reach of nonspecialists (Shapiro 1978; Shorter 1985).

With this scientific orientation has come a commitment to technology; doctors have learned to trust medical instruments over their own analyses and over patients' reports of illness. Laboratory reports have become the basis of diagnosis, and they take precedence over the patients' subjective descriptions of symptoms. Medical care relies on such an array of technical instrumentation that it can only be provided in a medical institution, an environment in which patients feel alienated and intimidated. Medicine has restricted its focus to objectively measurable symptoms and has, to a significant degree, chosen not to address patients as complex, integrated human beings. Among the many consequences that result from this decision is the widely recognized fact that physicians no longer feel the need to communicate with patients, develop relationships with them, listen to them, or hold their hands (Shorter 1985).

The appeal to technical measures lends an aura of objective truth to medical findings. In this way science supports physicians' claims to dominance over other health care workers and patients. It is, however, unclear how much of their judgment really rests on a firm scientific foundation. Contemporary medical practice involves a great deal of uncertainty and intuitive reasoning, in addition to the aspects that are derived from well-defined science. In claiming authority medicine presumes a degree of certainty and authority inappropriate to its actual level of knowledge. Some physicians recognize the precariousness of medical knowledge and talk about the importance of seeing medicine as an art as well as a science, but most interpret that to mean that clinical experience in the role of physician must be added to scientific data, thereby increasing their own authority. Significantly, neither subjective experiences of illness nor health care experiences from allied professions are recognized as providing the appropriate training in the art of medicine, because neither one begins with rigorous grounding in science.

Medical science, however, is not infallible. Instruments are limited in their readings: they can only report on what they are programmed to observe, and reliance upon them can blind practitioners to the consideration of other possibilities. The "scientific objectivity" of medicine tends only to observe what it looks for, what it expects to see. Hence even though many women have long complained of such conditions as menstrual cramps, nausea in pregnancy, labor pain, and infantile colic, these symptoms were declared purely psychogenic, that is, organically nonexistent, because medical authorities denied their possibility. When organic explanations were finally established for all of these conditions, each became belatedly recognized as a legitimate medical syndrome.[6] Unless medical practitioners are willing to take seriously patients' descriptions of their conditions, they may well be misdirected by the science of the day about how to interpret and respond to patients' complaints.

In addition, the use of mystifying, exclusionary language in science helps to defend its hierarchical structures and discourages challenges. Science accepts as valid only a particularly narrow sense of reason and knowledge; because the knowledge of personal experience is considered subjective, it is disqualified as not reliable. In this way the knowledge that belongs to patients, who are principally women, is discredited. As feminist and other philosophers of science have shown, however, science is far from objective (Harding 1986b; Hubbard 1990; Longino 1990); as an institution, the practice of science both reflects and supports the interests and ideology of the dominant groups in society. Rather than serving as a neutral social instrument, then, the practice of science has been party to continued patterns of social oppression. Therefore, the scientific roots of contemporary medicine provide no comfort from the fear that medical practices may be oppressive. Dominance relations are built into the organization of a scientific worldview.

My point is not that science is irredeemably corrupt or that medicine should abandon its dependence on science; rather, it is that medicine cannot claim a uniquely privileged position for decision-making by appeal to the superior scientific training of its students. I willingly grant that there is an important place for science in medicine, but I also believe that the particular practices of science demand very critical evaluation. Science can provide only certain aspects of the information necessary for proper decision-making on issues of health care. The question of the right treatment for a patient is not a question that can be wholly answered by science, because it also involves weighing the patient's own evaluations of the risks and benefits she may experience. It is a medical mistake to believe that science can provide all the relevant information for protecting or restoring the health of patients (Todd 1989). Expertise in the scientific aspects required for reaching a decision qualifies doctors to provide advice to those who try to make decisions about their health care, but it does not license them to appropriate that responsibility.

Paternalism and Trust

The third argument in favor of medical paternalism rests on the view that physician authority is an essential element in healing. Patients' beliefs in the effectiveness of their physicians does seem to contribute to their healing, because the placebo effect is one of the most powerful tools at a physician's disposal. It is not clear, however, that patients must be kept ignorant or dependent to achieve this end. Compelling evidence indicates that patients who take an active role as agents in their own health care are likely to be better off than those who are kept as passive recipients of authoritative treatment (Benfari et al. 1981; Howe 1981).

Moreover, if patient confidence in the healing power of the caregiver is to be effective, then it must be rooted in attitudes of trust.[7] Often, however, what passes for paternalism does not benefit the patient. The faith that patients place in the healing power of doctors, which sustains paternalism, should not, then, be arrived at through blind trust. In her ground-breaking account of trust and antitrust, Annette Baier offers a moral test for trust relationships, which is that "they be able to survive awareness by each party to the relationship of *what* the other relies on in the first to ensure their continued trustworthiness or trustingness" (Baier 1986, 259). Patients in general, and female patients in particular, have good grounds for suspicion in their dealings with physicians. If female patients explore what physicians rely on to ensure their continued trust, then it seems unlikely that the trust relationship can be sustained.

Although women are not the only patients with grounds for antitrust in their relationships with their physicians, they do have special grounds that extend beyond experiences that might be common to patients generally. Women, after all, have different roles and different experiences within the health care system than men do. Even though women are the major consumers of health care and constitute a significant majority of the workers in the health care delivery system, men hold the positions of power and authority in dispensing medicine. Most health care structures exhibit a model that seems to be based on the idea of a powerful, paternal authority directing obedient subordinates in the treatment of (ideally) compliant, passive patients. These professional patterns of dominance not only mirror but also reinforce social (and medical) expectations of men as knowledgeable authorities and of women as deferential servants who follow through, but do not initiate, treatment programs (see Chapter 11).

The gender imbalance within health care structures encourages doctors to accept prevailing social attitudes about women, illness, and reason in deciding on the treatments they prescribe for women. In medical literature, cases about "real," that is, organic diseases have traditionally been described in terms of male patients; conditions that are psychogenic, including neuroses, excessive anxiety, and physical symptoms with no identifiable organic basis (psychosomatic illness and hypochondria), are described with the use of feminine pronouns.

In general, it seems, the attitude is that men are to be believed in their reports of distress, but women are assumed to be "high-strung." Pharmaceutical advertisements in medical journals employ male models if they are advertising powerful pain relievers and female models if they are promoting tranquilizers.[8] Women are typically portrayed as psychologically unstable and weak, in need of calming or monitoring. Moreover, gender is not the only basis for the effects of dominance stereotyping in medicine: race, class, ethnicity, age, sexual orientation, and degrees of disability also influence the likelihood of a physician accepting a patient's report at face value.

Further, physicians have a large and growing interest in asserting their authority over women's health, and this interest cannot be attributed entirely to paternalistic concern. We can trace a long, historical pattern of medical attempts to extend authority over an increasing number of spheres of women's lives. Originally, physicians' interest in women's bodies coincided with their efforts to consolidate their professional status in society. Until the late nineteenth century, physicians were in competition for the care of the sick with many other sorts of healers, including those known as wisewomen, midwives, quacks, sectarians, and bonesetters; the profession engaged in periodic campaigns to eliminate competition through a variety of draconian measures. The most notorious of these occurred in the fifteenth and sixteenth centuries, when medical hostility combined with church-based misogyny and fostered mass murders of alternative healers (primarily women) under accusations of witchcraft (Daly 1978; Ehrenreich and English 1978). At that time, however, physicians were not particularly interested in caring for women or children; they were inclined to concentrate their efforts on middle-aged men and the elderly. Their intention was to maintain dominance over the field of health care, and they had little interest in tending those not highly valued by society. The care of women was still left largely to the informal workings of wisewomen and other healers in the widespread network of women's culture (Shorter 1985).

In the latter half of the nineteenth century, when competition among health care workers was particularly fierce, doctors recognized that women constituted a large market for their services; they understood that if they captured that market, they would then have access to the health needs of other family members. Therefore, they began to focus their attention directly on women, especially on the services surrounding pregnancy, and they moved to eliminate women's access to other health care providers.[9] Physicians succeeded in winning a monopoly over the delivery of health care, thereby driving other sorts of workers out of the field or into subordinate positions where they could only practice under the direct control of physicians. They seized control over women's fertility by lobbying for legislation to cut women off from all sources of abortion service and contraceptive information. Obviously, this control of women's bodies significantly improved the economic and hence the social and political position of physicians. Its benefits to women are much less clear.

Since that time physicians have gone on to expand their interest in treating women, seeing all aspects and stages of women's normal reproductive lives as material for medical treatment and claiming authority over more and more of women's ordinary experience. In appropriating the authority to define what is normal and healthy for women, they ensured women's continuing dependence on them. This pattern continues today. The development of new reproductive technologies promises continued expansion of medical services that were previously unimagined. In the United States, where competition has now become severe among profit-seeking hospitals, various health care institutions have begun to direct their marketing strategies at women; many have introduced women's health units as a means of attracting a larger female clientele. They reason, as did their predecessors at the turn of the century, that by attracting women through special services aimed specifically at them, they can gain access to other family members; because women are the medical gatekeepers in most families, if their loyalty can be captured by an institution, then they can be counted on to bring along others when the need arises (Worcester and Whatley 1988).

All this medical attention, however, is not necessarily a good thing for women; dangerous and medically unwarranted procedures are carried out on women's bodies at a frightening rate. Medical control of childbirth results in many more surgical interventions (and correspondingly higher mortality rates) in North America than in European countries where midwives are regularly included in the process. Women also find themselves exposed to excessive rates of surgery on their specifically female organs. For example, for many decades surgeons were inclined to subject all women with breast cancer to mutilating radical mastectomies even though there was no scientific evidence to establish that this treatment resulted in increased survival rates. Also, in a six-year study of communication patterns and the structure of decision-making between doctors and their female patients, Sue Fisher found that hysterectomies were recommended far more frequently than medical necessity demanded, reflecting the widespread medical attitude that if reproduction is finished, the uterus is a useless and dangerous organ, best removed (Fisher 1986). Lest there be any question about the ideological basis of this practice, Fisher offers a quote from a recent edition of a major gynecological text: "Menstruation is a nuisance to most women and if this can be abolished without impairing ovarian function, it would probably be a blessing not only to the woman but to her husband" (Fisher 1986, 37). She cites studies that indicate that if current trends continue, "more than half of the women in the United States will have their uteruses removed before they reach 65 years of age" (Fisher 1986, 33). It is revealing that although testicular and prostate cancers are a serious threat to men's health, there has been no comparable medical campaign to remove testicles or prostate glands as a matter of routine prevention once reproduction is complete.[10]

In the area of mental illness, there are further notable differences in the medical treatment prescribed for women and men: women are consistently treated more frequently and more aggressively than men.[11] Behavior that is considered healthy for adults has been deemed pathological for women (Broverman et al. 1981); psychiatrists have been willing to find unhealthy a good deal of ordinary female behavior, including lesbianism, political resistance, and the desire not to have children (Kitzinger 1987). Women seeking medical support from the injuries and distress caused by battering, rape, sexual harassment, incest, or racism are commonly treated with sedatives (or worse), to help them adapt to the ongoing situation (Stark, Flitcraft and Frazier 1983; Paltiel 1988). Furthermore, women are at least twice as likely as men to be prescribed psychotropic drugs for their complaints (Penfold and Walker 1983).

It seems, then, that the medical care that women receive for conditions unique to them as women—for example, those conditions associated with their reproductive functions or with characteristically female mental states—is often harmful to them. Furthermore, women are less likely than men to receive appropriate health care for conditions that are not sex-specific (McMurray 1990). Although decisions harmful to patients cannot properly be characterized as paternalistic, the ideology of paternalism and the general assumption of beneficent motives on the part of physicians work to rationalize and perpetuate such practices; claims of paternalistic intent and the importance of patient trust as an element in healing are frequently invoked as barriers to protect medical practice from close scrutiny. In general, the presumption of medical paternalism helps to ensure that the specific decisions governing the provision of health care to women remain largely in the hands of the medical experts.

The interest of physicians in defining and providing women's health care, then, is motivated by factors in addition to women's actual health needs. That does not mean, however, that all physicians are consciously determined to exploit women; I do not argue that there is some well-organized conspiracy among doctors to subordinate women deliberately. Medical care is provided within specific relationships holding between particular individuals, and many of the individuals involved in these relationships (both patients and physicians) are sensitive to the injustice of sexism in medicine. Many of the individual therapies that doctors offer women seem beneficial to patients from the physicians' medical point of view. Nevertheless, precisely because most practitioners view their role as being based entirely in concern for the well-being of their patients, they are often insensitive to their own participation in patterns of thinking that, overall, are harmful to women. Significantly, the historical and continuing records of women's experiences with medicine indicate that medical practice directed specifically at the health needs of women serves medical interests, and it is, far too often, harmful to women.

Hence we should be aware of the complexity of the values that underlie the medical services provided to women. This awareness makes it clear why women must regain control over the determination of their health-care needs and over the delivery of health-related services. Because paternalism encourages patients to trust and not question the authority of their physicians, it should not be accepted as common medical practice.

Feminist Alternatives

In medical contexts, attitudes about the value of a scientific background in medicine and the incapacitating effects of illness on a patient's ability to reason interact with general, social prejudices about women. Hence arguments in favor of authoritarian practice in medicine demand careful scrutiny, with attention directed to the standard sources of bias in these situations. To determine who is best qualified to decide about health care for patients, it is necessary to examine the underlying assumptions in the health care field about the nature of good decision-making.

The argument that patients should be relieved of the responsibility for deciding their own health care because, as a class, they suffer from diminished reasoning capacity cannot be sustained. Although in particular circumstances illness can compromise a patient's reason, physicians ought to try to avoid these effects as much as possible; when they do occur, physicians should help mitigate the effects of such diminished capacity by fostering decision-making processes sensitive to the patient's overall interests. Medical practice should be oriented to maximizing patients' ability to make reasonable, informed decisions about their health care. Hasty imposition of authoritarian, paternalistic intervention is more likely to inhibit than to support a patient's recovery of independence. Moreover, when paternalistic intervention is called for, the person authorized to act on the patient's behalf should be someone who can be counted on to return authority to the patient as soon as there is sufficient recovery to allow effective participation in the decision-making process. Ordinarily, this person will not be the patient's physician.

To the extent that patients are to place their trust in their physicians, that specific trust should be earned and not assumed. Trust can be built through sharing information, particularly the medical knowledge that might bear on the patient's expectations and deliberations. In the medical context earning a patient's trust requires that the physician have respect for the decision-making authority of the patient. A more open health care process, which involves rather than excludes patients from decision-making, is more likely to produce results in the best interests of patients than is the practice of paternalism.

As most bioethicists have recognized, physicians have technical expertise that is essential to sound medical decision-making, but they lack other kinds of knowledge necessary to make good decisions about particular patients' needs; physicians are not experts with respect to the centrally relevant knowledge of each patient's distress, values, or coping strategies. Their medical training does not provide them with special knowledge about the social context in which patients' needs for health care arise.

Thus feminists can agree with most of their nonfeminist colleagues in bioethics and insist that physicians should be directed to provide patients with the relevant information on which they rely, so that patients are informed adequately to make their own decisions.[12] Most patients do not need to know the technical terms involved or understand the biochemical theories that underlie medical diagnoses and treatment options. They do need to know what treatment is recommended (and why), whether plausible alternatives exist, what the likely consequences will be of each treatment option, what risks are involved, and what outcome they should expect if they decline treatment. All of these considerations can usually be made accessible to patients.

If more of the training that physicians receive were to cover communication skills, then they would be better able to provide patients with the relevant information; patients would then have the information needed for reasonable decision-making, and paternalism on the basis of superior information would not (normally) be necessary. There is a danger, however, that if physicians become more skillful at communication, then they may be more effective at exercising paternalism, because they could more easily manipulate patients to comply with their agenda. As Alexandra Todd observes, "If communication skills alone increase without adequate attention paid to deeper problems in the scientific, medical model, participants, even though becoming more interactionally competent, will do little to improve health care. In fact, the risk exists that if communication alone improves, patients' trust will increase—creating a situation that could be unhealthy" (Todd 1989, 146). Therefore, feminist analysis demands a change in the ideology that governs the patient–physician interaction, not just reforms in the details of the specific encounters. Physicians' knowledge is distorted by their own biased expectations and those of the scientists from whom they learn.

Communication involves (at least) two parties, and ethicists interested in the realm of health care should be concerned with the role of each participant when examining relationships between patients and physicians. Feminist ethics recommends that we not only advise physicians about how they should behave but also place priority on helping patients to obtain the information they need and to learn how to weigh and interpret the medical advice they receive.

In traditional approaches, when the sources of potential physician bias are uncovered, the conclusion is to reject paternalism and endorse the patient's prima facie right to autonomy. As we have seen, however, many feminists are not comfortable with appealing to the notion of autonomy as the alternative to paternalism. The concept of autonomy carries too many associations of isolation and independence to capture feminist conceptions of agency. In its place we could explore some of the more relational concepts that different feminists have proposed, which might support the agency of patients without abandoning them to their rights.

One example worth pursuing has been offered by Sarah Hoagland (1988). She proposes "autokoenony" as an alternative concept, which stands for "the self in community" and captures the sense of being free from dominance without suggesting self-domination. Autokoenony refers to "a self who is both elemental and related, who has a sense of herself making choices within a context created by community" (Hoagland 1988, 145). An autokoenonous person interacts with others and makes decisions in consideration of her own place and the agendas of others in the community. In the medical context, autokoenony suggests an understanding of patients existing in a social world, where their ends and activities are defined in conjunction with others they trust. This view offers a more realistic perspective of patients choosing in the company of others who help shape their lives; when patients are confronted with difficult decisions, physicians and patients might include in the decision-making process those others who are trusted by the patient.[13] Patients who are isolated, that is, who have no others they can trust, could be helped to form relationships that would foster their decision-making in an interactive way. Self-help groups of patients with a common condition, for instance, usually provide patients with the opportunity to explore the complexities of their decisions in a nonhierarchical environment.

Finally, the ethical question here is not simply a matter of who has the right to make the decision about a patient's health care, that is, whether to endorse autonomy or paternalism in a particular case. It is a question of how to strengthen the patient's agency, how to help her to make medical decisions that will serve her well. This task requires radical rethinking of the patient–physician relationship and development of improved patterns of communication and mutual respect.

To understand the limitations in current practices of communication between doctors and their female patients, we can turn to Sue Fisher (1986) and Alexandra Todd (1989); they have helped identify the sort of information that is usually exchanged and the topics that are usually missing in these encounters. Showing concretely how doctors set and dominate the agenda in their conversations with patients, Fisher and Todd help us to understand why the current model is actually contrary to the goal of fostering patient agency.

It seems clear that we need to turn to a model different from paternalism when patients do experience diminished reasoning or difficulty in making medical decisions as they face incapacitating or frightening illness. Unlike paternalism, a practice derived from the unacceptable model of the patriarchal family, we might invent a practice of "amicalism," which would be built on the more ethically promising model of friendship.[14] Under amicalism, the intention would be to enlist friends or family, who both understand and care personally and specifically for a patient, in the task of medical decision-making, rather than treating medical choice as a contest between isolated patient and physician. When patients feel unable to make decisions on their own (or if they are demonstrably incompetent), they could be helped to communicate with others whom they have reason to trust—that is, those who have already demonstrated their commitment to them as individuals.

Clearly, there would be difficulties in such a model: for example, not all patients have good friends, friends are not always available, not all friendships are worthy of trust, and friends can disagree. Nonetheless, this seems a model worth exploring, because it captures some of the legitimate grounds for paternalism in medical contexts and avoids some of its dangerous and unacceptable aspects. From a feminist perspective, it is also closer to the ethical ideal for addressing the inequalities inherent in a situation of serious illness.

8

Research

The history of medical research is filled not only with glorious discoveries but also with shameful examples of abuses of power and evidence of many researchers' flagrant disregard for the well-being of the subjects involved. The torturous experiments of the infamous Nazi doctors are probably the most familiar; they constitute particularly abhorrent examples of unethical research, but they are not entirely isolated events. For centuries medical scientists used unconsenting, weak, and powerless people as subjects in their studies, although seldom before in quite such a vicious or systematic way.[1] The public revulsion and distrust that followed revelations of the Nazi abuse of medical authority led to the introduction of a series of ethical codes governing the conduct of research on human subjects, beginning with the Nuremberg Code.

Not all moral problems can be addressed by codes, however; nor is it always obvious what moral position best applies to particular situations. Therefore, bioethicists have seen the need for extensive discussions about the moral considerations that are relevant in evaluating medical research. Among the questions commonly addressed are general ones, such as what sorts of research are inherently unethical and what sorts of criteria should be invoked when specific projects are evaluated. Studies that involve live human or animal subjects, for example, demand investigation as to whether there is justification for using living subjects and whether adequate attention has been paid to their safety and well-being. In the case of human subjects additional worries arise, such as how the subject population has been selected and what measures have been used to obtain the informed consent of the participants.

In the nonfeminist bioethics literature the principal ethical questions that are raised about research with human subjects center on matters of participation and consent. Typical questions pursued concern who can be asked to participate in research projects, under what circumstances voluntary consent from subjects can be obtained, whether it is acceptable to proceed when the proposed subjects cannot consent, and what limits exist on the degree of risk to which subjects will be exposed. Sometimes questions are asked about the legitimacy of particular research programs, for example, using fetal tissue for treating adult diseases. Other questions, concerning such issues as the appropriate degree of spending on research, are also found in the literature.

Each question explored in the bioethics literature is important from a feminist point of view, but so are others that have been mostly absent in the nonfeminist debates. For example, feminists ask how research topics are actually chosen: which issues are investigated and which are neglected by medical researchers, whose interests are served by the projects pursued and whose interests are ignored, and who controls research decisions and to whom researchers are accountable. Recognizing that patterns of oppression in society extend into the practices of medicine, feminists take a special interest in any medical research that is conducted on women. Moreover, their study of women's health care leads them to raise ethical questions about what guidelines determine whether procedures should be classified as experimental or as established therapy. Further, many feminists recommend models of the subject–investigator relationship that differ from the conceptions that govern most research practices.

In this chapter I explore only a few of the many specific ethical questions that feminists might raise about medical research. I review some of the ethical problems posed by the existing practice of decision-making in the area of research on women and make some proposals about how this decision-making could be conducted in a more ethically acceptable manner. Toward this end, I recommend that oppressed groups be treated as special subject groups if they are enlisted in research projects, and I examine how a feminist perspective on science might shape the nature of medical research for women and others.

Oppression and Research

Central to most discussions of research in the mainstream bioethics literature is consideration of what constraints should govern the use of human subjects. It is important to set limits on the use that can be made of human subjects, because research involves costs for its subjects, exposing them at least to some degree of inconvenience and, frequently, to discomfort and risk; moreover, by definition outcomes are uncertain so some risks are inevitably present. Because often expected benefits are long-term and directed at some future others, it cannot be assumed that subjects will benefit directly from their involvement in a research program. Even in so-called therapeutic research, where subjects have some hope of personal benefit, no assurances can be offered to the patient-subjects as long as the treatment being evaluated is experimental.[2] Usually subjects cannot even be certain that they are receiving the new therapy, because scientific methodology recommends that the effectiveness of new treatments be measured by comparison with a randomly assigned control group, whose members do not receive the therapy being tested. (The scientifically preferred study requires a double-blind format, where neither the patient-subject nor her treating physician knows if she is getting the new therapy or a placebo alternative.) Whichever group a subject seeking therapy is assigned to, she risks a worsening of her condition: if she is in the group receiving the new therapy, then the therapy may turn out to be ineffective or even dangerous; if she is in the control group, then she may be denied active therapy altogether.

In nontheraupeutic research there is no prospect of personal benefit for subjects other than the satisfaction of helping others or, in some cases, payment for participation. Most bioethicists agree that the decision to expose research subjects to this risk can be justified only when there is hope that the knowledge obtained from the study will help provide better medical care to others in the future.

Because of the self-sacrifice implicit in participation in medical research, bioethicists have agreed that it would be exploitative and unacceptable to allow the use of human subjects without their consent. Hence they have been concerned to clarify the criteria necessary to ensure that proper consent is obtained from subjects; they have focused on the sort of information needed, the degree of understanding to be achieved, the competence of each subject to make such decisions, and, significantly, the degree of voluntariness that motivates compliance. The general principle common to these debates is that persons should only be involved as subjects if they freely choose to participate (or, when not competent, if there is reason to believe they would so choose if able). Any research that does not meet these standards is generally thought to be ethically unacceptable.

It is widely acknowledged that particular subject groups are especially vulnerable to exploitation by researchers, and hence special precautions must be used in considering research on these designated groups. Most bioethicists agree, for instance, that research on prisoners is questionable even if they offer consent, because the range of autonomous choice available to them is so restricted that their consent may not be meaningful. As a result, special guidelines have been instituted that restrict the use of prisoners in medical experiments. There is also widespread agreement that the vulnerability of children and their inability to give adequate informed consent require that specific regulations limit the involvement of minors in medical experimentation. Parallel arguments govern the use of mentally handicapped persons in experimental research. Because it is assumed that patients are in a weakened state and are excessively dependent on their physicians, special restrictions on patient involvement in medical experimentation have also been introduced.

For distinct but important reasons, there are grounds for viewing women as constituting another special group for the purposes of medical research. Precisely because women's oppression consists in the subordination of women's interests to those of others, we ought to be wary of any proposal to use women's services for some greater social good, lest we further extend their oppression. We have already observed that women's relatively powerless role in society and their disproportionate frequency of medical interactions make them especially vulnerable as patients. These features also place them at a particular disadvantage when they become involved as subjects in medical research. Hence researchers should be required to take special precautions against the possibility of exploitation when they conduct research projects on women. We need ethical guidelines that will govern women's participation in medical research to ensure that women's service to this research is not especially dangerous for the individuals involved. Because there is a moral responsibility to reduce and not increase existing oppression, we should also try to ensure that the research in question contributes to the overall well-being of women, not to any further harm for women. Similar arguments apply for research directed at members of other oppressed groups and research conducted on specific groups of women who might be especially vulnerable.

Experience reveals ample reason for worry. Medical manipulation has made women a readily available population for research by guaranteeing their disproportionate presence in medical institutions. The monopoly that medical practitioners have achieved over the management of all phases of normal female development has provided researchers with an easily accessible population of healthy subjects for use in nontherapeutic research. Further, researchers have always been inclined to conduct their research on those considered to be less important than most other members of society, and have frequently selected prisoners, institutionalized populations, the poor, or the elderly for their studies. As an oppressed population, women are likely to be considered relatively expendable, making them likely candidates for exposure to risks from which more valued members of society would be protected.[3]

Consider one example of how women's ready accessibility as patients proved irresistible to researchers. In 1964 charges emerged concerning the nonvoluntary use of twenty-two residents at the Jewish Chronic Disease Hospital in a cancer study. These patients were subcutaneously injected with live cancer cells to determine the rate at which the cells would be rejected. Testimony revealed that the researchers had already performed the same procedure on three hundred healthy subjects and three hundred cancer victims and found that although all subjects rejected the cells, the healthy ones did so much more quickly than did the cancer patients. To determine whether the slow rejection rate was caused by cancer or by the patients' weakened physical condition, the researchers sought out debilitated patients who were suffering from other diseases, so that they could measure their rejection rates—hence the conscription of patients from the Jewish Chronic Disease Hospital.

The hearings focused on the purpose of the research, the procedures that were followed in the hospital, the ability of the particular patients to give consent, whether or not they actually gave consent, and the adequacy of the information that was provided to the subjects. In their defense, the researchers argued that they were confident the cells would be rejected and that they knew the experiment to be safe. They did admit, however that because of the strong aversion the public has to cancer, they believed few people would be likely to agree to have cancer cells injected into their bodies if they understood the request; hence they deliberately refrained from informing the patients that the cells to be injected would be cancerous.

It does not appear that any concern was expressed about the other six hundred subjects who had been involved in prior trials, yet similar questions should be raised about them. The subjects used for the earlier tests included three hundred dying, cancer-patient "volunteers" from a hospital associated with Chester Southam, the principal investigator. The healthy subject population included a group of prisoner volunteers from the Ohio state penitentiary. It also included a group of women. In testimony Southam explained that in the early stages of the research a full explanation was given to all volunteers, but in recent years the actual nature of the material injected was not disclosed.

Southam solicited cooperation from the Jewish Chronic Disease Hospital by reporting that "for two years we have been doing the tests *routinely on all postoperative patients on our gynecology service*" (Katz 1972, 11, emphasis added). Although they sought signed permits from the prison volunteers "because of the law-oriented personalities of these men, rather than for any medical reason," he admitted that they did not obtain written "permission from our patients before doing these studies" (Katz 1972, 11). Although the hearings did not explore this issue, it is apparent that many women were enlisted as uninformed and hence unconsenting subjects, by virtue of their status as postoperative gynecological patients.

Since the time of those hearings there have been many debates in the bioethics literature (and in various governing bodies) about the legitimacy of using prisoners as research subjects; much tighter restrictions have been put in place to govern research on prisoners. There have also been many moral debates about the use of ill populations for research that has no chance of being therapeutic for them; here, too, tight controls have been adopted. None of the bioethicists who have addressed this case, however, has seen a problem with the fact that the researchers' "healthy" volunteers were women who were receiving postoperative care on the gynecological service. As long as ethicists remain silent about harms perpetrated on women, there is reason to worry that women will continue to be exploited for the purposes of medical research.

Feminist ethics reminds us that patriarchy devalues women; women who are no longer able to fulfill their designated role as childbearers are especially devalued. Thus women in a postoperative gynecological ward are particularly vulnerable to multiple exploitation. The researchers chose to conduct their study on terminal patients, prisoners, senile men, and sterile women—all groups that our society judges as less than fully valuable. This point is vividly brought home in an interview Southam granted to *Science*. He maintained that the experiment was completely safe, but when asked if he and his colleagues would have considered taking part in the experiment themselves, he replied: "I would not have hesitated if it would have served a useful purpose. But to me it seemed like false heroism, like the old question whether the General should march behind or in front of his troops. I do not regard myself as indispensable—if I were not doing this work someone else would be—and I did not regard the experiments as dangerous. But, let's face it, there are relatively few skilled cancer researchers and it seemed stupid to take even the little risk" (quoted in Katz 1972, 49). In other words, the actual subjects used—the prisoners; terminal cancer patients; chronically ill, old men; and women who had undergone gynecological surgery—were less valuable and more dispensable than he was.

This cancer study is not atypical. Researchers often choose to conduct their experiments on populations that are considered expendable by the dominant groups in society. The blatant hostility of Nazi scientists is an extreme case of the dangers of research in a racist society, but more subtle practices can be found in the annals of medical research. Consider, for instance, the notorious Tuskegee syphilis study (Pence 1990). It involved a group of poor, black men in Mississippi, who were subjected to decades of nontreatment for syphilis so that doctors could document the course of the disease (information already widely available); begun in the 1930s, the study was continued into the 1970s, long past the time that antibiotics had been found to be an effective treatment for syphilis. It ended only after media attention created a public outcry. The subjects were not informed that they were part of an ongoing study or offered the alternative of conventional therapy. It seems clear that racism supported the view that these men's lives were expendable.

Nonfeminist bioethicists have set too narrow a focus in their attempts to identify the conditions that contribute to the unjust exploitation of individuals in research, and they have been too optimistic in their assumptions about the criteria that are jointly sufficient to protect against such abuse. They have argued for restrictions on the basis of the limited competence of members of specified groups to give consent. Individual competence, however, is not the issue. Prisoners and many ill people do not actually lack competence. They are at special risk because they are embedded in coercive circumstances that challenge the very conception of "free choice"; because all their options are so limited, they can be more easily exploited by others who are more powerful. They are also in danger because their well-being is not valued by society; harms to them are not experienced as a significant loss to the community.

Oppression creates the same sorts of circumstances. Members of oppressed groups usually also have limited opportunities. They, too, are caught in an environment that is coercive and that limits their ability to choose some sorts of options. Moreover, like prisoners, children, and mentally ill populations, victims of oppression are devalued in a hierarchical society. Hence members of oppressed groups are particularly vulnerable to exploitation in research. Ethical concern should address the circumstances of consent, as well as the matter of individual competence. Oppression, like prison and poverty, constitutes a circumstance that limits one's ability to protect oneself from abuse.

To protect children, the aged, the very ill, mentally incompetent people, and prisoners from exploitation by researchers, various ethical guidelines propose that they not be asked to participate in research not directed specifically at benefiting the group to which they belong. Similar restrictions should be applied to women and members of other oppressed groups. Any research program that proposes to recruit women qua women should aim to improve the health of women specifically and not simply be an opportunistic use of the women as readily available subjects. In other words, there needs to be an explicit reason for using women as subjects, such as the need to find out how women in particular are affected by the treatment being evaluated. Women should not be recruited for research that is irrelevant to their care as women, as they were in Southam's cancer study. Similar arguments should govern the use of people of color, religious minorities, disabled people, and so forth in research. If the research would be equally valid and equally beneficial to members of the oppressed group if conducted on a nonoppressed population—that is, if being female (or black, native, or disabled) is judged to be irrelevant to the outcome—then oppressed groups ought not to be employed.

Women as Subjects

Although much of the medical research that involves women as subjects has been explicitly concerned with matters of women's health, there are further concerns feminists should raise about the focus of this research. We need to consider, for instance, which conditions are investigated and which are left unexplored. It is troublesome that even though women's patterns of disease and their responses to treatment are not always the same as men's, most research into conditions that are shared by men and women focuses on male experiences as the norm. Hence women's experiences with heart disease, cancers of their nonreproductive organs, diabetes, and so forth are often inadequately researched (McMurray 1990). Anticipating that women will respond differently from men and hence "distort" the data, therapeutic studies on conditions that affect both men and women almost always select males as the subject of choice. This decision leaves practitioners without adequate information for the specific treatment of women. Further, the variations of diseases among black, native American, and disabled populations are also largely understudied, so doctors are especially unprepared to respond to the health needs of women who belong to other oppressed groups.[4] It is a matter of serious moral concern that there are so many urgent health needs of women that are seriously and inexcusably under-researched.

Another subject requiring ethical attention is that some of the studies specifically concerning women's health that have been undertaken have involved blatant violation of subjects' rights. For example, feminist researchers have uncovered the appalling story of a New Zealand study on women that is reminiscent of the notorious Tuskegee experiment (Haines 1990). Beginning in 1966, Herbert Green sought to prove his assumption that early signs of abnormal cell changes in the cervix were unlikely to lead to cervical cancer. To this end, he refrained from offering conventional forms of treatment to women who were diagnosed with this precancerous condition. The women involved were denied relevant information about the options for treatment. Although they were not asked to consent to participate in any study, they were monitored and subjected to repeated, invasive examinations to establish the "natural history of carcinoma in situ." The experiment continued for over twenty years; over that period nearly thirty women died of cervical cancer, and many others suffered a variety of health problems. The untreated women experienced vastly higher rates of invasive cancer and death than others with conventional treatment. Although many members of the medical community knew about the study and disapproved of it, it was not halted until women mounted sufficient political pressure to force a public inquiry. In the absence of organized political pressure, it seems, the medical community was willing to tolerate the needless death and suffering of many women, rather than restrict the "academic freedom" of one of their own.[5]

Moral concern should also be expressed that other research into the appropriate treatment of diseases that affect women uniquely has been inadequate or unacceptably late in its initiation, subjecting countless women to harmful and misguided treatment. For decades radical amputation was judged the appropriate therapy for any evidence of cancer or even the prospect of cancer in women's reproductive organs. Doctors told women that surgical removal of their breasts, uteruses, and ovaries was necessary if cancer was detected or suspected or if there was some reason to believe it might develop. (Prophylactic removal of reproductive organs was a widely recommended therapy even when no trace of cancer was found because of the possibility that cancer might develop in the future unless the site of growth was removed.)[6] Only recently have the appropriate scientific studies been carried out to evaluate the success of such "therapies."

Most of the medical research on specifically female health issues that is pursued has been concentrated on matters of reproduction. It is important to ask why medical researchers seem to be interested in only particular sorts of questions about women. It seems that much of the scientific research directed at oppressed populations aims to establish differences (and usually inferiorities) between the oppressed group and the dominant population of society; comparatively little research seems to be directed at meeting the explicit needs of oppressed groups. Although it is true that their reproductive organs constitute the major area of physiological difference between women and men, it is not necessary that concerns about women's health be confined solely to the health of their reproductive organs. By limiting their attention almost exclusively to means of exercising control over women's reproductive functions, medical researchers reflect a view of women as principally defined in terms of their childbearing function. In such ways, the research community and the agencies that fund it make their own contribution to the perpetuation of women's oppression.

Nevertheless, it must be emphasized that women themselves have a strong interest in the development of safe, reversible, reliable, and affordable ways to control their fertility, and they welcome measures that can ensure safer, less frightening childbirth experiences. Thus research into measures that permit safe, personal control over reproduction is, in principle, of benefit to women. As we have seen, however, much of the actual research on contraception and infertility that is pursued is not intended to increase women's control over their fertility. It is, therefore, necessary to distinguish between research aimed at giving women choice over their own fertility and research in support of state-sponsored population control policies. The value to women of research directed at controlling their fertility will vary greatly, depending on whether the products of that research will place control in the hands of women or in the hands of "experts."

In addition, feminists see grounds for moral concern in the specific details of much of this research. The case history of the development of birth-control pills, for example, reveals the need to ensure that particularly vulnerable women are protected from exploitation as research subjects: the earliest tests on "the pill" were carried out on poor and uneducated women in Puerto Rico and Mexico. Increasingly, drug companies are choosing to bypass the restrictive limits of human-subject research in the West and conduct their tests in less-developed nations, where research practices are much freer.

Moreover, when we look at some of the experiences women have had with innovative treatments in the area of their reproduction, we find a clear need to draw more stringent distinctions between research and therapy. Practices that are classified as experimental are monitored and controlled by far more exacting ethical standards than those that govern the delivery of established treatments. Understandably, patients believe that unless they formally consent to participate in a research program, they are receiving proven therapies. This presumption, however, is often wrong. In practice, the fine line separating therapeutic research from "established" therapies is quite permeable, especially in the area of women's health care.

In case after case we find that women receive treatments that have been falsely represented as safe, established, therapeutic practices, with no warnings or explanations about the innovative status of these procedures. For example, millions of women have used contraceptive drugs and devices that they believed had been tested and found safe, when in fact thorough testing had not been performed or, in some particularly infamous cases, data indicating danger were ignored or covered up (for example, the Dalkon Shield). The pill was widely marketed for more than a decade before federal hearings on its safety revealed some of the risks it posed and the hazards of long-term use.[8]

The failure to distinguish between research and therapy is particularly pronounced today in the are a of infertility treatment. Despite the serious hazards posed by the potent drugs involved (many have been associated with serious side effects, including death), adequate testing is often overlooked before such drugs are administered as routine therapy.[9] Fertility clinics, springing up around the world, offer "therapies" that are expensive, dangerous, painful, traumatizing, even life-threatening, and, for the most part, unsuccessful. Practitioners experiment with various modifications of the latest techniques without declaring their work as research and hence without needing to subject it to the careful scientific and ethical review required of research projects (or the stringent standards of informed consent that should be required of patient-subjects). Despite its high failure rate, in vitro fertilization is seen as an established therapy (a new medical miracle, in fact), not an experiment. By tolerating a blurring of the boundary between research and established therapy in this area of care, the medical community has limited women's ability to make informed decisions about their participation in data collection for new means of controlling fertility.

Although feminist analysis does not suggest that women alone are subject to such dangerous ambiguity, it does reveal that women are particularly vulnerable because of their unique need to control their fertility. Contraceptives and fertility treatments are overwhelmingly directed at women and constitute an enormous source of profit for their manufacturers.[10] Women's relatively powerless positions in society make it a matter of particular importance that we guard against the likelihood that their health is sacrificed to the financial interests of the pharmeceutical industry.[11]

Therefore, we must be especially vigilant in demanding proper scientific review of medical treatments aimed exclusively at women. Drugs and procedures designed to help women control their fertility should be carefully studied before being promoted as accepted therapy. Whatever the medical innovation, ethical concern for the well-being of patients demands adequate testing of new products and techniques before release and promotion in the marketplace. It also demands that patients be informed that many drugs involve risks that cannot be known for many years and that use of these new therapies should be understood as participation in an ongoing testing program.

When conducting an ethical analysis of a research proposal, the likely effects of the practice in question on society as a whole and on women and members of other dominated groups in particular should be taken into account. Therefore, research into means by which powerful men may increase control over the reproductive rates of women should be challenged, as should research that supports dominance structures by allowing the pursuit of racial and gender supremacy, research that threatens the environment, and research that supports unethical behaviors.[12] The political implications of research cannot be overlooked in any ethical review. Thorough ethical evaluation of medical research requires consideration of how the knowledge that is sought is likely to affect those who are especially disadvantaged in society.

The Organization of Research

Feminist critiques of science also have objected to the common interpretation of the methodological demand that science be neutral and objective as a requirement for a clear division between the researcher and the object of study. They remind us that the scientific method was developed as a means of dominating nature: Francis Bacon, the "father" of modern science, appealed to metaphors of rape and torture to make nature reveal "her" secrets (Merchant 1980). Modern scientific norms use less-provocative language, but they maintain a clear division between scientific subject and scientific object. Nature is still objectified, and scientific knowledge is pursued for the purpose of controlling and exploiting nature. The knower is envisioned as distinct from and dominant over what is to be known.[13]

Feminists propose alternative models for scientific research. For example, Evelyn Fox Keller's (1983) analysis of the distinct approach to research taken by Nobel prize winner Barbara McClintock explores McClintock's commitment to closing the gap between herself and the subject of her research. By identifying with the biological material and forming an emotional bond with it, Keller argues, McClintock was able to perceive processes that were missed by colleagues who relied on the standard scientific model of distance between researcher and scientific object. McClintock developed a "feeling for the organism" and learned to "listen to the material," providing a model of science that connects the knower with the known (Keller 1983).

In most scientific projects research subjects are generally viewed as passive objects of investigation, not active participants in the project; common presumptions about scientific methodology suggest that experimental results may be compromised if subjects become knowledgeable participants. In general, the contribution that subjects may make to a given research project is limited to their availability as test sites for investigation. Research is controlled by the investigators, who may care personally for the well-being of their subjects, but who also have other interests (for example, contributing to the growth of scientific knowledge, helping humanity, or achieving fame and professional advancement); these other interests may well conflict with those of the experimental subjects.

Science projects an image of dispassionate, neutral objectivity, a search for truth wherever it is to be found. In reality, however, science is an expensive, competitive institution. Researchers do not pursue whatever projects come into their heads but those for which they can receive funding. Needing to attract grant money and produce results, they shape their research interests to serve the orientations of funding sources. In this way projects are tied to the special interests of those with the power and resources to support them. A significant amount of scientific research is, for example, funded by national defense departments and linked to military interests. In the area of health care, much of the research is funded by pharmaceutical companies or, more recently, by the newly developing biotechnology industry. Even public money spent on health research reflects the political clout of special interests: although cancer prevention promises to save far more lives than treatment, vastly greater resources are directed at finding a cure for cancer than at preventing it, because the former promises great profits to industry, whereas the latter threatens to reduce them.

When feminists review the statistics associated with in vitro fertilization, they wonder why money is not spent on preventing infertility, rather than trying to correct it after the fact. Renate Klein (1989) offers the explanation that biotechnology promises fame and prestige to the doctors, scientists, and corporations involved and establishes a product for international export. She reports that a doctor associated with a private in vitro fertilization clinic in the United States anticipates that eventually the process could generate six billion dollars a year. It seems that financial concerns dictate that research must continue to the point where the money that has already been invested in reproductive technologies can be recouped and profits generated.

The forces directing other aspects of medical research are also skewed toward high-tech solutions; Western culture expects and celebrates technological responses to human problems. Careers and institutional reputations are made on technological breakthroughs, and technology promises the opportunity of significant profits to innovators. Therefore, in health care generally, multiple forces direct research at technological interventions in the face of health crises. Little support is available for the less-dramatic, less-rewarding work associated with prevention and the management of disease (Ratcliff 1989).

The rhetoric of medical research speaks of fighting wars against cancer and heart disease, not of finding ways of avoiding the need for battle. As the urgency to address the growing threat of AIDS in the population is felt in the research and health care communities, the focus is on the miracle of finding the cure and the vaccine. Relatively few resources are provided for learning better how to avoid or respond to the secondary infections from which AIDS sufferers usually die. Given our failure to prevent disease, technological innovations can be of great support to those who actually suffer from catastrophic illness, but society does not adequately weigh the trade-offs involved. Research toward developing various technologies is readily funded, and when successful, the resulting techniques are quickly incorporated into our health care schemes, but nowhere within the research phase is the measure taken of the implications for specific discoveries in the overall distribution of resources. Thus we now have the situation where public hospitals continue to invest in expensive technology and find themselves having to close beds, because there are insufficient funds left to staff the hospitals adequately.

Technological medicine is expensive and only accessible to those who live in developed countries, and often only to the wealthy among them. By committing Western research attention to technological health care, we essentially abandon responsibility for the health care needs of those in the developing world and often, too, for the needs of the poor among us. Because research inevitably leads to changes in health policy, efforts should be made to anticipate and review the likely effects of these changes; once available, technology becomes virtually irresistible.

Recommendations

The myth of the neutral, apolitical scientist can no longer be accepted. Research is a social and political activity, which has repercussions in our collective lives. Unless explicit attention is paid to the need for more democratic representation among the decision-makers responsible for research programs, the science that is carried out will continue to be, by and large, a science that supports the interests of the dominant groups in society. Scientists should recognize their complicity in perpetuating existing power structures and seek to increase their connection with, rather than distance from, the subjects of their work. They should see themselves as accountable to the population at large, not merely the institutions and corporations that support their work.

Current ethical standards in Canada and the United States demand that researchers gain the "informed consent" of their subjects; that is, they must explain what will happen to the subjects, including an indication of whatever risks are anticipated. Researchers are expected to inform their potential subjects that they are free to refuse participation, and they must ensure that their subjects understand the relevant information and genuinely consent. Nevertheless, these measures are not adequate to ensure that the research is ethically acceptable. We must also recognize that research reflects and supports particular social interests and may jeopardize others. Therefore, it is necessary to examine the potential social and political implications of research, as well as its acceptance by research subjects.

Review by the institutions in which researchers work and by funding agencies is usually the only constraint placed on the judgment of the researchers, but these measures are not sufficient to capture all relevant concerns. Research institutions and funding agencies are far from representative; they are controlled by members of the dominant class of society, and the values they pursue inevitably reflect the class, gender, and racial backgrounds of the powerful. Research pursued on women is research that has usually been chosen by privileged men (and, occasionally, by women trained by such men). Specific research may serve women's interests, but as things are now arranged, that only occurs when women's interests happen to coincide with those of the people who control research policy or when an explicit commitment to altruism shapes the decisions made in a particular case. Even so, it is most likely that the interests served will be those of relatively privileged women (white, heterosexual, middle-class, and educated); other women may have quite distinct interests, and no mechanism governing research choices is in place to address this diversity of interests.

Hence it is important that we recognize that medical research is a political activity; as such, it should be responsive to the principles of participatory democracy. Decisions about the direction of research should be made publicly and in a manner that ensures accountability to the specific communities at risk. Representatives of different interest groups in society, especially those of oppressed groups, should have input into the process of setting goals and guidelines for research. Whenever a research project may affect or unjustly ignore an oppressed segment of society, it is essential that the voices of that group be heard.

This is a very complicated task, because a group may be affected indirectly as well as directly. People who were born with birth defects, for example, may suffer from research proposed in the area of genetic screening if it leads to mandatory screening against their conditions, because such screening may result in less tolerance and social support for anyone who has been born with these now "preventable" diseases. Poor women and women of color will be harmed by fertility research on privileged women if the result is that eggs are "harvested" from more valued women, matured, fertilized in the lab, and transplanted into more vulnerable women for gestation and delivery. Social policy must be sensitive to such possibilities when research plans are contemplated; ethical reviews should explicitly consider whether there is social evidence that the technique in question might be applied in ways that will further existing patterns of oppression.

Therefore, research should be evaluated not only in terms of its effects on the subjects of the experiment but also in terms of its connection with existing patterns of oppression and domination in society. We need to develop mechanisms to address the hazards that are involved when the repercussions of a research project make the relatively powerless among us yet more vulnerable. One useful means of achieving this sensitivity would be to include representatives of oppressed groups in the decision-making structures.[14] It is not easy to identify everyone who should participate in this task, but we cannot assume that the voices of relevant groups are already included in our institutional reviews simply by virtue of the presence of a female, (or more rarely, a black or disabled) academic on the committees.

The research community needs to develop respectful lines of communication with community health care groups that act in an advocacy capacity for the populations they represent.[15] Feminist ethics demands that representatives of all oppressed groups be included in the setting of our medical research agendas.

Three

Feminist Expansions of the Bioethics Landscape

9

Ascriptions of Illness

According to Marilyn Frye, "one of the most characteristic and ubiquitous features of the world as experienced by oppressed people is the double bind—situations in which options are reduced to a very few and all of them expose one to penalty, censure or deprivation" (Frye 1983, 2). In this chapter I argue that medical authorities have created a series of double binds for women, by characterizing as pathological various bodily and mental states that are typical of women. They have, for instance, declared that normally both menstruation and its cessation (in either pregnancy or menopause) are appropriate subjects for medical treatment. In addition, most women are judged as being too fat or too thin, as eating too much or too little (or both, if they are bulimic), or as neglecting or overindulging in exercise; each of these different states is claimed to constitute a threat to health. Further, psychiatrists and other mental health workers consider the norms of "healthy" womanhood to be ones that are unhealthy for adults (Broverman et al. 1981), so non-feminist therapists "help" women conform to the standards of femininity—that is, to behavioral norms that they judge to constitute evidence of illness for adult existence.

In other words, women are caught in multiple double binds with respect to the norms of health and illness. Medical experts have claimed the authority to determine the range of the concepts of health and illness. They have used this authority to declare that many of the conditions that constitute normalcy for women are unhealthy and therefore, suitable subjects for medical management.

The decision to view as diseases such elements of women's lives as menstruation, pregnancy, menopause, body size, and feminine behavior forms an integral part of women's general oppression. Because being judged ill characteristically constitutes grounds for distinct treatment in society, the definition of ordinary female experience as pathological serves as a justification for treating women differently from men. Moreover, classifying the ordinary events of women's lives as illnesses licenses wide-scale medical management of women under claims of beneficence. Feminists are understandably critical of the wholesale classification of ordinary female experience as illness.

Nevertheless, there are medically dangerous anomalies associated with each of these aspects of women's lives; moral critiques of excessive medicalization with respect to female existence do not imply that all experiences of menstruation, pregnancy, menopause, and so forth should be automatically accepted as healthy. Particular women sometimes experience these events as intolerably painful, frightening, or otherwise distressing, and medical experts often have therapies available that can help reduce the pain, risks, or disability such women suffer. It is important, then, for feminist accounts to acknowledge that serious complications can occur with any aspect of a woman's reproductive life and to recognize that medical intervention is sometimes the safest course for her to pursue. It would be a mistake for feminists to insist that because menstruation, pregnancy, and so forth are ordinary events in women's lives, we should never apply the label of illness to particular instances.

When is it appropriate to apply the language of illness and disease to menstrually defined conditions? I attempt to answer this question by reviewing some of the history behind the medical decisions to designate these particularly female conditions as illnesses and by considering the implications of some of the proposed definitions of "health" and "illness" in the bioethics literature. In particular, I try to determine whether feminist analysis suggests that we should welcome or resist the recent decision of the American Psychiatric Association to add premenstrual syndrome (PMS) to its official diagnostic list.[1]

The Historical View of Menstruation as Illness

A brief review of the history of medical attitudes toward menstruation helps to define the context of contemporary debates surrounding PMS. Menstruation has always been recognized as an important element of difference between the sexes, but perceiving it as an explicitly medical event is a fairly recent phenomenon. Until the nineteenth century, it was common to believe that women's reproductive organs were analogous to men's and had comparable roles to play. The principal differences between men and women were thought to derive from the supposed lower body temperatures of women. Aristotle, for instance, considered menstrual blood to be semen that was insufficiently cooked.[2] Hippocrates thought that menstruation was a means of cleansing impurities from the body, making it an important element of overall health, and that men could accomplish the same end through sweat because of their greater body heat (Martin 1987). In the second century Galen proposed that it was necessary for both men and women to shed impurities from the body through blood; menstruation was the method women used for this end, and men could achieve the same thing by having their blood let (Martin 1987). Throughout the eighteenth century, it was common to see menstruation as natural and good for the body. Far from treating it as an illness, physicians warned women against indolence at the time of menstruation, encouraging them to maintain their regular activities (Lander 1988).

During the era of the Enlightenment, cultural values shifted and increased emphasis was placed on rationality; in a climate of growing pressures for democracy, it became socially necessary to provide justification for the different political treatment of men and women.[3] Intellectuals felt challenged to establish a physiological basis for the social construction of gender difference, so that society could maintain the legitimacy of male dominance.[4] The nineteenth century brought a concerted effort to prove that women differed from men in kind as well as by status. Menstruation, which is unique to women and nearly universal among them, was seen as providing the needed evidence. Therefore, in the nineteenth century menstruation came to be defined as pathological.

This change in thinking was reinforced by other cultural shifts. Industrialization and urbanization in America changed the role of women in the home. Men were increasingly involved in work away from home, but women were still largely relegated to the domestic sphere;[5] thus began the modern sexual division of labor. At the same time, middle-class women were freed from the burden of making many household products, because these could now be purchased as commodities. They had time and energy to define new interests. Many women became politically active in the abolition movement and the growing suffrage movement, and as colleges began to admit women, many pursued higher education. It was a period of mounting feminist awareness and activism.

Simultaneously, gynecology was becoming established as a distinct medical specialty. Speaking with scientific authority, the doctors of the era argued for the view that women were disabled during menstruation and probably also for a week or so before its onset; many insisted that the only way to preserve women's health was to have them retire from regular activities during that period. In 1859 the French historian Jules Michelet summarized the scientific evidence of his day as follows: "Woman . . . is generally ailing at least one week out of four. . . . But the week that precedes that of the crisis is also a troublesome one. And into the eight or ten days which follow this week of pain, is prolonged a languour and a weakness. . . . So that, in reality, 15 or 20 days out of 28 (we may say nearly always) woman is not only an invalid, but a wounded one" (quoted in Lander 1988, 48).

The mid-nineteenth century, then, brought with it a new medical interest in menstruation and women's reproductive organs; the focus of that interest was to establish menstruation as disability that demands rest and withdrawal from ordinary activities. Scientific evidence was collected to prove that the womb was in competition with the brain for blood and energy; hence it was argued that study, political activity, or any sort of serious mental work was harmful to a menstruating woman. By the end of the century physicians were in the forefront of the campaign to drive women out of the universities and to restrict their participation in the suffrage campaigns that increasingly brought women into the political sphere. Although some female practitioners gathered evidence to the contrary, the prevailing medical attitude was that menstruation created invalids out of women and made them particularly unfit for activities demanding significant mental effort. No thought was given, apparently, to adapting the demands of the universities or workplace to these supposed special needs of women.

Working-class women, of course, did not have the luxury of taking to their beds for three to twenty days a month. The medical authorities who declared that menstruation incapacitated middle- and upper-class women seemed to recognize the incongruity; they suggested that working-class women coped with their need to work while menstruating by becoming more masculine and hence less in need of special care. (Such masculinization was thought to be an unfortunate way of having to respond to need and not something to be pursued by more affluent women, who had other choices.) Black and native women, it was argued, had different constitutions and hence did not need coddling (Ehrenreich and English 1978). Further, it was assumed that nonwhite women did not face the demands posed by mental work.

As long as there were economic reasons to keep middle-class women out of the workplace, menstruation was seen as a legitimate justification for "protecting" them from harm; it was not generally recognized as a prohibition on their free choices. During the time that women's political involvement combined with their growing pursuit of education, the demands of the womb during menstruation were judged a serious threat to their active intellectual pursuits. When economic needs shifted and society needed women to return in force to the workplace, however, medical authorities revised their views on menstruation and encouraged continuous activity throughout menstruation. Medical science willingly provided the rationale for both sorts of claims (Martin 1987; Lander 1988).

PMS

In the twentieth century medical knowledge of menstruation has become far more sophisticated than it was in the nineteenth; so, too, have the political responses to feminism. It is no longer argued that menstruation per se incapacitates all women from activity while it occurs. The economic demands of moving women in and out of the workplace have continued, however, and medical views on menstruation have kept pace with changing social and economic currents. Instead of menstruation itself, PMS has become the condition of choice to serve this function in contemporary life.

Although, as we have seen, many nineteenth-century physicians expressed concern for women's fragility during the week preceding menstruation, credit for identifying the specific condition of premenstrual distress is generally given to Robert T. Frank. Frank saw the premenstrual period as problematic for women and had concern about their ability to work during this time; he coined the term "premenstrual tension" to identify a pathological degree of anxiety that occurred premenstrually and argued that affected women should be given time away from work. His work on premenstrual tension was published in 1931, that is, when the gains that women had made in the workforce during the war were being undermined by the Depression and when women were being pressured to give up paid employment so that men could take their jobs (Martin 1987). When demands for women's participation in the labor force resumed in World War II, medical authorities changed their minds again and denied the debilitating nature of menstruation, ignoring the current theories about premenstrual tension. In the post-war period of the 1950s, however, when women were again encouraged to leave the paid labor force to make way for returning male soldiers—and when the economy demanded increased reproduction in the form of the post-war baby boom—premenstrual distress reappeared in the medical literature.

At this time the condition was renamed premenstrual syndrome (PMS) to incorporate a broad range of symptoms; it was widely publicized by Katharina Dalton, a physician who perceived herself as a sufferer of the condition. Dalton founded the first PMS clinic and became a major advocate of recognition of PMS as a disease. According to her analysis, PMS is triggered by a specific hormone deficiency and therefore can be corrected through hormone therapy. She claims that PMS costs British industry 3 percent and American industry 8 percent of its total wage bill, because women cannot work properly when premenstrual; they are said to be more accident-prone and are so unpleasant to live with that husbands are less efficient when their wives suffer from PMS.[6] In other words, she established that PMS is a "public" as well as a "private" threat.

Like most other proponents of PMS as a medical disease, Dalton argues that it has no specific symptomology but covers an "indefinite variety" of symptoms. To date, more than 150 symptoms have been associated with PMS, covering physical, emotional, and behavioral changes (Lander 1988). There is no medical agreement about which of these symptoms should be included or about etiology or treatment. Dalton's own theory of PMS is widely rejected by the medical community, which warns that her proposed therapy of administering artificial hormones involves significant hazards and has never been subjected to clinical trials. Nevertheless, it is generally accepted that PMS is a "genuine illness," that is, a physically induced problem of a cyclical nature that merits medical intervention.

It does not seem accidental that widespread interest in PMS did not take hold until the late 1970s or early 1980s.[7] At that time feminism had again attained a strong hold on society, and women were entering the workforce in unprecedented peacetime numbers.[8] As women demonstrate their competence in spheres that were previously defined as the exclusive preserve of men and as they increasingly compete with men for equal treatment within those spheres, menstruation is again being portrayed as a liability; as in earlier eras, physicians have been quick to provide the biological and psychological evidence needed to sustain such claims.

Moreover, like menstruation itself in the nineteenth century, PMS is virtually inescapable for women. Given the diverse range of symptoms covered, researchers estimate that up to 95 percent of menstruating women "suffer from" it (Zita 1988). Jacquelyn Zita summarizes the medical perspective on PMS as a disease, noting that "the codification of symptoms results in the morbidification of a sex difference which renders all women inherently disadvantaged in a man's world" (Zita 1988, 94). In other words, PMS serves the political function of explaining and justifying women's different economic and political status.

Not Menstruating as Illness

Women cannot escape being labeled as diseased by not menstruating. For one thing, cyclical symptoms associated with PMS are found in women who are either too young or too old to menstruate and they are sometimes found to be worst in those who have had hysterectomies (Lander 1988). Several feminists argue that it is cyclicity itself that is seen as problematic in Western culture, even though men, too, are subject to various cycles (Martin 1987; Lander 1988; Zita 1988).

Menopause, which is commonly understood to be the cessation of menstruation, is viewed as a medical event that is fraught with risks and difficulties. Emily Martin (1987) documents the ways in which menopause is uniformly discussed in negative terms in textbooks: it is explained as the result of the ovaries becoming "unresponsive" and beginning to "regress" and of the hypothalamus giving "inappropriate orders." In these same texts, female systems are described as failing or faltering, and organs are described as "withering" and becoming "senile" (Martin 1987, 42).

Recently, menopause has officially gained the status of a disease, that is, a condition that should be medicated to prevent its symptoms from occurring. In recent years there has been a radical change in viewpoint and some would regard menopause as a possible pathological state rather than a physiological one and discuss therapeutic prevention rather than the amelioration of symptoms (Martin 1987, 51).[9] The World Health Organization has recently defined menopause as an estrogen-deficiency disease, which, it claims, requires significant readjustment in a woman's life (Martin 1987). Many physicians recommend artificial provision of hormones to maintain the pattern of menstruation, rather than tolerate the risks (osteoporosis) and inconvenience (vaginal sex requires more patience) of menopause. As with menstruation, society demands that menopause be hidden from view; the hot flashes often associated with menopause, which had been deemed healthy prior to the nineteenth century, are now supposed to be experienced as embarrassing. Menopause, however, occurs in all women who are healthy enough to reach their fifties, so there is something puzzling about its designation as an illness.

Women may also cease menstruating temporarily. The principal cause of such interruption is pregnancy, an event deemed by North American physicians to require significant medical supervision. Pregnancy, like menopause, provides a classic example of a medical double bind for women. Martin observes that most medical accounts reveal an ideological commitment to the idea that bodily processes should be interpreted as models of production, hierarchically organized according to economic principles. On such a model, women's reproductive organs are expected to produce a baby—that is seen as their clear function. Menstruation, then, gets interpreted as a failure of production (that is, as waste), despite the fact that for most of their lives, most women in our society do not wish to be pregnant (Martin 1987). Pregnancy, presumably, represents the successful use of the organs and processes that have been teleologically organized for the purpose of reproduction; theoretically, then, it should constitute health for women.

Medical attitudes toward pregnancy, however, define it as an event requiring a significant amount of specialized monitoring and constant preparation for radical intervention. Women are directed to modify their life-styles throughout pregnancy; they are to report for regular checkups, submit to increasingly sophisticated (and sometimes hazardous) tests, and promptly present themselves at the hospital when birth is imminent. Women are certainly not encouraged to think of themselves as healthy through the period of their pregnancies; rather, they are encouraged to become dependent on the technological expertise of their physicians. They are judged irresponsible (and sometimes even criminal) if they decline medical advice and supervision throughout pregnancy.

Thus all stages of a woman's experience with menstruation are subject to medical control. Surely, however, some state must be healthy for women, and only specific occurrences of menstruation, pregnancy, or menopause should be defined as indications of disease; the problem is how to determine which of these various states should be thought of as illnesses.

Body Size and Eating Patterns as Illnesses

A similar phenomenon can be observed with respect to medical attitudes towards women's body size. Ours is a culture that is fixated on women's bodies, where women's worth is often judged by the shape of their bodies. Although fashions in ideal body size have changed over time, the current norms dictate that women's bodies should be lean. The culture demands that women be attractive and, within this society, that means that they must be free of fat. Moreover, although thinness has long been a cultural ideal in North America, the 1960s and 1970s brought new standards for female size and increased pressure on women to fit these norms. North American women in the seventeen to twenty-four age group became five to six pounds heavier during this period; the models displayed in leading magazines and beauty pageants became increasingly thinner, however, which led to even greater pressure being put upon women to reduce.[10]

Significantly, it is not just the cultural fashion that demands women be thin. Medical authorities have added their voices to the chorus by warning women that obesity constitutes a serious hazard to their health. Large women are cajoled by their physicians, as well as by their partners, employers, coworkers, strangers in the street, and the general media, to lose weight for the sake of their health.[11] Physicians also express concern for male obesity, but men are allowed far more leeway in relation to the designated ideal (thirty-five pounds over the specified norms) than women are (fifteen to twenty pounds over the norms). The message comes through strongly for women: 95 percent of all people enrolled in weight-reduction programs are women (Szekely 1988), and 75 percent of all American women report that they consider themselves to be overweight (Bordo 1990).[12] Being fat is defined not only as a social failure but also as a medical condition. Unlike sufferers of other diseases, however, fat women are not thought to be innocent and unwilling victims; it is assumed that they are to blame for their condition and that their problem is a reflection and proof of a deficient character.

Women are directed to take responsibility for this disorder in their body size and learn self-control in their eating patterns. Dieting and exercise are the prescription of choice, but specialists have been willing to pursue more drastic forms of intervention in cases where individuals fail. Hospitalization to enforce dieting, the stapling of patients' mouths or stomachs, medication to destroy appetite, surgical removal of fat from below the skin, and amputation of most of the stomach or intestines are among the medical treatments performed on patients who fail on ordinary diet programs.

Current evidence suggests that the weight charts used to define obesity are dangerously low and that women are healthier if they are ten to fifteen pounds heavier than the charts specify (Szekely 1988). In fact, there is little evidence available to establish that excess weight is harmful to the health of women. Most research linking obesity to heart disease and diabetes, the two diseases most prevalent among overweight persons, has been performed on men and specifically identifies weight carried around the waist as dangerous, not weight distributed evenly through the body; the former is a pattern of weight gain characteristic of men, not women. Most significantly, the very prescription offered to women as a cure for the health hazards of their weight problem can be injurious to health. Dieting is seldom effective; the body seems to have a built-in tendency to rebound from its experience of starvation under dieting, so more than 95 percent of dieters gain back all the weight lost, plus some extra, within a year after losing it. Studies indicate that dramatic fluctuations in weight are far harder on the body than a steady state of being over the culturally defined norms for one's height and sex.

Failure to eat is also medically defined as a disease and is increasingly viewed as endemic among the young women of North America. Moreover, dieting seems to be the trigger for many instances of so-called eating disorders: Eva Szekely (1988) documents the connections between dieting, anorexia nervosa, and bulimia. More and more young women seem to be starving themselves to death by refusing food (anorexia nervosa), binging and purging (bulimia), or exercising excessively and burning more calories than they consume (or, frequently, a combination of the three). Women who are diagnosed as suffering from eating disorders are labeled as diseased and required to undergo therapy and, often, hospitalization. Psychiatrists are called in to address this frightening phenomenon, and various etiologies and prescriptions are promoted.

To be sure, eating disorders can be unhealthy and may be fatal. As Eva Szekely (1988) argues, however, these conditions are not radical departures from ordinary female experience. They are the embodiment of individuals' taking the cultural norms of femininity to their horrifying, logical conclusions. Susan Bordo (1990) argues that dieting and exercise play a normalizing role for women in our culture. She views the preponderance of eating disorders among women in our culture (some 90 percent of sufferers are female) as deriving from the classic "double bind," wherein women are told both to consume whatever they desire and to exercise control over their bodies.

In a culture that tells people it is their responsibility to look after their health and blames them for failures connected to life-style, there is growing pressure on individuals to pursue fitness, thinness, and the healthy look of youth. Because these purported norms of health are also the norms of femininity, here, too, we find medical prescriptions for female well-being linked to the cultural ideals of womanhood, even when these ideals support sexist attitudes and values. Women are judged ill if they eat too much or too little; drastic medical intervention is called for on either ground. The norms are internalized and few women, it seems, are able to perceive themselves as having "normal" or "healthy" eating patterns. Perhaps, then, the problem is best seen as lying with the norms of health, not the women. Alternatively, if it is true that most women have eating problems, then it seems likely that the problem is cultural, in which case medical control may not be the best means of addressing such issues.

The Application of the Concepts of
Health and Illness

Discussions of the proper use of the terms "health" and "illness" are common in the literature of medical ethics, where it is widely recognized that the linguistic decision to label a specific condition a disease has significant social and political implications and that the particular extensions of these concepts vary significantly across cultures. In our own pluralistic society, the disease status of certain conditions is a matter of serious controversy, especially with respect to conditions associated with behavior judged to be "dysfunctional" and socially unacceptable, such as alcoholism, drug addiction, all forms of mental illness, and homosexuality.

There are some areas of broad agreement among competing analyses of the terms. "Health" is generally acknowledged to be "an almost universally valuable state" (Gorovitz 1982, 60). Health and physical vigor are idealized and valorized (Wendell 1989). In our own highly competitive society, for instance, it has been argued that health and the relief of disease and disability are especially important, because disease interferes with equality of opportunity (Daniels 1985; Caplan 1989).[13] It is agreed that the extension of the terms "health" and "illness" shape important social roles: they set the boundaries for the domain of medical authority and determine the responsibilities and privileges of those individuals who are designated as ill. Those perceived as ill may be excused from certain obligations that would otherwise fall on them and may be entitled to special care and treatment; but they may also be subject to stigmatization, paternalism, and disqualification from particular activities. Society has granted to physicians the authority to assign these powerful labels and to develop the means for countering the effects of what they define as illness.

The best-known and most-debated definition of "health" is incorporated into the Preamble to the Constitution of the World Health Organization (WHO), which defines "health" as "the state of complete physical, mental and social well-being and not merely the absence of disease or infirmity." The breadth of this definition is of concern, because the Preamble goes on to assert that the enjoyment of the highest attainable standard of health is "one of the fundamental rights of human beings" and "governments have a responsibility for the health of their people which can be fulfilled only by the provision of adequate health and social measures."

If any of the member states of WHO took this definition seriously, then they would accept an enormous burden of social responsibility for their citizens, far out of proportion with the health services that are currently provided by any government. There are reasons to be grateful that none does take this injunction literally. As Daniel Callahan (1973) argues, defining health as covering such broad areas of human existence allows medical authorities far too great a sphere of influence. Furthermore, Callahan is concerned about the readiness expressed by WHO to extend the medical model of health and disease from the domain of physical health, where we can tie our value judgments to relatively well defined physiological norms, into the domain of mental or social norms, where attitudes of approval and disapproval are dangerously ungrounded. He urges us to restrict our use of the terms "health" and "illness" to the physical sphere, where he presumes that these can be scientifically defined.[14]

Christopher Boorse (1975) also supports a restriction of these concepts to the physical sphere; he argues that on physical questions, "health" and "disease" can be objectively defined by appealing to neutral, scientific standards, without reference to moral values or social norms. On his account, values enter when we try to determine which diseases should be classified as illnesses, because illnesses constitute a burden to their bearer and provide the basis for special treatment. Other theorists agree that ascriptions of "health" and "illness" reflect a significant degree of normativism but deny that even "disease" can be objectively determined.[15]

A particularly searching and cogent analysis of the value-laden use and political implications of these concepts is offered by H. Tristram Englehardt, Jr., in his book *The Foundations of Bioethics* (1986). Englehardt begins a chapter titled "The Languages of Medicalization" with a directness feminists can appreciate: "Medicine medicalizes reality. It creates a world. It translates sets of problems into its own terms. Medicine molds the ways in which the world of experience takes shape; it conditions reality for us" (Englehardt 1986, 157). The reality that medicine creates is socially accepted; given the power and authority that are awarded to medical expertise, its reality is generally socially dominating. Defining a problem as medical, he says, creates expectations and influences personal destinies. It changes social relations.

Englehardt provides a detailed description of the cultural phenomenon of medical reality as "the result of a complex interplay of descriptive, evaluative, explanatory, and social labeling interests" (Englehardt 1986, 163). He calls these the four languages of medicine (or modes of medicalization) and uses them to explain "how hidden value and policy judgments shape the 'medical facts'" (Englehardt 1986, 164).

The first, description (of symptoms), seems to be the most straightforward of the four, but even here we find that the task is always "infected by expectations" (Englehardt 1986, 175). In the second language, evaluation, there is a presumption that adverse values are attached to whatever is recognized as a diseased state. Like others who accept a normative definition of illness, Englehardt takes it as given that to be considered a disease, deformity, or disability, a condition must be recognized as a problem, something that is disvalued and beyond the power of the affected individual simply to will away.

Explanation, the third medical language, is particularly significant in the medical structuring of experience. Medicine is a purposeful activity that is directed at manipulating reality through making predictions (diagnosis) and offering treatment (providing preventive strategies and cures). In modern medicine physiological theory has been made central to both of these projects, to the extent that theory now outweighs patients' experience of illness in the attention of practitioners. Englehardt argues that since the nineteenth century, medicine has sought to correlate two distinct domains of medical description: the clinical world of symptoms and the laboratory world of theory. With increasing success at reconciling these domains, medical reality has changed, so that anatomical or physiological truth values, rather than the phenomenological experience of illness, have become the determinants of medical value.[16] Physicians rely on the explanatory role of medicine in determining the legitimate ascriptions of sickness, as well as its special social privileges and burdens, because "diagnosis is a complex means of social labeling" (Englehardt 1986, 185).

The fourth medical language involves the construction of certain aspects of experience as specifically medical phenomena. The power to control certain dimensions of meaning is not unique to physicians.

Ethicists, clergy, legislators, and judges (among others) also engage in social labeling and constructions of value and reality. Vigorous, public debates are waged about whether drug addiction, antisocial behavior, alcoholism, and so forth should be viewed as illnesses, wickedness, or insubordination and, correspondingly, which institution shall have authority over them. Construction decisions involve value judgments, because there are always other possible interpretations for addressing matters that are perceived as problems, which would require different sorts of institutional responses. Such decisions are subject to dispute in a pluralistic society and are matters of communal interest. Englehardt proposes that medical reality be democratized and communal negotiations held to determine the ultimate construals of reality (as medical, legal, moral, or other).

Feminist Perspectives on the Health/Illness Debate

Feminists share with Callahan and Boorse a concern about extending medical authority into mental and social spheres. There are significant risks in imagining that medical training creates expertise in areas of social and emotional life. Medical authorities, with their relatively homogeneous class backgrounds, should not be authorized to make unilateral decisions about life-style questions, such as the "healthfulness" of homosexuality.

Most feminists (for example, Todd 1989) are suspicious, however, of the worldview that imagines personal lives can be neatly fragmented into physical, mental, and social components so that one element can be "treated" in isolation from the other two. There is overwhelming evidence that physical health and illness are influenced by and themselves influence mental and social situations. Most feminists support a more holistic approach to health than the purely physical restriction would allow. Illness can be associated with poverty, oppression, ignorance, and stress and often cannot be eradicated without addressing the social conditions underlying its occurrence.

Moreover, various bureaucratic structures refuse to consider factors other than health as legitimate grounds for support of individuals in need. For example, legislation often makes abortion available only if it can be shown that continued pregnancy is a serious threat to a woman's health; many communities make welfare available only to individuals who can prove they are unemployed due to illness or disability; maternity benefits and the right to return to work are often available to workers only if pregnancy is defined as an illness subject to the provisions of a long-term disability plan; and access to and funding for treatment programs for alcoholism, addiction, violence, and so forth often are dependent on the classification of these behaviors as illnesses. In a society that restricts provision of most forms of social assistance to those who have been designated as ill, it is strategically important that we maintain a broad understanding of the conditions that constitute illness.

Feminist analysis suggests that we change the terms of the social debate, however, and recognize the complexity of human existence; social need should not have to be screened through the filter of medical values and authority. Many circumstances can undermine a person's ability to compete on an equal footing in the marketplace, as it is now arranged; often these features are structural and not adequately captured by the medical model of illness, which perceives the sick individual as the problem in need of adjustment.

The feminist ideal would involve society's recognition of this fact and development of means to respond to the many different kinds of human need, without having to force every sort of problem into the medical model. Until such social change is accomplished, however, we must be cautious about movements to restrict the support available under the rubric of health language. The linguistic question of the scope of the term "health" cannot be settled in isolation from the social structures surrounding the debate.

Feminists can find much of value in Englehardt's account of health and illness. His description of how medicine creates reality parallels claims that are commonly made by feminists.[17] By making explicit the various components of medical language and revealing that there is room for value ascriptions to enter at all four levels, Englehardt helps us understand the power of medical views, so that we can better appreciate the complexity of the task of challenging those views. His analysis demonstrates that the scientific expertise of physicians—which is the foundation for medical hegemony—is actually necessary for only one of the four modes of medical language (explanation); moreover, that element has, arguably, received a disproportionate share of attention, because the "objective" clinical evidence of disease is now given precedence over the subjective experience of illness. This imbalance values medical interpretations of illness over the direct experience of patients. It both represents and reinforces existing patterns of power and authority.

Feminists are also likely to share Englehardt's belief that the question of who has the authority to make the decisions of what constitutes illness is important because much hangs on the outcome of those decisions. Moreover, feminists can agree with him that the construction of illness is of such social significance that the process of determining which problems are defined as diseases should be democratized. The determination that a problem should be classified as a disease and be subject to the medical control entailed by that ascription is a matter of communal, not merely professional, interest.

Feminists are likely to disagree with Englehardt, however, over what constitutes the relevant community for making such decisions. They would not be willing to agree that the community at large should decide whether conditions that are unique to women constitute diseases but would want this matter to be resolved by discussion within the women's community itself. The significance of relative positions of power in the outcome of "democratic" processes would make most feminists uneasy with a process that did not grant special status to the input of an already oppressed group on a question that primarily affects its own members (see Chapter 3).

The specific category of oppression is important here, because I do not argue for a general theory wherein any group that is diagnosed as ill should have the authority to reject that label. I do not argue that people who are addicted to alcohol or drugs, for instance, or those who are diagnosed as having violent and uncontrolled personalities should have the sole authority for deciding whether their condition merits treatment or any form of intervention. Instead, my argument is that ascribing unique and universal illnesses to an oppressed group may be either a symptom or an effect of their oppression; it may also serve to entrench their subordinate status further. When a group is characterized as ill, they are subject to stigmatization, expectations of passivity, and judgments that they are not fully competent. Because oppressed groups are already subject to these negative judgments, it is especially important that they reclaim the power to decide whether a condition that uniquely affects them should be seen as a disease. Labeling as illness a condition distinctive to such groups inevitably carries political implications.

Moreover, feminists are likely to take issue with Englehardt's assumption that no controversy is involved in identifying a particular condition as problematic and that disagreement will be limited to debate over the condition's construction as a medical (rather than legal or moral) matter. The negative perception of a condition as problematic may itself be controversial. Medicalizing menstruation, menopause, PMS, and pregnancy is objectionable in part because their medical categorization rests on the presumption that these ordinary events of women's lives are negatively valued. Sexism construes the details of being female as undesirable, and medicine institutionalizes that negative evaluation by treating both menstruating and not menstruating as pathological.[18] It is not that feminists seek to construct menstruation, menopause, and so forth as problems in some sphere other than the medical one (as may be the case with respect to drug dependency, for example); rather, they reject altogether the analysis that views these states as inherently problematic.

Sometimes, specific occurrences of female conditions are properly evaluated as negative (for example, dangerous aspects of pregnancies, excessive menstrual bleeding, or severe pain), but these are anomalous, not typical, female experiences. Even so, some feminists have questioned constructing these events as illnesses. They share with bioethicists a concern about the social consequences of that labeling, and they also are sensitive to the phenomenology of being medically classified as ill. When people are diagnosed as ill, the bodily parts that are judged to be diseased become subject to medical expertise and control; as patients, individuals often experience alienation from those parts of themselves (Martin 1987; Zita 1988). This is especially problematic for women, because important elements of their oppression are the objectification of their bodies and the alienation that is created in the process. With the issue of ascribing illness to women, as with other social policies affecting women, feminists must ask who benefits from the designation and who is harmed by it.

PMS Revisited

Although PMS has been medically defined and pursued under particularly suspect conditions, many women have welcomed the label; they believe that it offers them an explanation of symptoms they experience as troublesome and a strategy to gain control over these symptoms. Its designation as a disease provides them with a reassuring legitimacy for being especially irritable and angry—moods not normally acceptable in women—on a regular basis. It also explains the discomfort of such common experiences as premenstrual tender breasts and bloated abdomens. It is validating to have one's symptoms taken seriously by the agents who are socially authorized to determine medical reality; the alternative has all too often been to dismiss complaints as trivial and to treat the women who report distress at these experiences as unreliable informants about their own states. In a culture that commonly views women as weak, irrational, inadequate, and deceptive, it is reassuring to have one's complaints respected (rather than ridiculed). Many women find that the self-help therapies suggested in the women's health press do provide relief from symptoms that trouble them; others pursue more active intervention from medical experts. If designations of illness are to be democratized and left to those affected (as I have proposed—at least, within oppressed groups), then we can see that many women have chosen to have PMS classified as an illness. Nevertheless, many feminists remain ambivalent about this conclusion.

Englehardt's four medical languages help explain why it might be inappropriate to accept the designation of PMS as an illness, despite the fact that many women choose that categorization. Beginning with the descriptive language, descriptions of PMS are so broad that they encompass virtually all recurrent "symptoms." Curiously, however, there is remarkably little mention of the positive experiences that feminist researchers have found associated with PMS, such as greater creativity (Martin 1987). As Jacquelyn Zita observes, "The observation language used and the interest behind much PMS research are directed towards the description and depiction of negatively evaluated changes in women" (Zita 1988, 80).

The evaluation language used in medical discussions of PMS should also be challenged. PMS is largely characterized in behavioral terms, and the behavior that is problematized is a change from the prescribed norms of feminine passivity, compliance, and accommodation (what Zita terms "benign femininity"). Women affected by what is called PMS have been found to be less able (or willing) to tolerate discipline and monotony in their lives. They become irritable, depressed, and angry at the constraints they face. When premenstrual, many women find themselves enraged by details in their lives that they apparently accept at other times. As Emily Martin (1987) proposes, however, perhaps this should be seen as evidence of the flaws not in women but in a society that relegates most women to oppressive, repetitious, soul-destroying, exploitative labor. Feminism reveals that the details that enrage women are the effects and evidence of their subordinate status; from the perspective of feminism, there is no reason to classify such premenstrual insight as negative.

Normally, explanation is the language that most clearly establishes the authority of medical expertise in ascribing to a condition the category of illness. It is the mode by which links are drawn between the observed clinical symptoms and an explanatory physiological theory, and it is the basis of the scientific objectivity that Callahan and Boorse thought was central to the proper use of the term "illness." With PMS, however, there is no agreement on etiology, only largely discredited theories (such as Dalton's). By calling PMS a syndrome, rather than an explicit disease, medical authorities implicitly admit that there is no theoretical explanation available by which treatment might be determined.[19]

Turning to Englehardt's fourth medical language, it becomes apparent that the medicalization of PMS constructs a picture of reality wherein virtually all women are viewed as disadvantaged in a man's world that is intolerant of female cyclicity. Changes in feelings, attitudes, and moods, however, are not always bad. Perhaps many more women could accept premenstrual changes and even come to welcome them if society allowed them the space to experience them differently. If, for example, the world of work were constructed to appreciate that people experience various cyclical changes and if variations in routine could allow for the inevitable differences in effectiveness that follow, then many (although not all) premenstrual complaints would likely disappear (Martin 1987). When encouraged to think positively about bodily changes, some women have even reported an ability to appreciate the phenomenon of menstrual cramps, perceiving this as a time to focus on their bodies and maintain contact with natural cycles in an otherwise artificially structured world.

Moreover, even if we allow that premenstrual changes can be considered problematic, there are further disadvantages in having them categorized as medical problems. This attitude contributes to the common tendency of our society to conceive of bodies, especially women's bodies, as objects for medicalization. Medical objectification of women's bodies is particularly worrisome, because it takes place in the context of a sexist society, which already objectifies women by reducing them to their bodies (and sometimes simply to particular body parts) and then reduces those bodies to their sexual or reproductive functions under patriarchy.

When their bodies are socially conceived as objects, women become alienated from them as parts of themselves, experiencing them as things to be shaped, decorated, cared for, and maintained as socially desirable objects. In the field of medicine women's bodies, especially the distinctly female aspects of their bodies, have been systematically divided into sites for surveillance and intervention. Medicalized constructions of PMS rest on the dubious (and alienating) assumption of a medicalized interpretation of women's bodies.[20]

Thus although many women do find aspects of their menstrual cycle to be unpleasant (and many will continue to do so, however we redescribe the phenomenon), we should question the conclusion that medical care is the most appropriate source of relief when cyclical changes are perceived negatively. Given encouragement, many women find relief from the pain and distress of menstruation and premenstrual changes through relaxation or visualization exercises, changes in routine, and attention to positive change. For both women and men, experience of one's body is affected by the cultural attitudes and the strategies that are learned. There are many possible ways of interpreting the body; medical models that classify the changes associated with being female as negative represent a particularly repressive option for women.

These warnings are not meant to imply that there are no such things as problematic premenstrual changes or to suggest that no women suffer from severe premenstrual or menstrual changes that might properly be relieved by medical means. It is not an argument against women seeking medical assistance in the pursuit of such relief. It does constitute, however, an argument against accepting the view that premenstrual and menstrual changes are necessarily undesirable and that medicine is the best place for women to turn if they do judge these changes negatively.

I propose, then, that we reserve the labels of disease and illness for atypical experiences of menstruation or premenstrual change that are unquestionably harmful to the women concerned: for example, an abnormal flow, extraordinary discomfort, significant irregularity, or unusual pain. To identify the symptoms that signal genuine diseases that may be associated with menstruation, it must first be determined what constitutes normal menstruation; this subject has not yet been adequately explored, perhaps because most researchers have preferred to see all menstruation as pathological. Only when physicians and women recognize the significant variation in healthy menstrual patterns will anyone know with confidence what constitutes evidence of disease associated with menstruation.

Acceptance of the medical model of PMS as a disease that affects 95 percent of women helps establish a sex difference for women that is disadvantaging in our society, just as medical views of menstruation did in the late nineteenth and early twentieth centuries.[21] The medical model of PMS perpetuates the image of women's bodies as objects out of control and requiring constant medical management, rather than recognizing the normalcy of change in women's experiences. Returning to Marilyn Frye, we should remember her warning that the arrogant perceiver controls by "the mis-defining of 'good' and 'health'. If one has the cultural and institutional power to make the misdefinition stick, one can turn the whole other person right around to oneself by this one simple trick." (Frye 1983, 70)

When we ask who is harmed and who benefits from the decision to treat PMS as a disease, we see many ways in which women may be harmed, and we observe that large profits are reaped by medical specialists and drug companies from the commodification that follows this decision. We note that as the birth rate has declined in Western nations, gynecologists have shifted their attention to the medicalization of PMS, menopause, and menstrual irregularities, thereby assuring themselves of a steady stream of clients. Once again, it is not at all clear that medical interests coincide with those of women.

Hence feminists should reject the notion of PMS as a universal disease of women, although they need not deny that particular women suffer from premenstrual changes that cannot be controlled without expert advice. Our society needs to accept the evidence of cyclical change as normal; until it does, feminists will have to struggle to make sure that such change is appreciated as a valuable part of the working and family lives of women. Rejecting the norm of PMS as a medical problem common to all women helps women reestablish an element of control over their bodies, their lives, and the social perceptions by which they are judged.

10

Medical Constructions of Sexuality

Human beings are clearly capable of enormous variations in sexual behavior; choices about how sexuality is organized and promoted are made within particular cultural groups. In contemporary Western society the authority to regulate sexual practices has largely been granted to medical specialists, on the basis of their presumed expertise in these matters. By delegating to doctors the task of determining the acceptable ways of being sexual, society has extended significant power to medical experts. Although the use of this medical power demands ethical evaluation, the topic has rarely been pursued in the traditional forums for medical ethics research. In this chapter I review some of the arguments that various feminists have offered about the structure of sexuality in our culture and make some suggestions for a feminist ethical evaluation of medicine's role in constructing sexuality.

The Pursuit of Control of Sexuality

Feminists generally agree that the ways in which we practice and experience human sexuality are socially constructed.[1] Catharine Stimpson and Ethel Person, for example, state: "Sexuality is a biological process that both follows certain development patterns and that responds to the mediation of culture. Biology may set the outer boundaries of sexual possibility, but cultures work effectively within them" (Stimpson and Person 1980, 1). In other words, although sexual activity has a biological basis and is found in all societies, the particular forms it takes, the meanings it carries, the sorts of partners with whom it may be shared, and so forth are learned and transmitted according to local norms and customs. Moreover, within any particular culture, the forms and meanings of sexuality vary with each individual's gender, class, and position within other hierarchies. The actual forms of behavior and desires that are identified within a culture as sexual cannot, then, be understood as wholly instinctual, automatic responses to biological phenomena, any more than the culturally defined and widely varied approaches to food selection and preparation found among humans of different traditions can be explained as simply "natural" responses to hunger.

Throughout the history of Western civilization, the major institutions of each era have sought to regulate sexual practices. All of the principal religious institutions have directed and restricted sexual choices: both Judaism and Christianity impose rigorous sexual restrictions on their followers, promoting monogamous marriage aimed at reproduction, and these restrictions are especially rigid in their applications to women. Other religions may be even less tolerant: under some conservative interpretations of Islamic law, for instance, women are largely restricted to their homes and barred from most public functions, for fear that their free movement might "provoke" sexual responses in men other than their husbands.

In most societies the rule of law is added to the authority of the church in regulating sexuality. Gerda Lerner has shown that "women's sexual subordination was institutionalized in the earliest law codes and enforced by the full power of the state" (Lerner 1986, 9).[2] Historically, many sorts of sexual practices and specific combinations of partners have been subject to criminal prosecution—for example, sexual unions across racial or feudal class barriers. More recently, unmarried women were prohibited by law from access to contraceptives until 1969 in Canada (Collins 1985) and until 1972 in the United States (Joffe 1986).

The practice of regulating sexuality is not confined to history; Carole Joffe claims: "All modern societies struggle to define the proper relationship between the state and the private lives of the citizenry, and sexual behavior is often the central arena of this conflict" (Joffe 1986, 3). In contemporary Western society legislation and the power of the state is still invoked to prohibit or discourage various sorts of sexual practices. Among current laws governing sexual choices are those that prohibit rape or sexual assault, prostitution (or soliciting), sodomy, bestiality, incest, and sexual activity with minors. In most jurisdictions legal recognition is denied to same-sex marriages and marriages between close relatives. Added to these direct limits (where unauthorized sexual activities may be subject to explicit punishment) are laws that seek to inhibit other "undesirable" sexual practices through restricting access to abortion. Throughout much of the world, a vast network of publicly supported family-planning agencies has been set up, "whose purpose is to help people manage their sexual lives" (Joffe 1986, 3).

Other power relationships also shape sexual activity. Many parents believe it is their duty to limit and direct the sexual activity of their adolescent children. Furthermore, as feminists frequently note, most men still seek to control the sexual activity of women. Within hierarchical social structures—be they religious, political, or family-based—those who possess power tend to use it to influence the sexual lives of subordinate others. As Michel Foucault (1980) observed, sex is commonly used as a target for intervention and social control.

Because in modern society obedience to the rule of law, the church, or the family cannot be guaranteed, other motivations are necessary if there is a continuing desire to ensure compliance with preferred modes of sexual expression. In this era of liberal humanism, where "private," individual choice is thought to be sacrosanct, powerful reasons must be supplied in support of any measures aimed at regulating individuals' sexual choices. Sexual behavior is considered the paradigm example of private choice; therefore, any laws that are aimed at governing sexual expression must be of demonstrably sufficient public interest to merit overruling the prima facie rights of individuals to pursue their own choices of sexual satisfaction.

Today medicine and science provide the needed rationales for restrictive sexual laws. Moreover, when laws are inadequate to ensure conformity to preferred sexual norms or when the commitment to individual autonomy is too strong to tolerate legal restrictions, medicine and science provide the justification (and often the means) for other forms of social coercion. Medical researchers and clinicians, together with psychologists and sociobiologists, establish what is "normal" and "natural" in the sphere of human sexuality and determine where to set the boundaries at which deviance and pathology begin. Rather than just condemning nonconformist behavior, as their religious and legal predecessors did, medical authorities purport to treat and transform unacceptable modes of sexual being. Like their nonmedical predecessors, they rely heavily on their power to establish the norms of what is proper in the sphere of sexuality and to generate guilt and anxiety in those who do not comply.

John Bancroft, a physician involved in sex therapy, comments:

> There is no doubt that sexual values have been powerfully influenced by medical opinion. In the eighteenth and nineteenth centuries, warnings from doctors of the dire medical consequences of non-procreative sex— coitus interruptus or masturbation or homosexuality—added a particularly heavy load to sexual guilt that is still very much in evidence. Members of the medical profession may be less naive about compounding medical advice with morality nowadays, but more subtle versions undoubtedly continue. (Bancroft 1981, 167).

Bancroft recalls the mistaken and unfounded nineteenth-century medical opinion that masturbation was harmful to health and perceives that "the 'medicalization' of this point of view effectively obscured the real ethical issues involved" (Bancroft 1981, 170). Nevertheless, Bancroft's view of the "real ethical issues" seems to be restricted to whether practitioners should warn against behavior that, for subjective reasons, they consider harmful, if there is no scientific evidence in support of their belief. Although feminists can applaud his self-conscious reflection on the medical tendency to pass judgment on other people's sexual behavior purely on the basis of physicians' own subjective attitudes, they are less likely to rely on scientific measures of harm as a reliable foundation for such judgments. Among other concerns, most feminist critiques of specific sexual practices judge that power differentials between the parties to a sexual interaction are morally significant. Hence most feminists would find it curious that the contemporary example over which Bancroft agonizes is pedophilia, a sexual practice that is inevitably defined in terms of unequal power relations.[3]

Despite their significant influence, neither medical nor other authorities have total power in this area, and many people persist in the practice of sexual behaviors that are condemned by the scientific experts (as is evident in the resistance of much of the population to medically recommended safe-sex practices in the age of AIDS). Moreover, medical authorities are not monolithic in their pronouncements; they disagree among themselves on many questions. Their theories also face competition from other experts who recommend different theories about sexuality. As Michel Foucault perceived, there are always multiple discourses going on, "a proliferation of discourses, carefully tailored to the requirements of power" (Foucault 1980, 72).

Foucault observed that sexual repression is a complex process: the very discourse that purports to repress sexual orientations that are declared deviant actually creates the desires to pursue such practices. Thus medico-legal discourse about the wrongfulness of nonheterosexual sexualities in part brings about the desire to pursue such apparently "repressed" practices. Foucault concluded that discourses on sexuality, rather than actual sexual practices, should be seen as representing "the essential place to grasp the workings of power in modern Western societies" (Martin 1988, 7). It is significant, then, that discourses of sexuality belong primarily to the privileged domain of the professional class; by controlling these discourses, the professionals establish their control of society through the relatively invisible procedures of normalization, instead of relying on the more obvious techniques of prohibition.

Within this "myriad of discourses," medical authorities have claimed and retained a privileged position. They have been granted substantial social authority, which they readily use to shape and reinforce the attitudes of the majority regarding acceptable and "deviant" sexual behaviors; those behaviors that they classify as deviant are subject to being both medicalized and marginalized. Foucault also argued that this power runs deeper than we might predict: it has been used not only to organize the political agenda of those who seek to repress particular forms of sexuality but also to determine the agenda of those who fight for sexual liberation (Sawicki 1988).

Feminists, too, have observed that beliefs about the pleasures and dangers associated with different sexual practices are powerful forces in the social organization of society. As Catharine MacKinnon (1989) stresses, sexuality is not only socially constructed but also constructing. It determines social arrangements and creates individuals' senses of themselves and their relationships; that is, sexuality is an important element of the social structures that control a person's life choices and opportunities.

It follows, then, that physicians' established authority to support or undermine prevailing social attitudes about sexuality entails significant moral responsibility. Therefore, it is important to examine the ethical character of the medical community's role in shaping social attitudes about sexuality, and here, too, I believe it is necessary to pursue an explicitly feminist version of ethics for the task.

Institutionalized Heterosexuality

Heterosexuality is the socially approved and dominant form of sexuality in modern, Western society. Obviously, non-heterosexual forms of sexual activity are common, but the norm, both in the statistical and prescriptive sense, is taken to be heterosexual pairing. In fact, heterosexuality is so pervasively accepted as the sexuality of choice that it is often not even recognized as a choice. As Christine Overall argues: "As an expected, supposedly normal characteristic of adult and even pre-adult life, it is so pervasive that it melts into our individual lives; its invisibility as a social condition makes it seem to be just a matter of what is personal, private, and inevitable" (Overall 1990, 2).

Heterosexuality is not only the most widely practiced form of sexuality, it is often described as being natural, innate, and instinctual. Because the dominant ideology assumes that heterosexuality is biologically motivated, only the ways of being nonheterosexual are usually thought to demand explanation.[4] Homosexuality and other non-heterosexual practices (such as celibacy, bisexuality, masturbation, voyeurism, and bestiality) are classified as deviant, and medical researchers have sought to find the scientific cause of such deviance, vainly pursuing hormonal and psychological explanations (Bleier 1984). In so doing, these researchers accept and promote the widespread cultural prejudice that all nonheterosexuality is problematic and in need of medical analysis and treatment.

Because of the essential role that coitus plays in reproduction (at least, until recently), it has been common for both technical experts and the lay public to conclude that it is biologically natural—that it is, in fact, the only natural sexual practice. Such accounts, however, do not address the fact that humans engage in a great many sexual acts (including, often, coitus) that do not have reproduction as their desired end. Furthermore, many other possible social arrangements might achieve reproductive ends without accepting the specific forms of heterosexual relations that are characteristic of our culture. Therefore, there is no reason to privilege heterosexuality as constituting some exclusive, natural norm. More specifically, we need not as-

sume that the particular ways in which we find heterosexuality practiced in our society are the outcome of natural forces.

As Christine Overall describes it, the familiar form of heterosexuality is less a natural practice than a "systematized set of social
standards, customs, and expected practices which both regulate and
restrict romantic and sexual relationships between persons of different
sexes in late twentieth century western culture" (Overall 1990, 3). It
is not merely a way of expressing individual sexuality but amounts to
a political institution, which many feminists have called "compulsory" because of its pervasive power to demand conformity (Rich
1980). This institution of heterosexuality is maintained by a system of
rewards or "heterosexual privileges," which are available to those who
comply with its prescribed forms and include enhanced status, social
acceptance, and a measure of protection from the violence of
strangers. Correlatively, homosexual men and lesbians are subject to
the power of "heterosexism" or systematic discrimination against
them. The principal instrument of heterosexism is homophobia, by
which a pervasive fear of being identified as homosexual is instilled in
individuals. There is reason for such fear in our society: deviations
from heterosexuality are frequently punished through mechanisms of
ridicule, social ostracism, economic penalties (loss of job), removal of
children, and often physical violence ("gay-bashing"). In many jurisdictions, including my own province of Nova Scotia, heterosexism is
a matter of legal policy; deliberate decisions are made to exclude sexual orientation and preference from the list of characteristics that are
protected under human rights legislation.

There are several reasons for any ethicist to object to the institu-
tionalization of a specific form of sexuality and to the institutionaliza-
tion of heterosexuality in particular. Coercive approaches to human
sexuality restrict the freedom of everyone. Nonheterosexuals are especially vulnerable to this manipulation; they are intimidated and challenged in their pursuit of their own sexual choices, and they may be
subject to severe social, economic, and even legal penalties if they
are open about their sexuality. Many nonsexual choices they might
otherwise make, such as pursuit of a political, religious, or military
career, may be prohibited to them. As Cindy Patton reports: "Fear of
job loss continues to serve as a prior restraint curtailing some gay
people from seeking rigorous career paths . . . where the hint or
disclosure of homosexuality would not be tolerated and career sacri-

fices could be lost in the single moment of coming out" (Patton 1986, 125).[5] They may be subject to loss of their homes, children, family support, acceptance in their religious community, and friends if their homosexuality becomes known. The forces in support of sexual conformity are very powerful.

This means, however, that not only the freedom of homosexuals is restricted by coercive heterosexuality. Those who have opted for heterosexuality are also limited in their sense of freedom. After all, when there are so many powerful forces directed at making us heterosexual, it is difficult to sort out genuine choice from surrender to compulsion. As Christine Overall notes, "When there are so many pressures to be heterosexual, and when failure to conform is so heavily punished, it is difficult to regard heterosexuality as the genuine expression of a preference" (Overall 1990, 9). Catharine MacKinnon puts it more bluntly: "Those who think that one chooses heterosexuality under conditions that make it compulsory should either explain why it is not compulsory or explain why the word choice can be meaningful here" (MacKinnon 1987, 61).

Under institutionalized heterosexuality, few people deliberate about becoming heterosexual. Jeffrey Weeks observes: "Not many, perhaps, say 'I am a heterosexual' because it is the taken-for-granted norm, the great unsaid of our sexual culture" (Weeks 1987, 31). During or after adolescence, heterosexuals may feel some relief at determining that they are not really homosexual, but apart from particular subcultures, few are likely to contemplate their sexual identity for long.[6] Because of the risks entailed in public or private disclosure of their sexuality, lesbians and gay men must usually become quite certain of their sexuality before declaring it, but no such restraint guides heterosexuals. Therefore, there are clear, nonfeminist, ethical objections to the social pressure put on everyone by the coercive demands of institutionalized heterosexuality.

Feminist Objections to Heterosexuality

In addition to the standard objections to coercive heterosexuality, feminists have added some strong, gender-specific critiques. They argue that the institution of heterosexuality is not defined in a gender-neutral fashion, where any sort of sexual relationship between people of different sexes is envisioned. Rather, heterosexuality in our culture is characterized by sex-role patterns that involve different costs and benefits for men from those for women, and as numerous feminists have demonstrated, it generally benefits men far more clearly than it does women.

As an institution, heterosexuality is not simply a matter of sexual expression. It supports and represents the whole set of gendered relations that jointly constitute the sex-gender system structuring our society. Male dominance and female subordination are entwined with the very conception of heterosexuality and extend to all aspects of interaction. Hence MacKinnon argues that "sexuality is gendered as gender is sexualized" (MacKinnon 1987, 50), by which she means that gender is defined in terms of its role in heterosexuality, wherein male dominance and female subordination have been eroticized. Moreover, this ideology is pervasive. Ruth Bleier observes that "underlying all forms of the oppression of women in patriarchal cultures—physical, economic, political, legal, emotional, ideological—are the assumptions of the institution of heterosexuality or heterosexism: specifically, the assumptions that men own and have the right to control the bodies, labor, and minds of women" (Bleier 1984, 164).

Patriarchy rests on the assumption that gender relations reflect a "natural" order, which is defined in terms of stereotypical attitudes about masculinity and femininity. Expectations about acceptable and unacceptable types of sexual interactions play an important role in this structure. In her psychoanalytic account of sexuality Ethel Spector Person argues that gender orders sexuality: "Socialization into passivity or activity, subordination or autonomy, is decisive for the way sexuality (sensuality) is experienced and for the fantasies that attach to it. Thus, gender training . . . molds sexuality" (Person 1980, 50). Moreover, she suggests that "sexuality in turn, may be a mainstay for gender" (Person 1980, 50); "it is precisely because sexuality is so often the vehicle for the expression of power relations that sexuality is by its very nature a subject for political inquiry" (Person 1980, 58). Definitions of heterosexuality seem to be inseparable from gender assignments in Western culture.

In our society heterosexuality seems to require very specific gender roles. For example, many popular, social myths characterize men as sexual aggressors who pursue and, if necessary, overpower their potential sexual partners. It is commonly assumed that if men are to be judged attractive to women, they must display confidence, forcefulness, and authority; physical strength and the symbols of power (money, position, influence) seem to be important sexual assets for men.[7] Women, in contrast, are often expected to be passive in their sexual pursuits. They are advised to make themselves sexually attractive to men by displaying a degree of weakness, vulnerability, and self-abnegation.

The gender roles associated with heterosexuality ensure women's subordination in nonsexual realms as well. Women are expected to attract and maintain heterosexual partners, and the behavior assigned to them for doing so requires them to foster their attractiveness according to prevailing standards; they are taught to please men in general and their designated partner in particular, that is, to accommodate themselves generally to the needs and desires of men. Women are usually made responsible for the domestic tasks of caring for the home, the children, food, social contacts, and the emotional health of their relationship with their partner. At work, women are often expected to monitor and smooth the interpersonal relationships—to anticipate personal needs, to see to personal comforts, to provide a sympathetic ear, and to be attractive and pleasant to have around. Many jobs that are relegated mostly to women, such as nurse, secretary, day-care worker, and sales clerk, demand the caring, self-sacrifice, and attractiveness that are part of women's training for heterosexuality.

Even the sexual assumptions underlying the institution of heterosexuality display gender bias. Heterosexuality is usually equated with sexual intercourse, but as Janice Moulton (1979) argued, sexual intercourse is defined as male ejaculation in a female vagina, a description that explicitly acknowledges only male sexual activity. While men must climax if the event is to count as a (the) sexual act, women may be entirely passive and dissociated from it. When women are characterized primarily as holes for penile insertion, the most passive females may even be the preferred choices: therefore, some men pursue their heterosexuality by raping infants, young girls, elderly or disabled women who cannot fight back, or mentally disabled women who cannot provide testimony.

Male sexual response has been generally treated as essential to heterosexuality and much effort goes into promoting men's arousal in our culture; society is saturated with sexual imagery aimed at stimulating men. Women and their body parts are objectified to promote male sexual stimulation. Women, themselves surrounded by the culture of commodified sex, learn to see themselves as sexual objects, and many choose to market themselves accordingly.[8] The pervasive eroticization of women and the scientifically promoted expectations of insatiable male sexual interest inevitably effect the actual interactions between women and men.

Gender requirements are subject to change, however, and the area of sexuality is no exception. Today, for instance, many men are no longer satisfied with the prospect of reluctant or distracted partners; they prefer to have their women overwhelmed with passion for them, so women are now commonly expected to experience sexual stimulation in intercourse. Although for many years medical textbooks continued to accept and pass on the Freudian edict that vaginal orgasms are distinct from and superior to clitoral ones (Scully and Bart 1972), sexologists have now acknowledged that women's sexual arousal is largely connected to clitoral stimulation. The medical response to this knowledge was not, however, to challenge the supremacy of intercourse as the primary form of sexual satisfaction but to devise techniques to facilitate clitoral contact in intercourse, including, for at least one specialist, the surgical alteration of the clitoris and the vagina.[9]

Feminists identify other objectionable features in the institution of heterosexuality. Its norms direct women to put men first in their lives, a priority that is expected to be rivaled only by the demands of children (who are, after all, the expected outcome—if not the primary purpose—of heterosexual unions). These requirements separate women from one another, deflecting their energies from women's interests and projects to male-oriented commitments.

Janice Raymond characterizes "the wide range of affective, social, political, and economic relations that are ordained between men and women by men" as "hetero-relations" and calls the resulting situation "hetero-reality" (Raymond 1986, 7). On her view, the demands of hetero-reality go beyond the obvious sexual demands of heterosexuality; in hetero-relational society, "most of women's personal, social, political, professional, and economic relations are defined by the ideology that woman is for man" (Raymond 1986: 11). As an alternative, Raymond proposes that women pursue the politically powerful option of "Gyn/affection" or female friendship, defined as "woman-to-woman attraction, influence, and movement" (Raymond 1986: 9).

She argues that the ideology that sustains heterosexuality as the "natural" form of sexuality supports the broader ideology of hetero-reality, in which male rights of access to females are presumed.

Other feminists comment on how heterosexual expectations shape worldviews. Adrienne Rich (1980) introduces the concept of a lesbian continuum to indicate how any direction of attention by women to other women amounts to a challenge to institutionalized heterosexuality. She understands all forms of bonding among women, not only genitally defined sexuality (as the usual constructions of sexuality would have it), as constituting a challenge to compulsory heterosexuality, because they all undermine men's presumed right of access to women. She urges feminists to appropriate the terms "lesbian existence" and "lesbian continuum" to encompass a broad range of "woman-identified experience" as part of the process of dismantling the oppressive norms of compulsory heterosexuality.

Many other feminists agree that what is threatening about lesbianism is not just its construction as a form of sexual deviance but its removal of women's accessibility from male control. Sarah Hoagland, for example, says: "Lesbians love lesbians, so some lesbian energy and focus is not accessible to men" (Hoagland 1988, 5). Moreover, she adds, lesbianism undermines ideological assumptions about the role of power relations in sexuality: "By our very existence lesbians challenge the social construction of reality. . . . Heterosexualism is a way of living that normalizes the dominance of one person and the subordination of another" (Hoagland 1988, 7).

Radical feminists argue that heterosexuality, at least as we know it, is at the root of women's oppression, because it makes dominance relations sexual and defines sexual relations as constructed on dominance. Socialist feminists are more open to the possibility of a noninstitutional form of heterosexuality, but many of them argue that the institution of heterosexuality is deeply entwined with the system of capitalism, and these institutions work together to oppress women. Most feminists agree that lesbian relations and other nonheterosexual ways of being for women challenge far more than society's ordinary sexual expectations. They also undermine the ideology that says women are intended for men. If there is any truth to these accounts and the institution of heterosexuality is the central element in the oppression of women, then those who shore up and protect the power of heterosexism must be seen as complicit in maintaining the institutions of female subordination.

Medicine's Distinct Role

Medicine constitutes a particularly powerful instrument of support for the coercive institution of heterosexuality. Its practitioners and theorists have helped to entrench heterosexism and to promote homophobia in several distinct ways. Psychiatry has been especially prominent in enforcing heterosexual norms, and it has been supported in this role by most other specialties, including gynecology, family medicine (through conservative assumptions about the nature of families), epidemiology (through its campaigns against the dangers of promiscuous sex), and even pediatrics.[10] In general, medical commentators have displayed a great willingness to provide evidence of the pathological nature of defections from the norms of heterosexuality.

As the designated judges of health matters, medical specialists, especially psychiatrists, define categories of "healthy" and "unhealthy" sexual orientations and practices, in conjunction with psychologists, sociologists, sociobiologists, and others who claim disciplinary authority in the field of sexology. Medicine remains prominent within the diverse collection of specialties associated with the study of sex, because the entire field of sexology claims respectability through its association with medicine (Weeks 1987). In other words, medicine offers its own prestige as a basis of legitimation for all sexologists.

Modern society has become so accustomed to medical pronouncements about the nature of sexuality that it is worth remembering that medical discussion of the concepts of homosexuality in general and lesbianism in particular is scarcely more than a hundred years old (Kitzinger 1987). For most of this period, medical interest in homosexuality has been chiefly directed at categorizing homosexual orientation as an illness and pursuing interventionist treatments to bring it under control. Until very recently, the dominant medical view was that homosexuality is a mental disorder to be treated by psychotherapeutic, and sometimes physically manipulative, techniques.

The psychiatric profession listed homosexuality as a form of personality disorder in the first two editions of its official *Diagnostic and*

Statistical Manual of Mental Disorders (DSM), making it subject to medical intervention and treatment. A newly politicized gay liberation movement became involved in the issue of psychiatric labeling in the late 1960s and early 1970s; it was effective at lobbying for change and, when the third edition emerged in 1980 (DSM III), homosexuality was no longer listed as a disorder. The third edition does, however, include a category of illness called "homosexual conflict disorder," which refers to the experience of ambivalence over one's homosexuality. Because it is difficult for homosexuals to avoid feeling some degree of ambivalence about their sexuality in a society as deeply homophobic as ours, psychotherapists can confidently assume that homosexuals do experience some dissonance with regard to their sexual orientation. Thus despite apparent progress on the psychiatric institution's response to homosexuality, there is still ample space for psychiatrists to equate homosexuality with illness.

Moreover, medicine extends its authority in the enforcement of dominant modes of sexuality beyond mere labeling; it also possesses the power to enforce its vision. In particular, psychiatrists have at their disposal many techniques by which they can manipulate behavior they oppose and coerce conformity to norms they support. When nonheterosexual forms of behavior are placed under the rubric of psychiatric problems, those who are so classified experience some fundamental changes in their lives: as psychiatric patients, they are expected to reveal the most intimate details of their lives, they lose credibility in their own analysis of their needs and situation, and they may find themselves hospitalized or placed on a regimen of powerful, mind-altering drugs. They may also be required to undergo the controversial electroconvulsive therapy ("shock treatment"). In addition to other consequences that arise from this experience, the self-confidence of those who have been labeled as mentally ill and their ability to function autonomously are likely to be seriously compromised by the experience. Cooperation with their medical managers, which is usually demonstrated only by submission to medical authority, is often the only path out.[11]

For feminists, it is significant that psychiatrists and other sexologists not only have promoted heterosexuality and licensed repression of nonheterosexual options but also have specifically "reflected and promoted the interests of men in a sexually divided society" (Jackson 1987, 52). The norms of heterosexuality endorsed by medical and other sexology experts actively support male dominance and privilege and promote female subordination. Feminists observe that scientific studies of sexuality became prominent in the late nineteenth and early twentieth centuries, when feminism began to challenge existing heterosexual norms. Typically, those studies supported patriarchal understandings of heterosexuality as "natural" and hence inevitable. These early studies were explicitly antifeminist in their arguments and seemed designed to try to stem the tide of feminist challenges to male privilege (Jackson 1987).

Early sexologists responded to feminism by linking it to the newly defined disease of lesbianism, in order to frighten women away from association with this "illness" (Kitzinger 1987). Most mental health professionals no longer presume any woman's interest in feminism should be read as a thinly veiled expression of lesbianism, and lesbianism per se is no longer defined as an illness. In any event, expert opinion is not required to establish the link between feminism and lesbianism, because belief in the connection has become well-entrenched in the popular culture, and in a homophobic climate this belief is effective in driving many women away from identifying themselves as feminists. Curiously, however, the threat of pathology is now reversed: the experts now argue that feminism is unhealthy for lesbians. Lesbians who are committed to feminism are seen as suffering from a disabling form of homosexuality, characterized as "ego dystonic" homosexuality. It is considered unhealthy for lesbians to define their identity through group membership; individual distinctiveness is said to be less dehumanizing than political affiliation (Kitzinger 1987). Hence although psychiatrists have decided that lesbians can now be deemed mentally healthy, that is only the case if they do not attach themselves to feminism.

In other words, both feminist interest in lesbianism and lesbian interest in feminism have been defined as forms of mental illness. Either way, explicitly political analyses of sexuality are perceived as pathological. Medical authority seems, then, to be directed toward suppressing political challenges to institutionalized heterosexuality and maintaining the status quo. "Progressive" medical thought now seeks to describe lesbians as "just the same" as heterosexual women and argues that their homosexuality constitutes a small and relatively insignificant part of the self (Kitzinger 1987). Its proponents reject the idea that political identity and activity that are defined around sexuality are compatible with mental health. In other words, they deny recognition of a difference that lesbian feminists consider critical to their identity.

Moreover, lesbianism is not the only sort of sexual behavior that may leave women exposed to medical intervention. Other violations of the norms of institutionalized heterosexuality have met with intrusive medical responses. In the nineteenth century clitoridectomies, ovariectomies, and even hysterectomies were used to control masturbation and nymphomania (Ehrenreich and English 1979), as well as hysteria, orgasm, insanity, use of contraception, and abortion (Barker-Benfield 1978) in women.[12] Women who were not monogamous and those who were too sexually demanding of their partners were often deemed abnormal and subjected to a range of therapies to limit their sexual drives to what physicians considered to be "normal" proportions. Even today, in our supposedly enlightened era of "liberated" sexuality, women who earn their living in the sex industry are often judged by labels of pathology; they are said to be in need of treatment to "normalize" their sexual responses. In addition, women who lack sexual interest in their husbands or who fail to achieve vaginal orgasms may still be subjected to psychoanalytic or physical manipulations to "help" them to conform to heterosexual expectations.

Further, while the theorists have developed the rationale and justification for maintaining existing norms defining sexual relations and while psychiatrists and gynecologists have assumed leadership in implementing these judgments, ordinary general practitioners have taken up the role of communicating sexual advice to the public. Physicians have been socially authorized to advise on sexual matters, although most of them actually have little training in the multidimensional aspects and varieties of human sexuality (and virtually no lessons on the politics of such studies). Many simply pass on their personal views about sexual matters under the guise of "scientific experts."

Other Forms of Medical Intervention

Medicine plays other key roles in maintaining the connections between sex, sexuality, and gender. Medically supported beliefs about the biological basis of these links are so deeply rooted that some physicians are now willing to shape biological sex to fit defined gender roles. In an important feminist critique, Janice Raymond (1979) examines the effects of the decision to medicalize the experience of believing one's biological sex does not fit one's deeper gender identity, defined as a disease called "gender dysphoria." The treatment for this disease is collectively called transsexualism, the changing of biological sex. Typically, this complex medical procedure involves radical surgery for anatomical sex conversion, major and permanent doses of artificial hormones, and intensive psychotherapy; it may also include cosmetic surgery on secondary sex characteristics, electrolysis, and speech therapy.

Transsexualism presumes that gender roles are fundamental; in defining this activity as a response to disease, the weight of medical authority is thrown behind the system of sex-role stereotypes. Raymond argues for a different interpretation: "Transsexualism is basically a social problem whose cause cannot be explained except in relation to the sex roles and identities that a patriarchal society generates" (Raymond 1979, 16). It is significant that many transsexuals abhor homosexuality and seek to "'normalize' their sexual relationships as heterosexual by acquiring the appropriate genitalia" (Raymond 1979, 122). The medical specialists they consult help them to accomplish this end—despite the severe health risks associated with the "cure" that is offered—presumably out of a shared belief in genitally defined heterosexuality.

Medicine has other techniques at its disposal to monitor and control sexuality in the general population. An important tool has been the promotion of "germphobia"—a term introduced by Patton (1986) to represent the emotional panic associated with fear of sexually transmitted germs. Germphobia serves two functions: it frightens people away from "deviant" sexual practices, and it entrenches medical power to determine what constitutes "healthy" sex. For many people, sexually transmitted diseases (STDs) are understood to be the appropriate punishment for sexual behavior that does not conform to the monogamous, heterosexual norm. Because treatment for these conditions is a medical matter, people are made accountable to medical practitioners should illness result from their nonconforming sexuality.

Although all illnesses are frightening because they likely will cause suffering and may even bring death, STDs often carry an extra burden of guilt, embarrassment, or shame. Whereas other illnesses may be viewed as the result of misfortune or bad genes and their victims are seen as innocent, STDs, which are understood to be the product of voluntary risk-taking, do not usually evoke such sympathy. Furthermore, as Susan Sontag (1989) has eloquently argued, illness is more than a private, physical event: it is also commonly interpreted as a metaphor. Some illnesses, (especially STDs) are associated with particularly devastating metaphors in both the medical and the public consciousness.

Germs were discovered to be responsible for transmission of venereal diseases in the nineteenth century. This medical understanding of the causal nature of STDs made it appropriate to discuss sex as a matter of science (rather than religion or vice). In addition, medical recognition of the role of germs in transmitting STDs supported public health measures promoting the roundup of prostitutes and enforcement of classist bias against the poor women who were identified as the agents of transmission (Corea 1985a; Patton 1986). Doctors sought to confine the disease to what was perceived as its appropriate class and offered a scientific justification for maintaining the "existing organization of sexual and social mores between and within classes, races, and genders" (Patton 1986, 57). Efforts were directed at controlling, not healing, the lower-class women who were blamed for the transmission of these germs, in order to protect male soldiers and affluent men; when the disease showed up in their wives, it was largely ignored (Corea 1985a). Stressing the hazards of sex outside marriage, public health practitioners were able to preach monogamy and heterosexuality as a matter of physical as well as mental health.

The discovery of antibiotics created a period in which medical threats against promiscuity lost much of their power—at least, for men who did not have to accept the remaining worry about unwanted pregnancy. Prophylaxis was largely ignored when cure seemed so accessible (Corea 1985a). The fact that STDs can be exceedingly difficult to diagnose in women was not treated as a matter of serious medical concern; for the most part, medical advice about prevention was directed exclusively at men (Corea 1985a).[13]

The discovery of AIDS, however, has brought the sexual authority of the public health specialist back into favor. Medical authorities have encouraged the media to generate a climate of fear, bordering on hysteria, with regard to AIDS. Although they seek to correct mistaken conclusions about the dangers of nonsexual transmission, most medical authorities have been very eager to discourage all forms of promiscuous sex. Monogamous, heterosexual sex is recommended as the medically safe option, and several physicians have leapt to the front of the campaign to stigmatize and ostracize those who have not had the good sense or strong moral character to conform to this pattern.[14]

AIDS is indeed a terrible disease, which is properly feared. We can question the response of the medical community to this new threat, however, because for the most part, medicine has directed social attention at fear, rather than at determining positive ways to respond to the threat. Medical reports categorize groups at special risk of the disease: gay men, intravenous drug users, Haitians, and poor black and Hispanic women and children. Fostering hostility to those "different" from the mainstream (white, middle-class, male-dominated, Christian, heterosexual, and theoretically monogamous), conservative physicians support their lay colleagues in encouraging public backlash against homosexuality and promiscuity. Most medical reports about the patterns of transmission uncritically foster existing social tendencies to characterize as dangerous people who are different from the majority; in so doing, they have helped to justify the prejudices of the dominant culture, encouraging its attempts to distance itself from what it perceives as difference, rather than helping to find ways of incorporating other types of people in the community.

Thus many physicians and medical researchers have used their scientific authority and expertise to legitimize their hostility to homosexuality and to other variations from monogamous heterosexuality. Most medical responses to the emergence of AIDS reflect evidence of medical collusion with the broader social agenda to control sexuality. Medical researchers and clinicians and public health authorities leapt quickly to the conclusion that AIDS is a "gay plague," a punishment for sexual activity that transcends acceptable practice. Their major conclusion has been that the crisis is best dealt with by restraining sexual desire and practice.

For the most part, Western researchers have ignored the incidence of AIDS among heterosexuals in Africa; they have obscured evidence that such social conditions as poverty and inadequate health care in the West are significant features in the spread of the disease (Patton 1986). For a long time it seemed that marginalized populations were the only victims of AIDS and that the best way of controlling the disease was to control those populations.

Even now, research resources are mainly directed at high-profile responses, such as the pursuit of a reliable test by which we can identify and isolate the dangerous individuals who are infected, a vaccine to protect the mainstream population from spread of the disease, and, ideally, the ultimate cure. Despite the large sums that have been made available for study of the disease, research into relief of its symptoms has not been a high priority (Patton 1986).

In contrast, gay and lesbian communities have sought to reinforce changes in sexual practice that support gay identity in face of the AIDS crisis (Patton 1986). They have concentrated on identifying and encouraging low-risk sexual practices that preserve physical pleasure and maintain sexual identity, thereby trying to transform sexual responsibility from a perceived limitation to an empowering aspect of agency. Speaking of the public health pronouncements on safe sex, Patton observes that "it has been all too easy in the process of developing sensible sex guidelines to confuse the sexual norms one might like to see with those that are actually risk-reducing" (Patton 1986, 138).

Relying on a variety of subtle and hence potentially insidious forms of manipulation, medicine has succeeded in replacing the church as the authoritative source of discourse on sexuality in the modern world; it has seized the role of specifying and thereby controlling the ways in which sex is discussed and experienced. Medicine has established its power to police and deter misguided sexualities by stressing the dangers of sexuality outside the norms of traditional forms of heterosexuality. Although the medical agenda of making people "normal" and well constitutes a far more sophisticated and perhaps effective approach than the more obvious attempts at sexual restriction enforced by the church and the state in earlier eras, it has a similar result. It, too, facilitates control over members of less powerful groups through the control of their sexual behavior.

Therefore, even the existence of a serious medical condition such as AIDS cannot be addressed in purely medical terms. Sexuality is not simply a medical question, even though it involves medical questions. Feminists must insist that dialogues on sexuality be recognized as having profound social, political, and legal dimensions, which make it impossible to speak of the "merely" medical aspects of sexuality. The biological and psychological expertise that belongs to medical theorists and practitioners is a significant feature of public and private considerations about sexuality, but it should not be privileged relative to other important sorts of knowledge. Given the intimate connection between sexuality and power in our culture, it is ethically unacceptable for physicians or other health care providers to offer sexual advice without acknowledging the political complexities and the variety of perspectives that are also relevant to these issues.

11

Gender, Race, and Class in the Delivery of Health Care

Oppression and Illness

It is widely recognized throughout the field of biomedical ethics that people's health care needs usually vary inversely with their power and privilege within society. Most bioethical discussions explain these differences solely in economic terms, observing that health and access to health resources are largely dependent on income levels. Poverty is an important determining factor in a person's prospects for health: being poor often means living without access to adequate nutrition, housing, heat, clean water, clothing, and sanitation, and each of these factors may have a negative impact on health (Lewis 1990). Further, the poor are more likely than others to work in industries that pose serious health risks (Stellman 1988) and to do without adequate health insurance (Tallon and Block 1988). And the poor suffer higher rates of mental illness and addiction (Paltiel 1988) than do other segments of the population. Financial barriers also often force the poor to let diseases reach an advanced state before they seek professional help; by the time these individuals do receive care, recovery may be compromised.

It is not sufficient, however, just to notice the effects of poverty on health; it is also necessary to consider who is at risk of becoming the victim of poverty. In a hierarchical society such as the one we live in, members of groups that are oppressed on the basis of gender, race, sexuality, and so forth are the people who are most likely to be poor. Moreover, not only does being oppressed lead to poverty and poverty to poor health but being oppressed is itself also a significant determining factor in the areas of health and health care. Those who are most oppressed in society at large are likely to experience the most severe and frequent health problems and have the least access to adequate medical treatment.[1] One reason for this vulnerability is that oppressed individuals are usually exposed to high levels of stress by virtue of their oppressed status, and excessive stress is responsible for many serious illnesses and is a complicating factor in most diseases. Another important factor to consider, as we shall see, is that the same prejudices that undermine the status of the oppressed members of society may affect the treatment they receive at the hands of health care workers.

North American society is characteristically sexist, racist, classist, homophobic, and frightened of physical or mental imperfections; we can anticipate, then, that those who are oppressed by virtue of their gender, race, class, sexual orientation, or disabilities—and especially, those who are oppressed in a number of different ways—will experience a disproportional share of illness and will often suffer reduced access to resources. Moreover, the connection between illness and oppression can run in both directions; because serious or chronic illness is often met with fear and hostility, it may also precipitate an individual's or family's slide into poverty and can therefore lead to oppression based on class.

The damaging connections between oppression and illness are profoundly unfair. Because this situation is ethically objectionable, bioethicists have a responsibility to consider ways in which existing medical institutions can be modified to challenge and undermine these connections, rather than contribute to them. Ethical analyses of the distribution of health and health care must take into consideration the role that oppression plays in a person's prospects for health and well-being.

Patients as Members of Oppressed Groups

Throughout this book I have argued that women constitute an oppressed group, which is at a clear disadvantage in the health care system. Women are the primary consumers of health care, but the care they receive does not always serve their overall health interests. In a report presented to the American Medical Association, Richard McMurray (1990) reviewed recent studies on gender disparities in clinical decision-making; he found that although women are likely to undergo more medical procedures than do men when they present the same symptoms and condition, they have significantly less access than men do to some of the major diagnostic and therapeutic interventions that are considered medically appropriate for their conditions. In some cases the discrepancies were quite remarkable: for example, despite comparable physical needs, women were 30 percent less likely than men to receive kidney transplants, 50 percent as likely to be referred for diagnostic testing for lung cancer, and only 10 percent as likely to be referred for cardiac catheterization. The studies were unable to identify any biological difference that would justify these discrepancies. In addition, even though biological differences are sometimes significant in the course of various diseases and therapies, McMurray found that medical researchers have largely ignored the study of diseases and medications in women; for instance, cardiovascular disease is the leading cause of death in women in the United States, but research in this area has been almost exclusively conducted on men.

Therefore, as a group, it appears that women are particularly vulnerable to poor health care. Although they receive a great deal of medical treatment, the relevant research data are frequently missing, and specific treatment decisions seem to be biased against them. When women are medically treated, they are often overtreated, that is, subjected to excessive testing, surgery, and prescription drugs (Weaver and Garrett 1983). Sometimes they are simply not offered the treatment that physicians have judged to be preferable; for example, most professionals who work in the area of fertility control encourage women seeking birth control to go on the pill, despite its known risks. Interestingly, the majority of practitioners choose barrier methods for themselves and their spouses (Todd 1989); they do not seem to trust ordinary women to be conscientious in the use of the safer, less medically intrusive methods.

Physicians are trained in the stereotypical views of women as people who are excessively anxious, devious, and unintelligent; they are taught not to take all women's complaints seriously (Ehrenreich and English 1979; Corea 1985a; Todd 1989). Researchers have found that physicians are often condescending toward their women patients, and many deliberately withhold medical information from them out of concern for their inability to interpret it correctly (Corea 1985a; Todd 1989). Having medicalized the very condition of being female (Chapter 9), many doctors have seized opportunities to intervene and modify those bodies in ways they are unwilling to apply to men—for example, psychosurgery, an exceedingly controversial therapy, is performed twice as often on women as on men, and ultrasound was widely practiced on women before being introduced as a therapy for men (Corea 1985a).

Nevertheless, not all women experience the health care system in the same ways. There are many important differences among women that result in different sorts of experiences within the health care system; in particular, differences that are associated with race, economic class, and ethnicity compound the difficulties most women experience in their various encounters with health care workers. Alexandra Todd observed that "the darker a woman's skin and/or the lower her place on the economic scale, the poorer the care and efforts at explanation she received" (Todd 1989, 77). Other factors that contribute to the sort of health care a woman is likely to receive include age, sexuality, body size, intelligence, disabilities, and a history of mental illness. It is a matter of serious moral concern that social factors play a significant role in determining the quality of health care a woman receives.

If we expand our scope to that of a global perspective, then it is obvious that women in other parts of the world face distinct health problems, such as those created by malnutrition, often to the point of starvation, and by the absence of a safe source of drinking water; many women must cope with the ravages of war or the hazards of living under brutally repressive political regimes. Third World women must frequently rely on unsafe drugs, which have failed to meet minimum safety standards and therefore are dumped in developing countries by manufacturers determined to make a profit from them (McDonnell 1986). Some prominent concerns of bioethicists, such as the need to obtain informed consent for treatment and research, are deemed to be the products of Western ideals and are likely to go unrecognized in nations where all personal liberties are severely curtailed; elsewhere, the ethical "niceties" are often ignored in the face of the pressing demands posed by crippling poverty and illiteracy.

The injustice represented by the differing health options and standards of care based on different levels of power and privilege is not restricted to the Third World. Inadequate prenatal care and birth services are common to poor women everywhere, and the lack of safe, effective birth control and abortion services is more a matter of politics than of economics. In North America women of color are at a higher risk than white women for many life-threatening conditions; for example, black American women are four times more likely to die in childbirth and three times more likely to have their newborns die than are white women (Gordon-Bradshaw 1988, 256). Black women in the United States are twice as likely to die of hypertensive cardio-vascular disease as are white women; they have three times the rate of high blood pressure and of lupus as do white women; they are more likely than white women to die from breast cancer (despite having lower rates of incidence); they are twelve times more likely than white women to contract the AIDS virus; and they are four times more likely than white women to die of homicide (Davis 1990).

In the United States the poor usually have (at best) access only to inadequate health services. Many people who find themselves employed full time but receiving annual incomes well below established poverty lines fail to qualify for Medicaid support (Tallon and Block 1988). Those who do receive subsidized health care must confront the fact that many physicians and hospitals refuse to accept Medicaid patients. In 1985, for example, four out of ten physicians who provided obstetrical service refused to take Medicaid patients (McBarnette 1988).

Canadians have so far avoided the two-tiered system of private and public health care. In Canada poor women are not turned away from hospitals or doctors' offices,[2] but they may not be able to afford travel to these facilities. Rural women are often restricted from access to needed health care by lack of transportation. Many Canadian communities lack suitably qualified health care specialists, and some provinces simply refuse to provide needed services, especially abortion, thus making it unavailable to women who cannot travel to a private clinic in another jurisdiction. Despite its guaranteed payment for health care, then, the Canadian health care system still reflects the existence of differential patterns of health and illness, associated with both race and income level (York 1987; Paltiel 1988).

In both countries the services available to women through the health care system are predominately those that meet the needs of the most privileged and articulate women, namely, those who are white, middle-class, educated, and urban. The health needs of other women are likely to be invisible or to slip through the cracks of the structures and funding of the system. In most cities, for example, prenatal programs, exercise counseling, mammography facilities, and hormone replacement therapy for menopausal women are available, but other urgent services, such as programs for alcohol- or drug-dependent women, are less easily found. Although some private programs exist for affluent women with substance-abuse problems, poor women have virtually no place to which they can turn. Further, if they should manage to find a program that is not too alienating to their experience to be of value, then they may face the problem of finding child care for the duration of the program, and if they are poor, then they are liable to lose custody of their children to the state when they admit to having a problem with addiction.

Although most urban centers offer nutritional guidance to affluent women trying to lose weight (even if their main goal is to fit the cultural ideals and medically mandated norms of slimness), few programs help women on welfare learn how to stretch their inadequate welfare checks to provide nutritious meals or to locate the resources for a healthy diet. Battered women who arrive at emergency rooms are patched up by the specialists on duty and perhaps referred to local, short-term shelters—if space can be found.[3] Preventive health care, which would help the abuser find nonviolent ways of behaving, is usually not available. As a result, many women get trapped in the cycle of returning home to their violent partner, returning to hospital with increasingly severe injuries (where they encounter frustrated staff members, who frequently blame them for repeat episodes), and recuperating in a temporary shelter. In the meantime, their children become intimately acquainted with violence as a means of addressing personal tensions and become primed to continue the pattern in the next generation.

In bioethics literature the issue of justice is often raised, but most discussions focus on whether or not everyone has a right to health care and, if so, what services this right might entail. Accessibility is viewed as the principal moral concern, but even where there is universal health insurance (for example, in Canada), the system is not designed to respond to the particular health needs of many groups of women. Being subject to violence, at risk of developing addictions to alcohol or other mood-altering drugs, and lacking adequate resources to obtain a nutritious food supply are all factors that affect peoples' prospects for health and their ability to promote their own well-being. Such threats to health are a result of the social system, which promotes oppression of some groups by others. Health care alone will not correct all these social effects, but as long as the damage of oppression continues, it is necessary to help its victims recover from some of the harms to their health that occur as a result of their oppressed status.

Bioethicists share with health care professionals and the rest of the community an ethical responsibility to determine how the health needs generated by oppressive structures can best be met. Medical care per se will not always be the most effective means of restoring or preserving the health of oppressed persons. Investigation of how best to respond to these socially generated needs is a topic that must be added to the traditional agenda of health care ethics.

The Organization of Health Care

Much of the explanation for the different ways in which health care providers respond to the needs of different social groups can be found in the very structures of the health care delivery system. The dominance structures that are pervasive throughout society are reproduced in the medical context; both within and without the health care delivery system, sex, race, economic class, and able-bodied status are important predictors in determining someone's place in the hierarchy. The organization of the health care system does not, however, merely mirror the power and privilege structures of the larger society; it also perpetuates them.

Within existing health care structures, women do most of the work associated with health care, but they are, for the most part, excluded from making the policy decisions that shape the system. They are the principal providers of home health care, tending the ill members of their own families, but because this work is unpaid, it is unrecorded labor, not even appearing in statistical studies of health care delivery systems; it carries no social authority, and the knowledge women acquire in caring for the ill is often dismissed by those who have power in the system. Furthermore, support is not made available to provide some relief to women carrying out this vital but demanding work.

In the formal institutions of health care delivery, women constitute over 80 percent of paid health care workers, but men hold almost all the positions of authority.[4] Health policy is set by physicians, directors, and legislators, and these positions are filled overwhelmingly by men. Despite recent dramatic increases in female enrollment in medical schools, most physicians are men (78.8 percent in Canada and 84.8 percent in the United States as of 1986);[5] further, female physicians tend to cluster in less influential specialties, such as family practice and pediatrics, and they are seldom in positions of authority within their fields. Most medical textbooks are written by men, most clinical instructors are men, and most hospital directors are men.[6] The professional fields that women do largely occupy in the health care system are ones associated with traditionally female skills, such as nursing, nutrition, occupational and physical therapy, and public health. Women who work in health administration tend to be situated in middle-management positions, where their mediating skills may be desirable but their influence on policy is limited.

Research, too, is largely concentrated in male hands. Few women have their own labs or the budgets to pursue projects of their own choosing. The standards by which research is evaluated are those that have been developed by privileged men to meet their needs. They do not incorporate considerations that some female scientists and most feminist philosophers of science find important, such as including space in the design of a project for a measure of participant control, reducing the separation between subject and object, and resisting restrictive, medicalized analysis.

When we focus directly on issues of race and economic class, the isolation of health care provider from consumer becomes even more pronounced. Although many members of minority races and plenty of poor people are involved in the delivery of health care, very few hold positions of authority. Working-class and minority employees are concentrated in the nonprofessional ranks of cleaners, nurses' aides, orderlies, kitchen staff, and so forth. Women from these groups generally have the lowest income and status in the whole health care system. They have no opportunity to shape health care policy or voice their concerns about their own health needs or those of persons for whom they are responsible. One result of this unbalanced representation is that there has been virtually no research into the distinct needs of minority women (White 1990). Both those empowered to do medical research and those expected to respond to identified health needs come almost entirely from the socially defined groups and classes most removed from the experiences of women of color and of poor and disabled women.

The gender and racial imbalances in the health care system are not accidental; they are a result of specific barriers designed to restrict access to women and minorities to the ranks of physicians. Regina Morantz-Sanchez (1985) documents how the medical profession organized itself over the last century to exclude and harass women who sought to become doctors, and Margaret Campbell (1973) shows that many of these mechanisms are still with us. Blacks, too, have been subject to systematic barriers, which keep them out of the ranks of physicians. For example, it is necessary to serve as an intern to become licensed to practice medicine, but until the 1960s, few American hospitals would grant internship positions to black physicians; those blacks who did manage to become qualified to practice medicine often encountered hospitals that refused to grant them the opportunity to admit patients (Blount 1990). Because black women must overcome both gender and race barriers, they face nearly insurmountable obstacles to pursuing careers as physicians (Weaver and Garrett 1983; Gamble 1990). Therefore, although blacks make up 12 percent of the population of the United States, they account for only 3 percent of the population of practicing doctors, and black women constitute only 1 percent of the nation's physicians; further, blacks represent only 2 percent of the faculty at medical schools (Gamble 1990).

Racism and sexism in health care have been exacerbated by the fact that different oppressed groups have long been encouraged to perceive their interests as in conflict, so that race often divides women who might otherwise be expected to unite. Darlene Clark Hine (1989) has shown that racial struggles have plagued the nursing profession since 1890. For much of that period, white nurses acted on their own racist views and fought to exclude black women from their ranks. Although their racism is not excusable, it is perhaps understandable: Hine explains that white nurses felt compelled to fight for professional status and autonomy. Acting within a predominantly racist culture, they feared that their claims for recognition would be undermined if they were to welcome black nurses into the profession on an equal footing. In other words, because the combined forces of racism and sexism made it especially difficult for black nurses to obtain respect as professionals, white nurses chose to accept the implicit judgments behind such attitudes and to distance themselves from their black colleagues, rather than joining them in the struggle to counter racial prejudice.

Moreover, the racial struggles of nurses are just one symptom of a larger problem. The hierarchical structures that operate throughout the health care system motivate each social group to pursue the pragmatic strategy of establishing its relative superiority over yet more disadvantaged groups, rather than working collectively to challenge the structures themselves. Although white nurses did seek to dissociate themselves from black nurses and claimed greater commonality with the higher-ranked (white) male physicians, black nurses were themselves driven to seek distance from other black women who were employed in the system as domestic staff or nurses' aides, by claiming an unreciprocated identity with white nurses. Within hierarchical structures, all participants have reason to foster connections with those ranked higher and to seek distance from those ranked lower. This motive breeds an attitude that encourages submission to those above and hostility and a sense of superiority toward those below; in this way, all but the most oppressed groups become complicit in maintaining the hierarchical structure of the health care system. Thus the organization of the health care system itself helps reinforce the oppressive structures and attitudes of society at large.

The Effects on Health Care

In addition to the obvious injustice involved in distributing health care jobs on the basis of sex, race, and class, this practice also has serious repercussions for the quality of the health care that is actually provided. When health decisions are made by predominantly white, affluent, well-educated men, there is great danger that professionals will act on the basis of the familiar gender, racial, and class stereotypes of their society. They are likely to accept the culturally defined view of women as stupid, ignorant, and dishonest, especially with regard to women of color who are also poor and uneducated. Patients from cultures different from that of the practitioner may find communication difficult, particularly in the face of existing prejudices; their care is likely to suffer as a result.[7] If the people in the health care system who are most like the patient are those consigned to low-level, demoralizing, dead-end jobs—that is, those most likely to be alienated from their work and hence least likely to demonstrate commitment to the health care "team"—then both patients and providers will assume great gaps in each other's expectations and values.

It should come as no surprise, then, that the health care system is least effective at providing for the needs of people who are multiply oppressed in society. Such consequences may be quite unconscious and wholly unintended. It is part of the very nature of oppression that those with the power to set the social agenda and define the realms of knowledge view the world from their own perspective. Hence in the realm of health care, the professionals who make the decisions about policies and priorities are most attuned to needs that arise among the types of people they know best—other people with power and privilege in society. Researchers tend to pursue grants to study conditions that threaten people like themselves, such as heart disease, cancer, and infertility. They have less incentive to worry about the health effects of poverty, oppression, or racially associated conditions (e.g. sickle cell disease).

At the same time, the health consumers, who are ultimately responsible for their own health and the health of those they care for, are offered little support in their role. The very people with the greatest health needs are likely to find the whole system alien. For example, in almost all families women bear the primary responsibility for the health needs of their families, but each must negotiate a male-dominated health care system that is chiefly oriented to expensive, hospital-based care. These women must learn how the system is organized, where to seek appropriate care, and how to linguistically and culturally translate their concerns into information that will be meaningful to health professionals (Zambrana 1988). Women of color, immigrant women, and poor women, as well as disabled women and lesbians, are at a significant disadvantage in this task, as long as the delivery system is controlled by individuals whose backgrounds are so different from the consumers'.

Those who set up the major medical facilities seem to have designed them to meet the health crises of a typically middle-class life. For instance, usually neither child care facilities nor transportation are provided as health resources, although both may be essential for some patients if they are to receive care. Hospital menus reflect the dietary preferences of the mainstream in North American society and seldom take account of the tastes of minority cultures. White physicians and nurses frequently adopt paternalistic, patronizing attitudes toward minority patients. If patients do not follow "orders," then they are described as noncompliant and are treated with anger and hostility, even if the reason for failure was that there was a breakdown in communications, that the patient could not afford the drug prescribed, that the patient could not be excused from work for the follow-up tests, that the patient had to skip an appointment to care for a sick child, or that the patient's exam was scheduled on a day that the patient's religion declares sacred. Without a more diverse group of health care providers at all levels of the system, such misunderstandings may be difficult to detect and will be virtually impossible to eradicate.

Moreover, many social problems that are connected to health may not be addressed at all. The actual needs of various women are often discounted in favor of more medically defined expectations. For example, Alexandra Todd found that *"women come to doctors for help in understanding how to adjust their bodies to their social lives. Doctors' technical answers assume that women should adjust their social lives to their bodies"* (Todd 1989, 96).

Chronic health problems that arise from the circumstances of oppression seldom receive the care required. Thus low priority is usually assigned to responding to the needs of people who suffer from current or childhood experiences of sexual, emotional, or physical abuse. Therapy for such conditions requires intensive and sympathetic interaction between patient and therapist, perhaps invoking methods different from those traditionally practiced in the medical model.[8] Often only pills or lectures are offered to survivors of physical or sexual assaults; here, too, a patient's social status generally determines the treatment available to her, as was admitted in a recent textbook of psychiatry: "In the past, long-term intensive, insight-oriented therapies usually have been reserved for intelligent, achievement-oriented patients with middle- or upper-class backgrounds and values. Psychotherapeutic approaches for lower-class patients have tended to be more authoritative, behavioral, supportive, symptomatic, short-term, and infrequent in nature, and usually combined with drugs" (cited in Paltiel 1988, 196). There is no evidence that things have improved for the poor in the present.

If we wish the situation to be fairer in the future, then we need to investigate means of responding more effectively to differing needs and situations. One important step in that task would be to broaden the base of the network of "experts" who shape the definition of health needs in our society. We can assume that, by virtue of their very success in their roles, those currently recognized as authorities on health matters are removed from the perspective of many of the members of society who face the most serious health risks.

Gender, Race, and Class as Ideological Influences in Health Care

Beyond the basic injustice apparent in the differential opportunities and care that result from an unequal health care system, indirect moral costs are also created. The hierarchical organization of our health care system not only reflects the sexist, racist, and classist values of society but also lends support to them.

That the demographic patterns of the health care system are reflections of those found in the larger society compounds their effect. When the patterns of gender, race, and class distribution that are found in health care are repeated in most other major social institutions—including universities, the justice system, the business community, and the civil service—they appear inevitable. In health care, as throughout society, the most prestigious, rewarding, and powerful positions are occupied by privileged white males, who are supported by a vast pyramid of relatively undervalued, white, professional women; unskilled laborers of color have been relegated to the realm of "merely physical" work.[9]

This arrangement is of moral concern not just because of its obvious unfairness but because it provides an ideological foundation for maintaining a hierarchically structured, stratified society.[10] Within the realm of health care, authoritarian structures are rationalized as necessary to the goals of achieving good health. The metaphors that structure participants' experiences within the system appeal explicitly to models of dominance: doctors "command" health care teams, "battle" illnesses, and "lead campaigns" against dangerous life-styles. Their expertise entitles them to give "orders" to workers in the affiliated health professions (nurses, physical therapists, pharmacists, and so forth) and to patients. These arrangements are justified in terms of their end, health. Because the end is of unquestionable value, the means are usually considered acceptable to the degree that they achieve this goal. Thus medicine's worthy goals and remarkable accomplishments are said to demonstrate the benefits of retaining power and privilege for a socially vital elite. That numerous critics have questioned the success of this model in the actual achievement of health has done little to dissuade the medical establishment from encouraging the public to accept its structures as necessary (York 1987). When feminists and other critics challenge the legitimacy of social hierarchies, the medical model can be held up as evidence of the value of hierarchical structures in achieving important social goals.

Moreover, when the physicians are overwhelmingly male, white, able-bodied, and upper- or middle-class, social messages about the appropriate holders of authority are delivered with the technical medical information they control. When predominately white, female nurses accept the authority of mostly male doctors and follow their directions, they convey gender messages to patients and health care workers alike. When these nurses assume professional superiority and authority over nonprofessional hospital workers of other races, the patterns of racial oppression are also sustained. In these ways, the role patterns of the health care system rationalize society's sex and race inequalities and confirm the existing stereotypes that maintain these inequalities.

There are further reasons for concern over the close correspondence between system and social power in an oppressive society. Decisions about illness in members of oppressed groups may be tainted by the social expectations that accompany discriminatory practices. Such decisions often reflect cultural stereotypes, which themselves derive from unjust social arrangements. At the same time, those decisions may serve to legitimize particular damaging stereotypes and the social divisions that depend on them.

For example, white health care experts (and others) have identified alcoholism as a pervasive problem in the native American community; they have preached abstinence as a response. Generally, these judgments are made without examining the devastation that white culture has wrought on native community values and without extending any support for traditional, native healing options as alternative paths to recovery. Often health care workers have uncritically accepted the stereotypical view of "drunken Indians" and suggested

that natives are either weak-willed or have some genetic propensity to
alcohol dependency; either way, their misfortune is a reflection of
some deficiency within them, not society. Most health professionals
are committed to the individualistic medical model, which views diseases as belonging to individuals; although they may acknowledge a
role for genetic or sociological factors, they believe that the individual
is the proper site for health care treatment.

Other conceptions are available, however, and it is useful to reflect
on alternatives in these circumstances. Some native healers suggest
that alcoholism in their communities is really a social disease of the
community, which should be understood as connected to the brutal
separation of their people from their culture. Their account leads to
an alternative strategy for recovery and a distinct form of health care;
where the medical model treats the individual, native healers believe
it is necessary to heal the community.[11] Nevertheless, only the medically authorized response receives approval and support from those
with the power to allocate health care resources.

The social harms extend further. Because the authority of health
care decision-making is concentrated in nonnative hands, native people who identify themselves as alcoholics are required to adapt to
treatment programs that have been designed for a white, urban population. They are deemed to be failures if the programs do not succeed
in curing them. Because the problems usually continue, native people are seen to fulfill their culturally generated stereotypes; their severely disadvantaged economic and social position is then explained
away by experts who speak authoritatively of native peoples' "natural"
propensity to alcohol abuse. As long as health care decision-making
resides in the hands of an elite, nonnative few, we can anticipate its
continued failure to recognize and address the real needs of the native community.[12] These failures, in turn, support the cultural prejudices that view natives as inferior members of modern society who
cannot hope to rise above their designated status on the socio-
economic scale.

Similar self-fulfilling prophecies can be found in other consequences of a socially unbalanced health care structure. For instance,
one of the truisms of modern health care is the recognition that stress
is an important contributing factor in illness, but the standard social
understanding of stress is that it is connected with positions of power
and authority. When, for example, experts compile lists of events
that contribute to stress, they focus on events that occur in men's

lives, such as being drafted, promoted at work, or having one's wife begin work. Experiencing an abortion, a rape, or a change in child-care arrangements usually does not appear on these lists, and hence these events may well be ignored as stress factors in a woman's life when she seeks medical care (Paltiel 1988). The paradigmatic picture of a stressful occupation is that of a high-powered, business executive. An American study on stress and the workplace found, however, that lower-status workers, especially clerks, are more likely to experience stress-related health effects than are senior managers; the most stressful, damaging jobs are the ones that combine high work demands with low control over the job (Paltiel 1988). Poor women, with no control over their jobs and with unsatisfiable responsibilities for their children's well-being, suffer more from stress than either professionals or managers, but they receive little support or relief for their problems. Instead of genuine strategies to help relieve their stress, they are often offered platitudes and judgmental lectures about their coping behaviors (which frequently include smoking, drinking, or use of drugs). Because those who control the provision of health services have such different life experiences from those of their female patients on social assistance, they are not likely to recognize the stress factors that afflict such women, and they have little advice for responding to poverty-induced stress, when it is acknowledged.

Furthermore, physicians use their authority to entrench their social attitudes toward women on a broad scale. For example, nineteenth-century physicians espoused theories about the competition between women's brains and their uteruses to support policies for keeping women out of universities and "protecting" them from political activity. Today many doctors promote estrogen replacement therapy for menopausal women, despite the risks of cancer associated with the treatment program, because of their belief that women should want to avoid the embarrassment of aging. Over the years, some physicians have gone to great lengths to make women fit their stereotypically defined social roles; they have responded to individual women's disaffection from feminine roles of procreator, housewife, mother, or companion with genital surgery, psychosurgery, psychotherapy, hormone therapy, or tranquilizers, depending on the fashion over the years (Ehrenreich and English 1979; Mitchinson 1991). Few doctors, however, have responded to women's complaints by challenging the roles to which women were (are) required to adapt.

The power and authority that society has entrusted to doctors give them the opportunity to destroy many of the patriarchal assumptions about women collectively and the racist, classist, homophobic, and other beliefs about various groups of women that are key to their oppression. Few physicians, however, have chosen to exercise their social power in this way. Many doctors have accepted uncritically the biases of an oppressive society, and some have offered evidence in confirmation of such values. As a group, physicians have held onto their own power and privilege by defending the primacy of the authoritarian medical model as a necessary feature of health care. Most have failed to listen honestly to the alternative perspectives of oppressed people who are very differently situated in society.

The medical model organizes our current attempts at defining and responding to health needs. It has been conceived as a structure that requires a hierarchically organized health care system, in which medical expertise is privileged over other sorts of knowledge. It grants license to an elite class of experts to formulate all matters of health and to determine the means for responding to them. As we have seen, however, there are several serious moral problems with this model. First, it responds differently to the health needs of different groups, offering less and lower-quality care to members of oppressed groups. Second, its structures and presuppositions support the patterns of oppression that shape our society. Finally, it rationalizes the principle of hierarchy in human interactions, rather than one of equality, by insisting that its authoritarian structures are essential to the accomplishment of its specific ends, and it tolerates an uneven distribution of positions within its hierarchy.

Some Conclusions

We need, then, different models to guide our thinking about how ways to organize the delivery of health care. In addition to the many limits to the medical model that have been named in the bioethics literature, the traditional model reflects and perpetuates oppression in society. I conclude by summarizing some feminist suggestions that I believe should be incorporated into alternative models, if they are to be ethically acceptable.

A model that reflects the insights of feminist ethics would expand its conceptions of health and health expertise. It would recognize social as well as physiological dimensions of health. In particular, it would reflect an understanding of both the moral and the health costs of oppression. Thus it would make clear that those who are committed to improving the health status of all members of the population should assume responsibility for avoiding and dismantling the dominance structures that contribute to oppression.

Such a model would require a change in traditional understandings of who has the relevant knowledge to make decisions about health and health policy. Once we recognize the need to include oppression as a factor in health, we can no longer maintain the authoritarian medical model, in which physicians are the experts on all matters of health and are authorized to respond to all such threats. We need also to recognize that experiential knowledge is essential to understanding how oppression affects health and how the damage of oppression can be reduced. Both political and moral understandings may be necessary to address these dimensions of health and health care. Physiological knowledge is still important, but it is not always decisive.

Therefore, a feminist model would resist hierarchical structures and proclaim a commitment to egalitarian alternatives. Not only would these alternatives be more democratic in themselves and hence more morally legitimate, they would also help to produce greater social equality by empowering those who have been traditionally disempowered. They would limit the scope for domination that is available to those now accustomed to power and control. More egalitarian structures would foster better health care and higher standards of health for those who are now oppressed in society; such structures would recognize voices that are now largely unheard and would be in a position to respond to the needs they express.

The current health care system is organized around the central ideal of pursuing a "cure" in the face of illness, wherein "cure" is interpreted with most of the requisite agency belonging to the health care providers. A feminist alternative would recommend that the health care system be principally concerned with empowering consumers in their own health by providing them with the relevant information and the means necessary to bring about the changes that would contribute to their health. The existing health care system, modeled as it is on the dominance structures of an oppressive society, is closed to many innovative health strategies that would increase the power of patients; a feminist model would be user-controlled and responsive to patient concerns.

Such a change in health care organization would require us to direct our attention to providing the necessities of healthy living, rather than trying only to correct the serious consequences that occur when the opportunities for personal care have been denied. Moreover, as an added benefit, a shift to a more democratized notion of health needs may help to evolve a less expensive, more effective health care delivery system; most patients seem to be less committed than are their professional health care providers to a costly high-tech, crisis-intervention focus in health care (York 1987).

A health care system that reflects feminist ideals would avoid or at least lessen the contribution that the system of health care makes in the maintenance of oppression. It would be significantly more egalitarian in both organization and effect than anything that we are now accustomed to. This system not only would be fairer in its provision of health services but would also help to undermine the ideological assumptions on which many of our oppressive practices rest. Such an alternative is required as a matter of both ethics and health.

To spell out that model in greater detail and with an appropriate understanding, it is necessary to democratize the discipline of bioethics itself—hence, bioethics, as an area of intellectual pursuit, must also recognize the value of incorporating diverse voices in its discussions and analyses. Like medicine or any other discipline, bioethics is largely defined by the perspective of its participants. If we hope to ensure a morally adequate analysis of the ethics of health care, then we should ensure the participation of many different voices in defining the central questions and exploring the promising paths to answers in the field. I hope this book facilitates that wider conversation and the transformations it may bring both to the provision of health care and to the study of health care ethics.

Notes, References, and Index

Notes

Introduction

1. Terminology is unsettled in this rapidly growing field. "Medical ethics" and "biomedical ethics" have been criticized for privileging the physician's role and concerns, "bioethics" for being overly concerned with the biological realm, rather than the more holistic human concerns that arise in the context of health care. The term "health care ethics" seems to avoid these problems but is less well established in the literature. When referring to the existing tradition, I rely on whichever of the first three forms seems appropriate, because they accurately represent the focus of most work in the field. When promoting the directions I would like to see the field take, I use the fourth term.

2. It has not totally escaped this criticism, however. Farley (1985) has offered a valuable critique from the perspective of feminist theology, and *Hypatia* devoted two issues (4: 2 and 3) to feminist ethics and medicine. There have also been numerous feminist critiques of two traditional problem areas in bioethics, abortion and reproductive technologies, and many feminist criticisms of medical practice that fall outside the traditional approaches to bioethics.

3. Harding's advice about science can be extended to bioethics: "In examining feminist criticisms of science, then, we must consider all that science does not do, the reasons for these exclusions, how these shape science precisely through their absences—both acknowledged and unacknowledged" (Harding 1986a, 650).

4. It must be acknowledged, however, that many others are not so altruistic. Medicine is filled with dreadful tales of abuse and incompetence, of sadism and flagrant exploitation of patients. Like other bioethicists, I do not address the sorts of cases that clearly violate ethical norms; rather, I restrict my discussion to the difficult cases where good intentions and well-developed professional skills may still not result in ethically acceptable practice.

Chapter 1. Understanding Feminism

1. Frye helps her readers understand the difference that perspective makes in recognizing barriers by introducing the metaphor of a bird cage. If one limits one's vision to the fine, individual strands of the cage, then it is difficult to identify any serious impediment, but if one focuses on the micro-level of the interwoven pattern of these fine strands, then the effect of the barrier is obvious. For a more complete discussion of the nature of oppression and the variety of forms it takes, see Young (1988).

2. See Frye (1983), 2–5, for a discussion of the characteristic place of the double bind in oppression.

3. See, e.g., Aiken et al. (1988) for an overview of the ways various academic disciplines have institutionalized male values and the difference a feminist perspective makes to their traditional pursuits. In philosophy see Harding and Hintikka (1983), Lloyd (1984), and Code, Mullett, and Overall (1988).

4. See esp. Lloyd (1984); see also Clark and Lange (1979) and Harding and Hintikka (1983).

5. See, e.g., Merchant's interesting exploration of these connections (Merchant 1980).

6. Here, too, feminist analysis warns against accepting superficial impressions. The differences in the norms of dress and appearance for men and women reflect and reinforce their differences in power and vulnerability.

7. On December 6, 1989, Mark Lepin walked into the engineering school of the University of Montreal with a semiautomatic assault rifle, separated the men from the women, accused the women of being feminists, and then murdered fourteen women before killing himself. He left a three-page suicide note in which he explained why he hated women and how he believed that they had ruined his life. Many commentators, both male and female, insist on viewing this event as the isolated attack of a lone madman and denied any connection with social attitudes, in which hatred and violence toward women are routinely tolerated. Most feminists experienced a personal shudder of terror on hearing of this event and saw no reason to separate it from the context in which women are regularly murdered for being women, often by their lovers or husbands.

8. For a particularly effective description of this change in consciousness, I recommend Bartky's paper "Towards a Phenomenology of Feminist Consciousness" (1975). She explains that a feminist consciousness does not lead us to see different things but to see the same things differently.

9. Some feminists do feel conflict over this sort of resolution. They accept the criticism of their lesbian sisters that their ties to men keep them from directing their energies to women, from developing women-centered relationships and habits, and from breaking out of the patterns that feed

heterosexism. Still, ties of love are not to be discarded easily, not even for political reasons. Here we have a feminist double bind.

10. Antifeminists seldom miss the opportunity to refer to Margaret Thatcher, whom they consider a decisive counter-example to all feminist claims. They argue that her obvious power disproves all claims of systematic discrimination against women.

11. Badgley et al. (1984) determined that one in three males has been a victim of unwanted sexual attacks. For most, the attacks occurred when they were children or youths.

12. See Calhoun (1989) for an exploration of the difficulty in assigning blame for sexist acts in a pervasively sexist environment.

13. This arrangement has been noted by many feminists. See, e.g., Griffin (1971); Frye (1983), esp. 52–83; and Hoagland (1988), esp. 29–32.

14. Frye suggests that men set themselves against masculinity, asking that they think about how they can "stop being men" (Frye 1983, 127).

15. See, e.g., the discussion in Hoagland (1988), 117–20.

16. Among the various attempts to categorize variations in feminist thought, Jaggar's political classification is probably the most detailed and best known (Jaggar 1983). Tong (1989) offers a wider set of categories, based on a variety of criteria for classification. Harding (1986b) offers a different criterion of division, based on epistemological differences, and Alcoff (1988) offers one based on metaphysical differences.

17. This decision means that I leave vague a number of important theoretical issues: e.g., the origins of patriarchy, the connection among the various species of oppression, the primacy of economic versus sexual oppression. It does, however, allow me to get on with a more specific focus of developing a feminist approach to the ethics of health care.

18. There is significant ambiguity in most attempts to characterize the various approaches to feminism that have been categorized to date. The term "liberal feminism," in particular, is almost exclusively defined by those who reject it, and as Wendell (1987) has argued, critics have not been entirely fair in their definitions. Insofar as I associate myself with some of the insights of liberal feminism, I have in mind the version that Wendell defines.

19. This is because those with the greatest social power are best situated to protect their rights if they come into conflict with those of others; thus in North America it is common for middle-class, white males to be the most adept and successful claimants with respect to human-rights legislation purportedly initiated to support the rights of women and minorities.

20. I do not agree with the familiar analysis that suggests that the fall of Eastern Europe establishes the failure of socialism, because I do not think that any of the Soviet-bloc countries actually represented socialist ideals.

21. Ferguson (1989) is a notable exception on this score and for that

reason does not easily fit in the usual picture of socialist feminism, although she maintains the label.

22. Those I find most appealing tend to resist such labeling, however, simply calling themselves feminists; MacKinnon (1987), e.g., calls her theory "feminism unmodified."

23. See, e.g., hooks (1982) and Hull, Scott, and Smith (1982).

24. For documentation of some of the forms this takes, see Daly (1978).

25. Daly (1978) is often taken as representative of the view that an essential female nature is characteristic of women, although that nature is often so crippled by patriarchy as virtually to have disappeared; Grimshaw (1986) offers a representative challenge to this metaphysical assumption; and Riley (1988) offers a particularly clear example of postmodern concerns with the category of "woman." Alcoff (1988) offers an imaginative proposal for resolving the apparent contradiction between these positions and for incorporating the truths inherent in each.

26. Hoagland points to the sort of rethinking required here, by distinguishing between "power-over" and "power-from-within" or power as ability (Hoagland 1988, 117).

27. Furthermore, if we do not manage these changes, then there may be no world at all, because masculinist values have led humans to produce a terrifying arsenal of military weapons and have brought us to the brink of environmental catastrophe.

Chapter 2. Ethics, "Feminine" Ethics, and Feminist Ethics

1. Like many other moral theorists, I use these terms interchangeably. I will avoid the term "morality," which generally implies a rather authoritarian, specific set of rules, and focus instead on the theoretical underpinnings for any such rules.

2. Apparently, this handy feminist term originated with O'Brien in her influential book *The Politics of Reproduction* (1981). It has been widely adopted by feminist critics in many disciplines, and it is hard to imagine how we ever got along without it.

3. Because my thinking is most influenced by work in the Anglo-American tradition, the sort of philosophy most commonly pursued in North American institutions, my discussion is limited to the leading ethical traditions within that paradigm. Continental and non-Western styles of philosophy propose different ethical models from those explored here, but they are beyond the scope of this review.

4. A modern form of utilitarianism, known as rule utilitarianism, does

involve commitment to following moral rules. Its basic principle directs the agent to follow those rules that, if generally followed, would create the best consequences. Rule utilitarians evaluate rules according to the consequences they can be expected to produce and so are still properly categorized as believing in variants of consequential ethics. Unlike the case of strict deontological theories, rules that lead to disastrous consequences would not be the appropriate ones to follow under this theory.

5. In an intriguing essay Scanlon (1982) outlines a form of contractual reasoning he calls "contractualism," which aims to achieve reasonable agreement about moral matters with others, in contrast to the common contractarian aim of pursuing mutual advantage. His proposal avoids some of the more objectionable features of traditional contractarian positions, because it does not presume equality among contractors or demand aggregative measures of the good but allows comparison of individual gains, losses, and levels of welfare. This seems a more promising program for feminists, because it is free of many of the most objectionable features of social contract theory, but Scanlon acknowledges that his version of contractualism is "only in outline"; its ultimate promise remains to be determined.

6. E.g., see Rawls (1971). He argues that one can arrive at a just contract only if one does not know the special, distinguishing features of one's life, and hence each contractor must carefully consider the possibility of occupying each position that will exist within the society.

7. Okin (1989b) does believe that contractarian theory can be revised to meet feminist concerns. She develops a feminist critique of some of the leading contractarian theories and spells out a positive proposal of how feminist modifications can be made to Rawls's theory to produce a more acceptable theory. Her work shows that we need feminism to do the ethical work that contractual theories purport to accomplish.

8. As Spelman (1988) has pointed out, yet another set of virtues was defined for slaves who are presumed to be male. What virtues were expected of slave women remains undefined.

9. For excerpts representing views on women from these and other historical figures, with commentaries by feminists, see Osborne (1979).

10. See Okin (1989a) for a detailed discussion of the problems with Rawls's inattention to gender and for suggestions of how to add the missing feminist perspective to his theory.

11. See Okin (1989b) for an indication of how Nozick's theory would change if he paid attention to the existence and experiences of women. Campbell (1988) shows how Gauthier fails to address some feminist concerns.

12. The construction of a human scale designed on the basis of male development is not unusual. Scientists commonly take the male experience

as the norm, and women are characterized by their deviance from this norm. Sometimes juggling is necessary to make the outcomes fit the expectations; for example, early IQ tests had to be redesigned when girls consistently scored higher on them than boys did (Block and Dworkin 1976, 461–62).

13. Baier (1985b) has described the male ideal of morality as the search for "workable traffic rules for self assertors" (62).

14. Elsewhere (Baier 1987b), she recommends David Hume's pursuit of moral psychology, rather than universalizing theory, as a fruitful basis for moral reflection for women.

15. I do not mean to imply that the proposals offered by Gilligan, Noddings, and others for an ethics of care are simply emotive theories directing us to "act according to our feelings." They are more sophisticated than that, specifying the nature of the relationships subsumed under the obligation to care; further, neither offers any basis for directing "negative" care or harm at others.

16. For an interesting discussion of how one feminist has spelled out this connection, see Shogan (1988).

17. This position is spelled out most explicitly in Sandel (1982); see also MacIntyre (1981) and Taylor (1985).

18. Friedman (1989) and Okin (1989b) offer more detailed feminist critiques of communitarian theories.

19. For a selection of other authors who oppose the notion of a single, comprehensive, normative theory, see Clarke and Simpson (1989).

Chapter 3. Feminism and Moral Relativism

1. For a selective sample of the feminists who have criticized the conservative use of ethics against feminist challenges, see Daly (1984), Hoagland (1988), and Frye (1990).

2. For a more detailed description of the health risks associated with female genital mutilation, see Koso-Thomas (1987).

3. Clitoridectomy was prescribed for a large variety of medical reasons in many countries, including Canada and the United States, in the late nineteenth and early twentieth centuries (Ehrenreich and English 1979; Mitchinson 1991).

4. Some critics may consider it appropriate to call this position "feminist moral absolutism," because it is defined in terms of a nonrelative moral judgment on the wrongfulness of oppression. Although I appreciate the logic

of that view, I prefer to retain the label of "feminist moral relativism," because I want to stress the authority of properly organized communities to determine their specific understandings of morality. As long as communities do not rely on oppressive forces to achieve moral agreement, moral matters are relative to their collective deliberations.

5. The definition of "permissible" ends will be derived from the moral theory in which it is embedded; for the Kantian, it will be defined as rational ends.

6. That is not to say that women do not take an active part in the abortion debate. Women are among the most active campaigners for and against liberal abortion policies (Luker 1984; Collins 1985). Few women, however, are influential in the dominating institutions that largely determine the outcome of the struggle, including the legislatures, courts, and health care structures.

7. Consider, e.g., Tong's (1988) cautious mention of the practice, which occurs in a footnote: "Clitoridectomy, or female circumcision, is probably a practice that harms women. The health hazards of the practice are enough to constitute an argument against it. Nevertheless, the practice has been invested with weighty cultural baggage having to do with the passage from girlhood to womanhood and/or having to do with the integrity of native customs against the force of colonial powers' morality. Thus, any wholesale condemnation of clitoridectomy is problematic" (261, n.5). Daly, in contrast, has been willing to offer a detailed argument against this practice, as well as other forms of female mutilation (e.g., Chinese foot-binding, Western gynecological surgery) indigenous to cultures both local and foreign (Daly 1978).

8. Koso-Thomas (1987), e.g., writes from within Sierra Leone that "there is no doubt that the heavy weight of international opinion put behind any local effort will provide the moving force necessary to initiate strategy in any particular community" (98).

9. Barry has also argued that genital mutilation is a means of keeping women from forming sexual relations with each other, when confined to the intimate proximity of polygynous marriage (Barry 1979, 163–64).

10. It should be stressed, however, that this argument is made from outside the culture, where it is sometimes difficult to understand the complex dimensions of the power structures. The moral criticism offered here is conditional, based on the assumption that women's consent to this practice has been coerced. If that interpretation turns out to be wrong, unlikely though that seems, then the grounds for criticism would dissolve.

11. Koso-Thomas (1987) notes that "most traditional African women tend to have a strong negative attitude towards other women searching for a

way to help their suffering; they seem also to object to the growing interest shown by people in the developed world. This interest they interpret as interference in their culture" (14).

Chapter 4. Toward a Feminist Ethics of Health Care

1. These shortcomings have not altogether escaped the notice of theorists still strongly committed to the classical theories. Many ethical theorists try to develop variations on the classical theories that are more sensitive to context. I do not argue that such adaptations are impossible, that the theories are hopelessly incapable of addressing contextual details. My point is that context, and particularly the political context, is essential to the ethical enterprise, and theories will be of value only to the extent that they adopt this feminist perspective.

2. Proposed by Fletcher (1966).

3. See, e.g., Macklin (1987), esp. 50–51.

4. As noted in Chapter 2, several nonfeminist philosophers—e.g., Sandel (1982) and MacIntyre (1981)—have also been interested in developing an ethics oriented to building community. For reasons Friedman (1989) develops, feminists should be wary of these proposals and must pursue their own explicitly feminist conceptions of community.

5. This tendency seems to me esp. common in the contributions of physicians to medical ethics; it is less apparent in the philosophical discussions in the field.

6. Here, as elsewhere, there is space for alternative feminist analyses. Although most feminists have been deeply suspicious of the acceptability of the practice of contractual pregnancy, Shavel (1990) has offered a compelling feminist argument in favor of legalizing such arrangements.

Chapter 5. Abortion

1. Much of the philosophic literature on abortion characterizes the possible moral positions on the issue as falling within three slots along a continuum: conservative (no abortions are morally acceptable, except, perhaps, when the woman's life is at stake), moderate (abortions are permissible under certain circumstances), or liberal (abortion should be available "on demand"). See, e.g., Wertheimer (1971) or Sumner (1981).

2. Technically, the term "fetus" does not cover the entire period of development. Medical practitioners prefer to distinguish between differing stages

of development with such terms as "conceptus," "embryo" (and, recently, "pre-embryo"), and "fetus." Because these distinctions are not relevant to the discussion here, I follow the course common to discussions in bioethics and feminism and use the term "fetus" to cover the entire period of development from conception to the end of pregnancy through either birth or abortion.

3. Bearing a child can keep a woman within a man's sphere of influence against her will. The Canadian news media were dominated in the summer of 1989 by the story of Chantel Daigle, a Quebec woman who faced injunctions granted to her former boyfriend by two lower courts against her choice of abortion before she was finally given permission for abortion by the Supreme Court of Canada. Daigle's explanation to the media of her determination to abort stressed her recognition that if she was forced to bear this child, she would never be free from the violent father's involvement in her life.

4. Feminists believe that it is wrong of society to make childbearing a significant cause of poverty in women, but the reality of our social and economic structures in North America is that it does. In addition to their campaigns for greater reproductive freedom for women, feminists also struggle to ensure that women receive greater support in child-rearing; in efforts to provide financial stability and support services to those who provide care for children, feminists would welcome the support of those in the antiabortion movement who sincerely want to reduce the numbers of abortions.

5. Among the exceptions here, see Overall (1987), who seems willing to specify some conditions under which abortion is immoral (78–79).

6. Critics continue to base the debate on the possibility that women might make frivolous abortion decisions; hence they want feminists to agree to setting boundaries on acceptable grounds for choosing abortion. Feminists, however, should resist this injunction. There is no practical way of drawing a line fairly in the abstract; cases that may appear "frivolous" at a distance often turn out to be substantive when the details are revealed. There is no evidence to suggest that women actually make the sorts of choices worried critics hypothesize about: for example, the decision of a woman eight-months pregnant to abort because she wants to take a trip or gets in "a tiff" with her partner. These sorts of fantasies, on which demands to distinguish between legitimate and illegitimate personal reasons for choosing abortion rest, reflect an offensive conception of women as irresponsible. They ought not to be perpetuated. Women seeking moral guidance in their own deliberations about choosing abortion do not find such hypothetical discussions of much use.

7. In her monumental historical analysis of the early roots of Western patriarchy, Lerner (1986) determined that patriarchy began in the period from 3100 to 600 B.C., when men appropriated women's sexual and repro-

ductive capacity; the earliest states entrenched patriarchy by institutionalizing the sexual and procreative subordination of women to men.

8. Some women claim to be feminist yet oppose abortion; some even
claim to offer a feminist argument against abortion (see Callahan 1987). For
reasons that I develop in this chapter, I do not believe a thorough feminist
analysis can sustain a restrictive abortion policy, although I do acknowledge
that feminists need to be wary of some of the arguments proposed in support
of liberal policies on abortion.

9. The state could do a lot to ameliorate this condition. If it provided
women with adequate financial support, removed the inequities in the labor
market, and provided affordable and reliable child care, pregnancy need not
so often lead to a woman's dependence on a particular man. That it does
not do so is evidence of the state's complicity in maintaining women's subordinate position with respect to men.

10. The IUD has proven so hazardous and prone to lawsuits, it has been
largely removed from the market in the United States (Pappert 1986). It is
also disappearing from other Western countries but is still being purchased
by population-control agencies for use in the developing world (LaCheen
1986).

11. For a more detailed discussion of the limitations of current contraceptive options, see Colodny (1989); for the problems of cost, see esp. 34–35.

12. See Petchesky (1985), esp. chap. 5, where she documents the risks
and discomforts associated with pill use and IUDs and the increasing rate at
which women are choosing the option of diaphragm or condom, with the
option of early, legal abortions as backup.

13. Eisenstein (1988) has developed an interesting account of sexual politics, which identifies the pregnant body as the central element in the cultural subordination of women. She argues that pregnancy (either actual or
potential) is considered the defining characteristic of all women, and because it is not experienced by men, it is classified as deviance and considered grounds for different treatment.

14. Thomson (1971) is a notable exception to this trend.

15. Because she was obviously involved in sexual activity, it is often concluded that the noncoerced woman is not innocent but guilty. As such, she
is judged far less worthy than the innocent being she carries within her.
Some who oppose abortion believe that an unwanted pregnancy is a suitable
punishment for "irresponsible" sex.

16. This seems reminiscent of Aristotle's view of women as flowerpots
where men implant the seed with all the important genetic information and
the movement necessary for development and the woman's job is that of
passive gestation, like the flowerpot. See Whitbeck (1973) and Lange (1983).

17. Some are so preoccupied with the problem of fetuses being "stuck" in

women's bodies that they seek to avoid this geographical complication altogether, completely severing the ties between woman and fetus. For example, Bernard Nathanson, an antiabortion activist with the zeal of a new convert, eagerly anticipates the prospect of artificial wombs as alternative means for preserving the lives of fetuses and "dismisses the traditional reverence for birth as mere 'mythology' and the act of birth itself as an 'insignificant event'" (cited in McDonnell 1984, 113).

18. Cf. Warren (1989) and Tooley (1972).

19. The definition of pregnancy as a purely passive activity reaches its ghoulish conclusion in the increasing acceptability of sustaining brain-dead women on life-support systems to continue their functions as incubators until the fetus can be safely delivered. For a discussion of this trend, see Murphy (1989).

20. This apt phrasing is taken from Petchesky (1985), 342.

21. E.g., Held (1987b) argues that personhood is a social status, created by the work of mothering persons.

22. Fetuses are almost wholly individuated by the women who bear them. The fetal "contributions" to the relationship are defined by the projections and interpretations of the pregnant woman in the latter stages of pregnancy, if she chooses to perceive fetal movements in purposeful ways (e.g., "it likes classical music, spicy food, exercise").

23. See Luker (1984), esp. chaps. 6 and 7, and Petchesky (1985), esp. chaps. 7 and 8, for documentation of these associations in the U.S. anti-abortion movement and Collins (1985), esp. chap. 4, and McLaren and McLaren (1986) for evidence of similar trends in the Canadian struggle.

24. See McLaren and McLaren (1986) and Petchesky (1985).

25. When abortion was illegal, many women nonetheless managed to obtain abortions, but only the relatively privileged women with money were able to arrange safe, hygienic abortions; poor women were often constrained to rely on dangerous, unacceptable services. In the United States court rulings have ensured that rich and middle-class women have, for the moment, relatively easy access to well-run clinics and hospitals, but because public hospitals are mostly unwilling to offer abortion services and federal law prohibits the use of Medicaid funding for abortion, many poor women still find legal, safe abortions out of reach (Petchesky 1985). In Canada, too, abortion services are most readily available to middle-class, urban, mature women. This suggests that financial circumstances may be a more significant factor in determining women's access to abortion than abortion's legal status.

26. Some feminists suggest we seek recognition of the legitimacy of non-medical abortion services. This would reduce costs and increase access dramatically, with no apparent increase in risk as long as services were provided by trained, responsible practitioners who were concerned with the well-be-

ing of their clients. It would also allow the possibility of increasing women's control over abortion. See, e.g., McDonnell (1984).

27. For a useful model of such a center, see Van Wagner and Lee (1989).

28. A poignant collection of some women's unfortunate experiences with hospital abortions is offered in *Telling Our Secrets*, produced by CARAL (1990).

29. Therefore, the Soviet model, in which abortions have been relatively accessible, is also unacceptable, because there the unavailability of birth control forces women to rely on multiple abortions to control their fertility.

Chapter 6. New Reproductive Technologies

1. It was not until 1965 that the United States overturned state laws that prohibited the sale of contraceptives to married couples, and not until 1973 that single persons could claim similar rights. In Canada regulations restricting the provision of contraceptive information and devices were removed in 1969.

2. Morgan (1984) reports that only one-third of the women in the world have access to the information and means necessary for contraception.

3. We should keep in mind that much of the promise of the new forms of reproductive technology remains unfulfilled at this time; most cannot achieve the control they are meant to accomplish.

4. A very useful description of the process involved in this technique and its variations can be found in Birke, Himmelweit, and Vines (1990).

5. Therefore, Klein (1989) concludes, "In reality, it is a *failed* technology" (1).

6. Multiple births are a relatively frequent occurrence in IVF and other technological responses to infertility; the preferred technological solution to this iatrogenic problem is the new technique of selective abortion, wherein some fetuses in the womb are given a lethal injection and the other(s) are allowed to continue their development.

7. Having a healthy baby with an uncomplicated birth is an extremely rare achievement for IVF technology. A survey conducted by the Australian government reported that fewer than 5 percent of cases resulted in an unproblematic, live birth (cited in Klein 1989).

8. For a discussion of some of the already apparent dangers of clomid use in the treatment of infertility, including deaths attributed to irresponsible prescriptions, see Klein (1989).

9. Beck-Gernsheim (1989) reports that over half of the women who give birth to IVF babies do so by cesarian section (36).

10. The province of Ontario is a remarkable exception; it does include IVF under the rubric of provincially funded medical services. In Britain only one clinic is fully funded under the National Health Service, and waiting lists are extremely long (Doyal 1987; Birke, Himmelweit, and Vines 1990).

11. When I raised this point in a panel discussion on the ethics of reproductive technologies at the University of Alberta, the gynecologist on the panel patiently explained the reason for this omission: primates are expensive research animals. Although I do not mean to imply that there are no ethical problems in the experimental use of animals, animal experimentation and careful documentation are usually demanded before any new medical technology can be implemented; but here, where the technology is directed exclusively at women, no such research was performed. Further, the women on whom this technology is practiced are not advised of this omission; many assume that they are undergoing an established treatment, rather than participating in a broad, uncontrolled clinical trial.

12. See Soules (1985). Much of the difficulty has to do with the unwillingness of practitioners to establish meaningful guidelines on what constitutes success. For women contemplating such therapy, "success" naturally is interpreted as meaning that the process produces a healthy baby, but for practitioners, success can mean success at any of the stages of the program. Even with the most generous interpretation, however, there is evidence that some clinics have been less than honest.

13. E.g., a man may be interested in producing a genetically linked child because genetic inheritance is likely to be his only real connection with the child, if he does not assume any child-rearing responsibilities, or a racist may choose this technology to ensure that only "racially pure" genes go into the creation of the child.

14. See, e.g., Holmes, Hoskins, and Gross (1981); Overall (1987); Corea (1985b); Klein (1989); Williams (1989).

Chapter 7. Paternalism

1. This is not to suggest any broad agreement in the traditional literature about the precise definition of "autonomy." The term remains one of the most controversial, in a discipline defined by controversy—see, e.g., Christman (1989). The range of understandings is quite extensive, especially as the term is sometimes invoked in the bioethics literature: e.g., Miller (1981) has delineated four distinct uses of the term that enter into discussions of medical ethics, and *Hastings Center Report* 14 no. 5 (October 1984) offers a symposium on autonomy, paternalism, and community that reflects a wide range of views on autonomy. Nonetheless, a common expectation in the

bioethics literature is that something like the Kantian conception of rational, individual self-rule is central to the idea of autonomy.

2. See Katz (1984), esp. chap. 1. He observes: "The contemporary proponents of informed consent come largely from the field of bio-ethics and most of them are non-physicians. . . . The resistance among physicians to joint decision making has not substantially diminished" (27).

3. See, e.g., the lament, offered by Shorter (1985), for the loss of physician mystique that has been brought about by the consumer health movement's demand for greater patient information and involvement in decision-making: "The crisis of postmodern medicine is that this art of curing illness is now being lost. It is not just because of the doctors. Their patients no longer seem able to muster the requisite faith that the doctor can cure, that his [sic] healing hand and all-knowing gaze will restore. . . . The patient's rights movement and the mass media have done their clients a grim disservice" (259).

4. Nonfeminist critics are also unhappy with the dichotomy of choosing between traditional characterizations of autonomy and paternalism. Bioethicists commonly modify and revise the classical conception of autonomy to fit the realities of the medical context. Alternative feminist conceptions can play a significant role in helping to reconceptualize the options here.

5. Paternalism in the face of a patient's actual incompetence at decision-making is generally characterized as "weak paternalism," because if patients are not fully competent, then they are lacking autonomy; under such conditions, there may be no real interference with autonomy.

6. See Lennane and Lennane (1973). More recently, other conditions, including breast pain, absence of sexual feeling in intercourse after hysterectomy, and postpartum depression, have been added to the list.

7. Childress (1982) observes that "paternalism presupposes trust" (47).

8. For more detail of the stereotypes of women that are used to sell tranquilizers and antidepressants to physicians, see Penfold and Walker (1983), 198–200.

9. As Todd (1989) observes, women were not passive dupes in this shift. Many women favored medical control of pregnancy and childbirth because it promised greater safety and less pain, although there is much dispute about how reliable those promises were at the time.

10. Corea (1985a) cites a report from the *Medical World News* on the proceedings of a cancer conference, where surgeons agreed that "they rarely hesitate to remove an ovary but think twice about removing a testicle." One doctor seemed to sum up the sentiments: "No ovary is good enough to leave in, and no testicle is bad enough to take out!" (14).

11. Women constitute more than two-thirds of the mental patient population in North America (Penfold and Walker 1983).

12. For a particularly effective argument to this effect, see Katz (1984).

13. Feminists are not alone in promoting a communal alternative to both autonomy and paternalism in medicine. See Hardwig (1990) and the "Fifteenth Anniversary Symposium: Autonomy, Paternalism, Community" in *Hastings Center Report* 14 no. 5 (October 1984). Feminist proposals are distinctive because they are sensitive to the need to evaluate the patient's family or community, before judging it a reliable agent to represent or make demands on the patient (see Chaps. 3 and 4). Because families and communities may be oppressively structured, feminists are wary of simply endorsing the status quo.

14. Several feminist writers have proposed friendship as an alternative basis for ethics; see, e.g., Raymond (1986), Code (1987), Held (1987b).

Chapter 8. Research

1. See Katz (1972). Further, Seidelman (1989) argues that the complicity of Nazi physicians in carrying out state racism is not anomalous but is an implicit part of the physician's role of gatekeeper and decision-maker, whose legacy is evident in current medical practice. See also Proctor (1988).

2. The terminology of therapeutic and nontherapeutic research is frequently used to distinguish between research programs that offer experimental therapy to subjects who may benefit from their participation (therapeutic), and those in which the subjects cannot be expected to benefit directly (nontherapeutic). The terminology is not always used consistently, however, and has itself been the subject of controversy. For a review of this controversy, see Lynch (1984).

3. It is not the case that women alone are exposed to risk by society. Some very significant risks are reserved exclusively for particular men, namely, those involved in military service. Male risks, however, differ in important ways from those usually assigned to women; in particular, they are universally recognized as risks and accorded honor and gratitude by society. Women's risks, in contrast, are generally denied and ignored. Even in war, male soldiers, not the women nurses, are glorified by their societies. The dangers to local women posed by invading, "courageous" soldiers are not even acknowledged.

4. As in other oppressive practices, the factors governing oppression can be compounded. Women who are multiply oppressed are at particular risk with health care designed for middle-class, able-bodied, white women. Duggan (1986) documents a study conducted fifteen years after Depo-Provera was introduced in Asia (where it is most widely promoted), in which it is apparent that dosages were designed for larger Western women, and half of the conventional dose would probably have been effective for Asian women.

5. In another phase of the study, private physicians did protect their own clients by not referring them to the unit involved. This resulted in disproportionate use of poor, mostly Maori women in the study, demonstrating again the multiple risks that multiple oppression produces (Haines 1990).

6. Some physicians have gone even further and recommended the removal of the healthy breast when the other is amputated, to allow plastic surgeons to create a nice, matched set through surgical reconstruction. Lorde (1980) quotes one physician, R. K. Snyderman as saying: "It is important when considering subcutaneous mastectomy to plan to do both breasts at the same time. . . . It is extremely difficult to attain the desired degree of symmetry under these circumstances with a unilateral prosthesis" (68). Clearly, inadequate research is not the only problem facing women for whom mastectomy is recommended.

7. "Third World populations are ideal research material for field trials, especially since the norms for such research are extremely stringent in the advanced countries and the public there is far too vocal and well-informed to allow rampant trials of potentially dangerous drugs" (Balasubrahmanyan 1986, 146).

8. Disturbingly, when this information was revealed, the American Medical Association chose to lobby the U.S. Food and Drug Administration to prevent it from demanding that detailed warnings be included in all packets of birth-control pills, thus contributing to women's continued ignorance about the risks they took in using the pill. See "Medical Innovation and the State—A Case Study of Oral Contraception," chap. 11B, in Katz (1972), 736–93.

9. Notorious cases of catastrophic consequences from insufficient research make clear the need for safety tests. Although scientific evidence of the safety of thalidomide use in pregnancy was lacking, it was widely marketed for a period in the 1960s, in Canada and in some European countries, as an agent to counteract morning sickness; this resulted in tragically high rates of serious birth deformities. Furthermore, for three decades DES was prescribed as a prophylactic measure to reduce the chances of miscarriage, although there was no evidence of its effectiveness in this role. Some twenty years later doctors discovered its carcinogenic effects on the women who took it and the offspring they were carrying at the time (Corea 1985a). Even now, DES continues to be marketed in the Third World without any warnings (Marcelis and Shiva 1986).

10. Oral and injectible contraceptives are the largest contraceptive market in the world and have been recognized by financial advisors as being "among the most profitable of all pharmaceuticals" (LaCheen 1986, 108).

11. We cannot, however, explain the risks women are expected to assume as solely the product of drug-company profit, because most of the

contraceptive research performed is funded by government, especially the American government; nevertheless, only 10 percent of research funds went to safety assessments in 1979 (Duggan 1986).

12. As examples of what constitutes research in support of unethical behavior, I would cite the research that is conducted to determine how to administer torture, by calculating precisely the degree of harm that victims can be expected to tolerate and physically survive; the research that goes into determining the advantages and disadvantages of various methods of capital punishment; and the research that is conducted with respect to the devastating arts of chemical and biological warfare.

13. See, e.g., Keller (1983) or Harding (1986b), where this argument is spelled out in greater detail.

14. For a model of this approach in a more formally political context, see Young (1989).

15. A model for development of such groups and for ways researchers can improve their communication with them is offered by Keck, Dauphinais, and Lewko (1989).

Chapter 9. Ascriptions of Illness

1. PMS was added to the appendix of the 1987 rev. ed. of the American Psychiatric Association's *Diagnostic and Statistical Manual III*.

2. For a more complete description of the Aristotelian theory of sexual difference and of the role of menstruation in supporting claims of male superiority in that theory, see Tuana (1988).

3. I take this argument from Martin (1987); she attributes it to Thomas Lacquer, "Female Orgasm, Generation, and the Politics of Reproductive Biology," *Representations* 14 (Spring 1984): 1–82.

4. This is not to suggest that earlier accounts lacked grounds for claiming that the woman was inferior. For some two thousand years, scientists followed Aristotle in believing that women were inferior to men because of their lower body heat and, further, that they contributed nothing to the seed from which fetuses developed, despite mounting evidence to the contrary. Nonetheless, by the nineteenth century it became necessary to acknowledge that women had more than a "flowerpot" role to play in reproduction, so new explanations for discrimination needed to be devised. (See Tuana 1988.)

5. Only 15 percent of American women worked outside the home in 1860 (Lander 1988).

6. Figures quoted in Martin (1987), 127; for a summary of the devastating consequences Dalton claimed for PMS on other family members, see Martin (1987), 130–31, and Zita (1988), 77–78.

7. The first American PMS clinic was opened in 1981.

8. Laws (1983), Martin (1987), and Zita (1988) all argue convincingly that the burgeoning interest in PMS should be recognized as a response to the second major wave of feminism.

9. Martin provides a quote from the 1965 edition of *Novak's Textbook of Gynecology*, 7th ed., describing the new thinking on menopause: "In the past few years there has been a radical change in viewpoint and some would regard the menopause as a possible pathological state rather than a physiological one and discuss therapeutic prevention rather than the amelioration of symptoms" (Martin 1987, 51).

10. From Garner et al. (1980). They also note that articles on dieting increased by over 70 percent in the leading women's magazines over the same period.

11. For some moving accounts of these sorts of experiences, see Schoenfielder and Wieser (1983).

12. Moreover, this message is learned early; a 1986 University of California study reports that over 80 percent of nine-year-old girls are already committed to dieting (Bordo 1990).

13. This is largely a matter of social choice, however. As the disabled among us stress, we have chosen to structure our world "as though everyone is physically strong, as though all bodies are 'ideally' shaped, as though everyone can walk, hear, and see well, as though everyone can work and play at a pace that is not compatible with any kind of illness or pain" (Wendell 1989, 111). Our world can be constructed otherwise.

14. Callahan is far from alone in his prescription to restrict the scope of disease language to physical conditions. Other notable proponents of this view include Szasz (1961) and Flew (1973).

15. See, e.g., Sedgwick (1973), Margolis (1976), or Culver and Gert (1982).

16. Such scientific measurement was perceived by Callahan (1973) and Boorse (1975) as the only reliable basis for defining illness; that is why they considered the physical sphere the only appropriate scope for the medical model of illness.

17. Consider, e.g., some remarks by Lander (1988): "medical doctrine reflects ideology as much as biology" and "a significant function of medical authority is to propound a particular view of reality, to help shape the self-conceptions of those who fall under its influence" (5, 6).

18. Even Englehardt (1986) apparently forgets his general understanding of the pervasiveness of value judgments on medical norms here, for he seems willing to perceive menopause—or, at least, the osteoporosis that accompanies it—as a disease that is probably an "error" of evolution (170).

19. Zita (1988) has provided a helpful analysis of the problems for med-

icine with respect to PMS and the grounds feminists have for being distrust-
ful of the existing proposals.

20. As Zita (1988) argues, "The 'medicalized female body,' a cyclically
diseased entity, becomes *what a woman is*" (94).

21. I want to be clear, however, that it is not just that 95 percent of the
population is affected that is problematic; a similar percentage may also suffer from tooth decay, which would not make having cavities healthy. What
is problematic here is that what has been called PMS is apparently part of
most women's normal patterns of menstruation, and this frequency is used
to suggest that all women are to some degree pathologically unable to function normally for a time each month.

Chapter 10. Medical Constructions of Sexuality

1. For a sampling of the many feminists who have expressed this view,
see Rich (1980); MacKinnon (1982); Bleier (1984); Valverde (1985); Jackson
(1987); Ferguson (1989); and Overall (1990).

2. Lerner (1986) sees the appropriation of women's sexual and reproductive capacities by men as the initial step in the development of patriarchy in
Western civilization. Further, she identifies this move as the foundation of
private property and the origin of dominance and hierarchy relations between other groups. Therefore, male control of women's sexual activity appears, on her analysis, to be the very foundation of power understood as
dominance.

3. Not all feminists would agree about the proper basis for evaluating
sexual practices. There have been intense disputes within the feminist community about the legitimacy of some feminists passing judgment on others'
sexuality. Ferguson (1989) characterizes the two poles of this dispute as pluralist or libertarian feminist (any consensual sex is permissible) on the one
hand and radical feminist (sex must be freed from its place in the structures
of domination) on the other hand. (Ferguson also offers a thoughtful resolution to this intrafeminist controversy.) Some pluralist feminists have defended forms of adult–child sex, but only insofar as the activity is consensual. The difficulty for most other feminists is that under current social
arrangements, the difference in power between adults and children is so
great that genuine consent on the part of children is difficult to achieve and
nearly impossible to identify.

4. Foucault (1980) reminds us that even this is a relatively recent inven-
tion; until the nineteenth century, people engaged in many different types of
sexual acts with various partners, but individuals were not perceived as hav-

ing a sexual identity as such. The identification of a person as a homosexual or, eventually and correlatively, as a heterosexual is a modern conception.

5. Until World War II, lesbians and homosexual men in Canada and the United States had little choice but to hide and try to deny their sexuality. At that time, gay and lesbian communities developed in many of the major urban centers, which offered their members an opportunity to be open about their life-styles. To remain within the safety of these communities, however, many lesbians and gay men have had to accept marginal, low-paying jobs, rather than seeking more visible jobs in which they would be vulnerable to dismissal because of their sexual identities (Patton 1986).

6. In many feminist circles, for example, heterosexuals often feel a need to explain their sexual choices, at least to themselves.

7. These themes are played out regularly in popular media and are a staple of the genre of popular romance fiction, which is marketed to women.

8. Many feminists have documented how the institution of heterosexuality sexually objectifies women in the minds of both men and women. For a particularly cogent philosophical analysis of the moral objections to this practice, see LeMonchek (1985).

9. Dr. James Burt reports having "helped" some four thousand women (as of 1975) have orgasms by reconstructing their genitals to make the clitoris more accessible to direct penile stimulation; often these operations were done without the patient's knowledge or consent, after childbirth (Corea 1985a).

10. Ehrenreich and English (1979) document how experts have linked parents' sexual relations to the psychological well-being of children (242–45).

11. For a particularly poignant, frightening account of one patient's encounter with psychiatry after declaring herself a lesbian, see Blackbridge and Gilhooly (1985); Gilhooly underwent years of coercive "therapy" to cure her of her lesbianism, despite the fact that lesbianism is no longer authorized as a mental illness at all. Quotes in their report and other first-person accounts found regularly in *Phoenix Rising* (especially in the special gay and lesbian issue, vol. 8, nos. 3 and 4) testify that hers is not an isolated case.

12. Ehrenreich and English (1979) also cite evidence that these practices continued well into the twentieth century, including a 1948 case of clitoridectomy to control masturbation in a five-year-old girl.

13. As Corea (1985a) reports, STDs are a principal cause of infertility in women; there are some 3 million new cases of chlamydia reported each year, although 80 percent of the women who are afflicted are asymptomatic. Although barrier contraceptive measures can provide significant protection to women and the pill may actually enhance users' susceptibility, the latter

is still highly recommended by many physicians as the contraceptive of choice. "It's estimated that by the year 2000, 15–20 percent of women in the reproductive age range will be infertile because of sexually transmitted disease" (quoted in Corea 1985a, 129).

14. Patton (1986) quotes two physicians from Dallas Doctors Against AIDS as saying: "Such a severe public health concern must cause the citizenry of this country to do everything in their power to smash the homosexual movement in this country to make sure these kinds of acts are criminalized" (4). Another physician, commenting on the AIDS crisis, writes in a professional journal that "from an empirical medical perspective alone, current scientific observation seems to require the conclusion that homosexuality is a pathologic condition" (*Southern Medical Journal* [1984]: 149–50; quoted in Patton 1986, 87).

Chapter 11. Gender, Race, and Class in the Delivery of Health Care

1. Writers who are concerned about oppression are likely to make the connection prominent; for example, Beverly Smith states: "The reason that Black women don't have good health in this country is because we are so oppressed. It's just that simple" (quoted in Lewis 1990, 174).

2. Nevertheless many provinces would like to reinstitute a "small" user fee. Quebec has recently announced plans to proceed with a five-dollar charge for each visit to a hospital emergency room.

3. Women who gain entry to shelters learn that there are limits to the amount of time any woman can stay; most also find that low-cost housing is not available for them to move into once their prescribed time is exhausted, especially if they have children in tow and welfare is their only means of support.

4. Canada census data statistics for 1986 list 104,315 men and 418,855 women employed in the areas of medicine and health. Brown (1983) reports that over 85 percent of all health-service and hospital workers in the United States are women.

5. The Canadian figure is from Statistics Canada census figures; the American figure is taken from Todd (1989).

6. To correct the apparently systematic gender bias in the provision of health care McMurray (1990) recommends that efforts be made to increase "the number of female physicians in leadership roles and other positions of authority in teaching, research and the practice of medicine" (10).

7. Roger Shuy observed: "Consciously or unconsciously, dialect speakers tend to get worse treatment, wait longer for service, are considered ignorant,

and are told what to do rather than asked what they would like to do" (quoted in Todd 1989, 16). See also Weaver and Garrett (1983), who report that a "lack of awareness of a patient's cultural preferences and style of action often generates antagonisms which lead to curtailed or aborted treatment" (99).

8. Laidlaw, Malmo and associates (1990) present a variety of nonmedical, feminist approaches to therapy for victims of such abuse.

9. Fortunately, there is now widespread social agreement that all social institutions should be transformed to reflect fairer selection procedures and to challenge the pervasive stereotypes that nurture oppression; many institutions have affirmative action programs in place to bring about such structural changes. Until such redistributions occur, however, the organization of the health care system will continue to promote attitudes that foster oppression.

10. I use the term "ideology" in its simplest sense: "a body of ideas used in support of an economic, political, or social theory" (*Webster's* 1989).

11. For alternative therapies developed within native culture, see Hodgson (1990). For a discussion of the special needs of black, female alcoholics, see Battle (1990). For an African discussion of alternative therapy in general, see Minh-ha (1989), 135–41.

12. For a clear explanation and detailed description of the cultural changes required to provide helpful health services to native Americans, see Hagey (1989).

References

Addelson, Kathryn Pyne. 1987. "Moral Passages." In *Women and Moral Theory*, ed. Eva Feder Kittay and Diana T. Meyers. Totowa, N.J.: Rowman & Littlefield.

Aiken, Susan Hardy, Karen Anderson, Myra Dinnerstein, Judy Note Lensink, and Patricia MacCorquodale, eds. 1988. *Changing Our Minds: Feminist Transformations of Knowledge*. Albany: State University of New York Press.

Alcoff, Linda. 1988. "Cultural Feminism versus Post-Structuralism: The Identity Crisis in Feminist Theory." *Signs* 13(3): 405–36.

Annas, George J. 1982. "Forced Cesareans: The Unkindest Cut of All." *Hastings Center Report* 12(3): 16–17, 45.

———. 1966. "Pregnant Women as Fetal Containers." *Hastings Center Report* 16(6): 13–14.

Badgley, Robin, chair, Committee on Sexual Offenses against Children and Youths (Canada). 1984. *Sexual Offenses against Children in Canada*. Ottawa: Canadian Government Publishing Centre.

Baier, Annette C. 1985a. *Postures of the Mind: Essays on Mind and Morals*. Minneapolis: University of Minnesota Press.

———. 1985b. "What Do Women Want in a Moral Theory?" *Nous* 19(1): 53–63.

———. 1986. "Trust and Antitrust." *Ethics* 96: 231–60.

———. 1987a. "The Need for More than Justice." In *Science, Morality and Feminist Theory*, ed. Marsha Hanen and Kai Nielsen. *Canadian Journal of Philosophy* 13 (supplementary vol.): 41–56.

———. 1987b. "Hume, The Women's Moral Theorist?" In *Women and Moral Theory. See* Addelson 1987.

Balasubrahmanyan, Vimal. 1986. "Finger in the Dike: The Fight to Keep Injectables Out of India." In *Adverse Effects: Women and the Pharmaceutical Industry*, ed. Kathleen McDonnell. Toronto: Women's Press.

Bancroft, John. 1981. "Ethical Aspects of Sexuality and Sex Therapy." In *Psychiatric Ethics*, ed. Sidney Block and Paul Chodoff. Oxford: Oxford University Press.

Barker-Benfield, G. J. 1978. "Sexual Surgery in Late-Nineteenth Century America." In *Seizing Our Bodies*, ed. Claudia Dreifus. New York: Vintage.

Barry, Kathleen. 1979. *Female Sexual Slavery.* Englewood Cliffs, N.J.: Prentice-Hall.

Bartky, Sandra. 1975. "Towards a Phenomenology of Feminist Consciousness." *Social Theory and Practice* 3(4): 425–39.

Battle, Sheila. 1990. "Moving Targets: Alcohol, Crack and Black Women." In *The Black Women's Health Book: Speaking for Ourselves*, ed. Evelyn C. White. Seattle: Seal Press.

Bayles, Michael. 1984. *Reproductive Ethics.* Englewood Cliffs, N.J.: Prentice-Hall.

Beck-Gernsheim, Elisabeth. 1989. "From the Pill to Test-Tube Babies: New Options, New Pressures in Reproductive Behavior." In *Healing Technology: Feminist Perspectives*, ed. Kathryn Strother Ratcliff. Ann Arbor: University of Michigan Press.

Bell, Nora K. 1989. "What Setting Limits May Mean: A Feminist Critique of Daniel Callahan's *Setting Limits*." *Hypatia* 4(2): 167–78.

Bell, Susan. 1987. "Changing Ideas: The Medicalization of Menopause." *Social Science and Medicine* 24: 535–42.

Benfari, R. C., E. Eacker, and J. G. Stoll. 1981. "Behavioral Interventions and Compliance to Treatment Regimes." *Annual Review of Public Health* 2: 431–71.

Benhabib, Seyla. 1987. "The Generalized and the Concrete Other: The Kohlberg–Gilligan Controversy and Moral Theory." In *Women and Moral Theory. See* Addelson 1987.

Birke, Lynda, Susan Himmelweit, and Gail Vines. 1990. *Tomorrow's Child: Reproductive Technologies in the 90's.* London: Virago.

Blackbridge, Persimmon, and Sheila Gilhooly. 1985. *Still Sane.* Vancouver: Press Gang.

Bleier, Ruth. 1984. *Science and Gender: A Critique of Biology and Its Theories.* New York: Pergamon Press.

Block, N. J., and Gerald Dworkin. 1976. "IQ, Heritability, and Inequality." In *The IQ Controversy*, ed. N. J. Block and Gerald Dworkin. New York: Pantheon Books.

Blount, Melissa. 1990. "Surpassing Obstacles: Pioneering Black Women Physicians." In *Black Women's Health Book. See* Battle 1990.

Boorse, Christopher. 1975. "On the Distinction between Disease and Illness." *Philosophy and Public Affairs* 5(1): 49–68

Bordo, Susan. 1990. "Reading the Slender Body." In *Body/Politics: Women and the Discourses of Science*, ed. Mary Jacobus, Evelyn Fox Keller, and Sally Shuttleworth. New York: Routledge.

Broverman, Inge, Donald Broverman, Frank Clarkson, Paul Rosenkrantz, and Susan Vogel. 1981. "Sex-Role Stereotypes and Clinical Judgments of Mental Health." In *Women and Mental Health*, ed. Elizabeth Howell and Marjorie Bayes. New York: Basic Books.

Brown, Carol A. 1983. "Women Workers in the Health Service Industry." In *Women and Health: The Politics of Sex in Medicine*, ed. Elizabeth Fee. Farmingdale, N.Y.: Baywood.

Calhoun, Cheshire. 1988. "Justice, Care, and Gender Bias." *Journal of Philosophy* 85(9): 451–63.

———. 1989. "Responsibility and Reproach." *Ethics* 99(2): 389–406.

Callahan, Daniel. 1973. "The WHO Definition of Health." *Hastings Center Report* 1(3): 77–88.

———. 1986. "How Technology Is Reframing the Abortion Debate." *Hastings Center Report* 16(1): 33–42.

Callahan, Sidney. 1987. "A Pro-Life Feminist Makes Her Case." *Utne Reader*, March/April, 104–14.

Campbell, Margaret. 1973. "Why Would a Woman Go into Medicine?" *Medical Education in the United States: A Guide for Women*. Old Westbury, N.Y.: Feminist Press.

Campbell, Richmond. 1988. "Moral Justification and Freedom." *Journal of Philosophy* 35(4): 192–213.

Canovan, Margaret. 1987. "Rousseau's Two Concepts of Citizenship." *Women in Western Political Thought*, ed. Ellen Kennedy and Susan Mendus. Brighton, Eng.: Wheatsheaf Books.

Caplan, Arthur L. 1980. "Ethical Engineers Need Not Apply: The State of Applied Ethics Today." *Science, Technology, and Human Values* 6(33): 24–32.

———. 1989. "The Concepts of Health and Disease." In *Medical Ethics*, ed. Robert M. Veatch. Boston: Jones & Bartlett.

CARAL/Halifax. 1990. *Telling Our Secrets: Abortion Stories from Nova Scotia*. Halifax, N.S.: CARAL/Halifax.

Cassell, Eric. 1976. *The Healer's Art: A New Approach to the Doctor-Patient Relationship*. Philadelphia: J. B. Lippincott.

Childress, James F. 1982. *Who Should Decide? Paternalism in Health Care*. New York: Oxford University Press.

Christie, Ronald J., and C. Barry Hoffmaster. 1986. *Ethical Issues in Family Medicine*. Oxford: Oxford University Press.

Christman, John, ed. 1989. *The Inner Citadel: Essays on Personal Autonomy*. Oxford: Oxford University Press.

Clark, Lorenne M. G., and Lynda Lange, eds. 1979. *The Sexism of Social and Political Theory.* Toronto: University of Toronto Press.

Clarke, Stanley G., and Evan Simpson, eds. 1989. *Anti-Theory in Ethics and Moral Conservatism.* Albany: State University of New York Press.

Code, Lorraine. 1987. "Second Persons." In *Science, Morality and Feminist Theory. See* Baier 1957a.

Code, Lorraine, Sheila Mullet, and Christine Overall, eds. 1988. *Feminist Perspectives: Philosophical Essays on Methods and Morals.* Toronto: University of Toronto Press.

Collins, Anne. 1985. *The Big Evasion: Abortion, the Issue That Won't Go Away.* Toronto: Lester & Orpen Dennys.

Colodny, Nikki. 1989. "The Politics of Birth Control in a Reproductive Rights Context." In *The Future of Human Reproduction,* ed. Christine Overall. Toronto: Women's Press.

Connelly, Patricia. 1978. *Last Hired, First Fired: Women and the Canadian Labour Force.* Toronto: Women's Press.

Corea, Gena. 1985a. *The Hidden Malpractice: How American Medicine Mistreats Women.* rev. ed. New York: Harper Colophon Books.

——. 1985b. *The Mother Machine: Reproductive Technologies from Artificial Insemination to Artificial Wombs.* New York: Harper & Row.

Culver, Charles M., and Bernard Gert. 1982. *Philosophy in Medicine.* New York: Oxford University Press.

Daly, Mary. 1973. *Beyond God the Father: Toward a Philosophy of Women's Liberation.* Boston: Beacon Press.

——. 1978. *Gyn/Ecology: The Metaethics of Radical Feminism.* Boston: Beacon Press.

——. 1984. *Pure Lust: Elemental Feminist Philosophy.* Boston: Beacon Press.

Daniels, Norman. 1985. *Just Health Care.* Cambridge: Cambridge University Press.

Davis, Angela Y. 1990. "Sick and Tired of Being Sick and Tired: The Politics of Black Women's Health." In *Black Women's Health Book. See* Battle 1990.

Diamond, Irene, and Lee Quinby. 1988. "American Feminism and the Language of Control." In *Feminism and Foucault: Reflections on Resistance,* ed. Irene Diamond and Lee Quinby. Boston: Northeastern University Press.

Doyal, Lesley. 1987. "Infertility—A Life Sentence? Women and the National Health Service." In *Reproductive Technologies: Gender, Motherhood and Medicine,* ed. Michelle Stanworth. Minneapolis: University of Minnesota Press.

Duggan, Lyn. 1986. "From Birth Control to Population Control: Depo-Provera in Southeast Asia." In *Adverse Effects. See* Balasubrahmanyan 1986.

Edwards, Robert G., and David J. Sharpe. 1971. "Social Values and Research in Human Embryology." *Nature* 231: 87.

Ehrenreich, Barbara, and Deirdre English. 1979. *For Her Own Good: 150 Years of the Experts' Advice to Women*. Garden City, N.Y.: Anchor Books.

Eisenstein, Zillah R. 1988. *The Female Body and the Law*. Berkeley: University of California Press.

Englehardt, H. Tristram, Jr. 1986. *The Foundations of Bioethics*. Oxford: Oxford University Press.

Farley, Margaret. 1985. "Feminist Theology and Bioethics." In *Theology and Bioethics: Exploring the Foundations and Frontiers*, ed. Earl E. Shelp. Boston: D. Reidel.

Fee, Elizabeth, ed. 1983. *Women and Health*. See Brown 1983.

Ferguson, Ann. 1989. *Blood at the Root: Motherhood, Sexuality, and Male Dominance*. London: Pandora Press.

Ferguson, Ann, Jacqueline N. Zita, and Kathryn Pyne Addelson. 1982. "On 'Compulsory Heterosexuality and Lesbian Existence': Defining the Issues." In *Feminist Theory: A Critique of Ideology*, ed. Nanneral O. Keohane, Michelle Z. Rosenberg, and Barbara C. Gelpi. Brighton, Eng.: Harvester Press.

Fisher, Sue. 1986. *In the Patient's Best Interest: Women and the Politics of Medical Decisions*. New Brunswick, N.J.: Rutgers University Press.

Flax, Jane. 1990. "Postmodernism and Gender Relations in Feminist Theory." In *Feminism/Postmodernism*, ed. Linda J. Nicholson. New York: Routledge.

Fletcher, Joseph. 1966. *Situation Ethics: The New Morality*. Philadelphia: Westminster Press.

Flew, Anthony. 1973. *Crime or Disease?* London: Macmillan.

Foot, Philippa. 1982. "Moral Relativism." In *Relativism: Cognitive and Moral*, ed. Michael Krausz and Jack W. Meiland. Notre Dame, Ind.: University of Notre Dame Press.

Foucault, Michel. 1980. *The History of Sexuality. Vol. 1, An Introduction*, trans. Robert Hurley. New York: Vintage/Random House.

Frances, Esther. 1990. "Some Thoughts on the Contents of *Hypatia*." *Hypatia*, 5(3): 159–61.

Freud, Sigmund. 1925. "Some Psychical Consequences of the Anatomical Distinction between the Sexes." In vol. 19 of *The Standard Edition of the Complete Psychological Works of Sigmund Freud*, trans. and ed. James Strachey. London: Hogarth Press.

Friedman, Marilyn. 1987. "Care and Context in Moral Reasoning." In *Women and Moral Theory*. See Addelson 1987.

———. 1989. "Feminism and Modern Friendship: Dislocating the Community." *Ethics* 99(2): 275–90.

Frye, Marilyn. 1983. *The Politics of Reality: Essays in Feminist Theory.* Freedom, Calif.: Crossing Press.

———. 1990. "A response to *Lesbian Ethics.*" *Hypatia* 5(3): 132–37.

Gamble, Vanessa Northington. 1990. "On Becoming a Physician: A Dream Not Deferred." In *Black Women's Health Book.* See Battle 1990.

Garner, David, Paul Garfinkel, Donald Schwartz, and Michael Thompson. 1980. "Cultural Expectations of Thinness among Women." *Psychological Reports* 47: 483–91.

Gauthier, David. 1986. *Morals by Agreement.* Oxford: Clarendon Press.

Gilligan, Carol. 1982. *In a Different Voice: Psychological Theory and Women's Moral Development.* Cambridge: Harvard University Press.

Gordon-Bradshaw, Ruth H. 1988. "A Social Essay on Special Issues Facing Poor Women of Color." In *Too Little, Too Late: Dealing with the Health Needs of Women in Poverty,* ed. Cesar A. Perales and Lauren S. Young. New York: Harrington Park Press.

Gorovitz, Samuel. 1982. *Doctors' Dilemmas: Moral Conflict and Medical Care.* New York: Oxford University Press.

Gould, Carol C., ed. 1984. *Beyond Domination: New Perspectives on Women and Philosophy.* Totowa, N.J.: Rowman & Allanheld.

Griffin, Susan. 1971. "Rape: The All-American Crime." *Ramparts,* September: 26–35.

Griffiths, Morwenna, and Margaret Whitford. 1988. *Feminist Perspectives in Philosophy.* Bloomington: Indiana University Press.

Grimshaw, Jean. 1986. *Philosophy and Feminist Thinking.* Minneapolis: University of Minnesota Press.

Hagey, Rebecca. 1989. "The Native Diabetes Program: Rhetorical Process and Praxis." *Medical Anthropology* 12: 7–33.

Haines, Hilary. 1990. "Following Doctors' Orders." *Women's Review of Books* 7(8): 20–21.

Hanen, Marsha, and Kai Nielsen, eds. 1987 *Science, Morality and Feminist Theory.* See Baier 1987a.

Harding, Sandra. 1986a. "The Instability of the Analytic Categories of Feminist Theory." *Signs* 11(4): 645–64.

———. 1986b. *The Science Question in Feminism.* Ithaca, N.Y.: Cornell University Press.

———. 1987. "The Curious Coincidence of Feminine and African Moralities: Challenges for Feminist Theory." In *Women and Moral Theory.* See Addelson 1987.

Harding, Sandra, and Merrill Hintikka, eds. 1983. *Discovering Reality: Feminist Perspectives on Epistemology, Metaphysics, Methodology, and Philosophy of Science.* Dordrecht, Neth.: D. Reidel.

Hardwig, John. 1990. "What about the Family?" *Hastings Center Report* 20(2): 5–10.

Harman, Gilbert. 1982. "Moral Relativism Defended." In *Relativism: Cognitive and Moral.* See Foot 1982.

———. 1985. "Is There a Single True Morality?" In *Morality, Reason, and Truth: New Essays on the Foundations of Ethics,* ed. David Copp and David Zimmerman. Totowa, N.J.: Rowman & Allanheld.

Harrison, Geoffrey. 1982. "Relativism and Tolerance." In *Relativism: Cognitive and Moral.* See Foot 1982.

Hawkesworth, Mary E. 1989. "Knowers, Knowing, Known: Feminist Theory and Claims of Truth." *Hypatia* 14(3): 533–57.

Held, Virginia. 1984. *Rights and Goods: Justifying Social Action.* New York: Free Press.

———. 1987a. "Non-contractual Society: A Feminist View." In *Science, Morality and Feminist Theory.* See Baier 1987a.

———. 1987b. "Feminism and Moral Theory." In *Women and Moral Theory.* See Addelson 1987.

Heldke, Lisa. 1988. "Recipes for Theory Making." *Hypatia* 3(2): 15–29.

Hine, Darlene Clark. 1989. *Black Women in White: Racial Conflict and Cooperation in the Nursing Profession, 1890–1950.* Bloomington: Indiana University Press.

Hoagland, Sarah Lucia. 1988. *Lesbian Ethics: Toward New Value.* Palo Alto, Calif.: Institute of Lesbian Studies.

Hodgson, Maggie. 1990. "Shattering the Silence: Working with Violence in Native Communities." In *Healing Voices: Feminist Approaches to Therapy with Women,* ed. Toni Ann Laidlaw, Cheryl Malmo, and associates. San Francisco: Jossey-Bass.

Holmes, Helen B., Betty B. Hoskins, and Michael Gross, eds. 1981. *The Custom-Made Child? Women-centered Perspectives.* Clifton, N.J.: Humana Press.

hooks, bell. 1982. *Ain't I a Woman? Black Women and Feminism.* London: Pluto Press.

———. 1984. *Feminist Theory: From Margin to Center.* Boston: South End Press.

Houston, Barbara. 1987. "Rescuing Womanly Virtues: Some Dangers of Moral Reclamation." In *Science, Morality and Feminist Theory.* See Baier 1987a.

Houston, Barbara, and Ann Diller. 1987. "Trusting Ourselves to Care." *RFR/DRF* 16(3): 35–38.

Howe, Herbert. 1981. *Do Not Go Gentle.* New York: W. W. Norton.

Hubbard, Ruth. 1990. *The Politics of Women's Biology.* New Brunswick, N.J.: Rutgers University Press.

Hull, Gloria T., Patricia Bell Scott, and Barbara Smith, eds. 1982. *All the Women Are White, All the Blacks Are Men, But Some of Us Are Brave: Black Women's Studies.* Old Westbury, N.Y.: Feminist Press.

Jackson, Margaret. 1987. "'Facts of Life' or the Eroticization of Women's Oppression? Sexology and the Social Construction of Heterosexuality." In *The Cultural Construction of Sexuality*, ed. Pat Caplan. New York: Tavistock Publications.

Jacobus, Mary, Evelyn Fox Keller, and Sally Shuttleworth. 1990. *Body/ Politics*. See Bordo 1990.

Jaggar, Alison. 1983. *Feminist Politics and Human Nature*. Totowa, N.J.: Rowman & Allanheld.

Joffe, Carole. 1986. *The Regulation of Sexuality: Experiences of Family Planning Workers*. Philadelphia: Temple University Press.

Jonsen, Albert, and Stephen Toulmin. 1988. *The Abuse of Casuistry: A History of Moral Reasoning*. Berkeley: University of California Press.

Kass, Leon. 1979. "'Making Babies' revisited." *Public Interest* 54: 32–60.

Katz, Jay, with the assistance of Alexander Capron and Eleanor Swift Glass. 1972. *Experimentation with Human Subjects: The Authority of the Investigator, Subject, Professions and State in the Human Experimentation Process*. New York: Russell Sage Foundation.

————. 1984. *The Silent World of Doctor and Patient*. New York: Free Press.

Keck, Jennifer, Henriette Dauphinais, and John Lewko. 1989. *Critical Paths: Organizing on Health Issues in the Community*. Toronto: between the lines.

Keller, Evelyn Fox. 1983. "Gender and Science." In *Discovering Reality*. *See* Harding and Hintikka 1983.

Kittay, Eva Feder, and Diana T. Meyers, eds. 1987. *Women and Moral Theory*. *See* Addelson 1987.

Kitzinger, Celia. 1987. *The Social Construction of Lesbianism*. London: Sage Publications.

Klein, Renate D. 1989. *Infertility: Women Speak Out about Their Experiences of Reproductive Medicine*. London: Pandora Press.

Koso-Thomas, Olayinka. 1987. *The Circumcision of Women: A Strategy for Eradication*. London: Zed Books.

Krausz, Michael, and Jack W. Meiland, eds. 1982. *Relativism: Cognitive and Moral*. *See* Foot 1982.

Kunisch, Judith R. 1989. "Electronic Fetal Monitors: Marketing Forces and the Resulting Controversy." In *Healing Technology*. *See* Beck-Gernsheim 1989.

LaCheen, Cary. 1986. "Pharmaceuticals and Family Planning: Women Are the Target." In *Adverse Effects*. *See* Balasubrahmanyan 1986.

Laidlaw, Toni Ann, Cheryl Malmo, and associates, eds. 1990. *Healing Voices: Feminist Approaches to Therapy with Women*. *See* Hodgson 1990.

Lander, Louise. 1988. *Images of Bleeding: Menstruation as Ideology*. New York: Orlando Press.

Lange, Lynda. 1983. "Woman Is Not a Rational Animal: On Aristotle's Biology of Reproduction." In *Discovering Reality. See* Harding and Hintikka 1983.

Laws, Sophie. 1983. "The Sexual Politics of Pre-menstrual Tension." *Women's Studies International Forum* 6(1): 19–31.

LeMonchek, Linda. 1985. *Dehumanizing Women: Treating Persons as Sex Objects*. Totowa, N.J.: Rowman & Allanheld.

Lennane, K. Jean, and R. John Lennane. 1973. "Alleged Psychogenic Disorders in Women—A Possible Manifestation of Sexual Prejudice." *New England Journal of Medicine* 288(6): 288–92.

Lerner, Gerda. 1986. *The Creation of Patriarchy*. New York: Oxford.

Lewis, Andrea. 1990. "Looking at the Total Picture: A Conversation with Health Activist Beverly Smith." In *The Black Women's Health Book. See* Battle 1990.

Lind, Alice. 1989. "Hospitals and Hospices: Feminist Decisions about Care for the Dying." In *Healing Technology. See* Beck-Gernsheim 1989.

Lloyd, Genevieve. 1984. *The Man of Reason: "Male" and "Female" in Western Philosophy*. Minneapolis: University of Minnesota Press.

Longino, Helen. 1990. *Science as Social Knowledge: Values and Objectivity in Scientific Inquiry*. Princeton: Princeton University Press.

Lorde, Audre. 1980. *The Cancer Journals*. San Francisco: Spinsters/Aunt Lute.

Lugones, Maria C., and Elizabeth V. Spelman. 1983. "Have I Got a Theory for You! Feminist Theory, Cultural Imperialism, and the Demand for 'the Woman's Voice.'" *Women's Studies International Forum* 6(6): 573–81.

Luker, Kristin. 1984. *Abortion and the Politics of Motherhood*. Berkeley: University of California Press.

Lynch, Abbyann. 1984. "The Therapeutic/Nontherapeutic Research Distinction: Why/Why Not?" In *Medical Priorities in Medical Research: The Second Hannah Conference*, ed. John M. Nicholas. Toronto: Hannah Institute for the History of Medicine.

McBarnette, Lorna. 1988. "Women and Poverty: The Effects on Reproductive Status." In *Too Little, Too Late. See* Gordon-Bradshaw 1988.

McCrea, Frances B. 1983. "The Politics of Menopause: The Discovery of a Deficiency Disease." *Social Problems* 31: 111–23.

McDonnell, Kathleen. 1984. *Not an Easy Choice: A Feminist Re-examines Abortion*. Toronto: Women's Press.

———, ed. 1986. *Adverse Effects. See* Balasubrahmanyan 1986.

MacIntyre, Alasdair. 1981. *After Virtue*. Notre Dame, Ind.: University of Notre Dame Press.

MacKinnon, Catharine. 1982. "Feminism, Marxism, Method and the State: An Agenda for Theory." *Signs* 7(3): 515–44.

————. 1987. *Feminism Unmodified: Discourses on Life and Law.* Cambridge: Harvard University Press.

————. 1989. *Toward a Feminist Theory of the State.* Cambridge: Harvard University Press.

Macklin, Ruth. 1987. *Mortal Choices: Ethical Dilemmas in Modern Medicine.* Boston: Houghton Mifflin.

McLaren, Angus, and Arlene Tigar McLaren. 1986. *The Bedroom and the State: The Changing Practices and Politics of Contraception and Abortion in Canada, 1880–1980.* Toronto: McClelland & Stewart.

McMurray, Richard J. 1990. "Gender Disparities in Clinical Decision-making." Report to the American Medical Association Council on Ethical and Judicial Affairs.

Marcelis, Carla, and Mira Shiva. 1986. "EP Drugs: Unsafe by Any Name." In *Adverse Effects. See* Balasubrahmanyan 1986.

Margolis, Joseph. 1976. "The Concept of Disease." *Journal of Medicine and Philosophy* 1(3): 238–55.

Martin, Biddy. 1988. "Feminism, Criticism, and Foucault." In *Feminism and Foucault. See* Diamond and Quinby 1988.

Martin, Emily. 1987. *The Woman in the Body: A Cultural Analysis of Reproduction.* Boston: Beacon Press.

Merchant, Carolyn. 1980. *The Death of Nature: Women, Ecology, and the Scientific Revolution.* New York: Harper & Row.

Miles, Steven H., and Allison August. 1990. "Courts, Gender and 'the Right to Die.'" *Law, Medicine and Health Care,* 18(1, 2): 85–95.

Miller, Bruce L. 1981. "Autonomy and the Refusal of Lifesaving Treatment." *Hastings Center Report* 11(4): 22–28.

Minh-ha, Trinh T. 1989. *Women, Native, Other.* Bloomington: Indiana University Press.

Mitchinson, Wendy. 1991. *The Nature of Their Bodies: Women and Their Doctors in Victorian Canada.* Toronto: University of Toronto Press.

Morantz-Sanchez, Regina Markell. 1985. *Sympathy and Science: Women Physicians in American Medicine.* New York: Oxford University Press.

Morgan, Kathryn Pauly. 1987. "Women and Moral Madness." In *Science, Morality and Feminist Theory. See* Baier 1987a.

————. 1991. "Women and the Knife: Cosmetic Surgery and the Colonization of Women's Bodies." *Hypatia* 6(3): forthcoming.

Morgan, Robin, ed. 1984. *Sisterhood Is Global: The International Women's Movement Anthology.* Middlesex: Penguin Books.

Moulton, Janice. 1979. "Sex and Reference." In *Philosophy and Women,* ed. Sharon Bishop and Marjorie Weinzweig. Belmont, Calif.: Wadsworth.

Murphy, Julien S. 1989. "Should Pregnancies Be Sustained in Brain-Dead

Women? A Philosophical Discussion of Postmortem Pregnancy." In *Healing Technology*. *See* Beck-Gernsheim 1989.

Nelson, Lawrence J., and Nancy Milliken. 1990. "Compelled Medical Treatment of Pregnant Women: Life, Liberty, and Law in Conflict." In *Ethical Issues in the New Reproductive Technologies*, ed. Richard T. Hull. Belmont, Calif.: Wadsworth.

Nicholson, Linda J., ed. 1990. *Feminism/Postmodernism*. *See* Flax 1990.

Nicholson, Susan T. 1977. "The Roman Catholic Doctrine of Therapeutic Abortion." In *Feminism and Philosophy*, ed. Mary Vetterling-Braggin, Frederick A. Elliston, and Jane English. Totowa, N.J.: Littlefield, Adams & Co.

Noble, Cheryl. 1982. "Ethics and Experts." *Hastings Center Report* 12(3): 7–9.

Noddings, Nel. 1984. *Caring: A Feminine Approach to Ethics and Moral Education*. Berkeley: University of California Press.

Nozick, Robert. 1974. *Anarchy, State, and Utopia*. New York: Basic Books.

Nsiah-Jefferson, Laurie, and Elaine J. Hall. 1989. "Reproductive Technology: Perspectives and Implications for Low-Income Women and Women of Color." In *Healing Technology*. *See* Beck-Gernsheim 1989.

Nye, Andrea. 1990. *Words of Power: A Feminist Reading of the History of Logic*. New York: Routledge.

Oakley, Ann. 1987. "From Walking Wombs to Test-Tube Babies." In *Reproductive Technologies*. *See* Doyal 1987.

O'Brien, Mary. 1981. *The Politics of Reproduction*. London: Routledge and Kegan Paul.

Offen, Karen. 1988. "Defining Feminism: A Comparative Historical Approach." *Signs* 14(1): 119–57.

Okin, Susan Moller. 1989a. "Reason and Feeling in Thinking about Justice." *Ethics* 99(2): 229–49.

———. 1989b. *Justice, Gender, and the Family*. New York: Basic Books.

Osborne, Martha Lee, ed. 1979. *Women in Western Thought*. New York: Random House.

Overall, Christine. 1987. *Ethics and Human Reproduction: A Feminist Analysis*. Boston: Allen & Unwin.

———. 1990. "Heterosexuality and Feminist Theory." *Canadian Journal of Philosophy* 20(1): 1–18.

———, ed. 1989. *The Future of Human Reproduction*. *See* Colodny 1989.

Paltiel, Freda L. 1988. "Is Being Poor a Mental Health Hazard?" In *Too Little, Too Late*. *See* Gordon-Bradshaw 1988.

Pappert, Ann. 1986. "The Rise and Fall of the IUD." In *Adverse Effects*. *See* Balasubrahmanyan 1986.

Patton, Cindy. 1986. *Sex and Germs: The Politics of AIDS*. Montreal: Black Rose Books.

Pearsall, Marilyn, ed. *Women and Values: Readings in Recent Feminist Philosophy*. Belmont, Calif.: Wadsworth.

Pence, Gregory E. 1990. *Classic Cases in Medical Ethics: Accounts of the Cases That Have Shaped Medical Ethics, with Philosophical, Legal, and Historical Backgrounds*. New York: McGraw-Hill.

Penfold, Susan P., and Gillian Walker. 1983. *Women and the Psychiatric Paradox*. Montreal: Eden Press.

Perales, Cesar A., and Lauren S. Young, eds. 1988. *Too Little, Too Late.* See Gordon-Bradshaw 1988.

Person, Ethel Spector. 1980. "Sexuality as the Mainstay of Identity: Psycho-analytic Perspectives." In *Women—Sex and Sexuality*, ed. Catharine R. Stimpson and Ethel Spector Person. Chicago: University of Chicago Press.

Petchesky, Rosalind Pollack. 1980. "Reproductive Freedom: Beyond 'a Woman's Right to Choose.'" In *Women—Sex and Sexuality. See* Person 1980.

———. 1985. *Abortion and Woman's Choice: The State, Sexuality, and Reproductive Freedom*. Boston: Northeastern University Press.

———. 1987. "Foetal Images: The Power of Visual Culture in the Politics of Reproduction." In *Reproductive Technologies. See* Doyal 1987.

Pfeffer, Naomi. 1987. "Artificial Insemination, In-vitro Fertilization, and the Stigma of Infertility." In *Reproductive Technologies. See* Doyal 1987.

Phillips, Paul, and Erin Phillips. 1983. *Women and Work: Inequality in the Labour Market*. Toronto: James Lorimer & Company.

Plant, Judith, ed. 1989. *Healing the Wounds: The Promise of Ecofeminism*. Toronto: between the lines.

Proctor, Robert. 1988. *Racial Hygiene: Medicine under the Nazis*. Cambridge: Harvard University Press.

Ramsey, Paul. 1972. "Shall We Reproduce?" *Journal of the American Medical Association* 220: 1484.

Ratcliff, Kathryn Strother, ed. 1989. *Healing Technology. See* Beck-Gernsheim 1989.

Ratzinger, Joseph Card, and Alberto Bovone. 1987. "Instruction on Respect for Human Life in its Origin and on the Dignity of Procreation: Replies to Certain Questions of the Day." Vatican City: Vatican Polyglot Press.

Rawls, John. 1971. *A Theory of Justice*. Cambridge: Harvard University Press.

Raymond, Janice. 1979. *The Transsexual Empire*. Boston: Beacon Press.

———. 1982. "Medicine as Partiarchal Religion." *Journal of Medicine and Philosophy* 7(2): 197–216.

———. 1986. *A Passion for Friends: Toward a Philosophy of Female Affection*. Boston: Beacon Press.

Rich, Adrienne. 1980. "Compulsory Heterosexuality and Lesbian Existence." *Signs* 5(4): 631–60.

Riley, Denise. 1988. *Am I That Name? Feminism and the Category of 'Women' in History.* Minneapolis: University of Minnesota Press.

Rodgers, Sandra. 1989. "Pregnancy as Justification for Loss of Juridical Autonomy." In *Future of Human Reproduction. See* Colodny 1989.

Ross, W. D. 1930. *The Right and the Good.* Oxford: Oxford University Press.

————. 1939. *Foundations of Ethics.* Oxford: Oxford University Press.

Rothman, Barbara Katz. 1986. "Commentary: When a Pregnant Woman Endangers Her Fetus." *Hastings Center Report* 16(1): 25.

Ruddick, Sara. 1984a. "Maternal Thinking." In *Mothering: Essays in Feminist Theory,* ed. Joyce Trebilcot. Totowa, N.J.: Rowman & Allanheld.

————. 1984b. "Preservative Love and Military Destruction: Some Reflections on Mothering and Peace." In *Mothering. See* Ruddick 1984a.

Russell, Diane. 1984. *Sexual Exploitation: Rape, Child Sexual Abuse, and Workplace Harassment.* Beverly Hills, Calif.: Sage Publications.

Sandel, Michael. 1982. *Liberalism and the Limits of Justice.* Cambridge: Cambridge University Press.

Sawicki, Jana. 1988. "Identity Politics and Sexual Freedom: Foucault and Feminism." In *Feminism and Foucault. See* Diamond and Quinby, 1988.

Scanlon, T. M. 1982. "Contractualism and Utilitarianism." In *Utilitarianism and Beyond,* ed. Amartya Sen and Bernard Williams. Cambridge: Cambridge University Press.

Scheman, Naomi. 1983. "Individualism and the Objects of Psychology." In *Discovering Reality. See* Harding and Hintikka, 1983.

Schoenfielder, Lisa, and Barb Wieser, eds. 1983. *Shadow on a Tightrope: Writings by Women on Fat Oppression.* San Francisco: Spinsters/Aunt Lute.

Scully, Diana, and Pauline Bart. 1972. "A Funny Thing Happened on the Way to the Orifice: Women in Gynecology Textbooks." *American Journal of Sociology* 78: 1045–49.

Seager, Joni, and Ann Olson. 1986. *Women in the World: An International Atlas.* London: Pan Books.

Sedgwick, Peter. 1973. "Illness—Mental or Otherwise." *Hastings Center Report* 1: 19–40.

Segal, Lynne. 1987. *Is the Future Female? Troubled Thoughts on Contemporary Feminism.* London: Virago Press.

Seidelman, William E. 1989. "Medical Selection: Auschwitz Antecedents and Effluent." *Holocaust and Genocide Studies* 4(4): 435–48.

Seller, Anne. 1988. "Realism versus Relativism: Towards a Politically Adequate Epistemology." In *Feminist Perspectives in Philosophy*. *See* Griffiths and Whitford 1988.

Shapiro, Martin. 1978. *Getting Doctored: Critical Reflections on Becoming a Physician*. Kitchener, Ont.: Between the Lines.

Shavel, Carmen. 1989. *Birth Power: The Case for Surrogacy*. New Haven and London: Yale University Press.

Shogan, Debra. 1988. *Care and Moral Motivation*. Toronto: OISE Press.

Shorter, Edward. 1985. *Bedside Manners: The Troubled History of Doctors and Patients*. New York: Simon & Schuster.

Sontag, Susan. 1989. *Illness as Metaphor and AIDS and Its Metaphors*. New York: Anchor Books.

Soules, Michael. 1985. "The In Vitro Fertilization Pregnancy Rate: Let's Be Honest with One Another." *Fertility and Sterility* 43(4): 511–13.

Spelman, Elizabeth V. 1988. *Inessential Woman: Problems of Exclusion in Feminist Thought*. Boston: Beacon Press.

Stanworth, Michelle, ed. 1987. *Reproductive Technologies*. *See* Doyal 1987.

Stark, Evan, Anne Flitcraft, and William Frazier. 1983. "Medicine and Patriarchal Violence: The Social Construction of a 'Private' Event." In *Women and Health*. *See* Brown 1983.

Stellman, Jeanne Mager. 1988. "The Working Environment of the Working Poor: An Analysis Based on Worker's Compensation Claims, Census Data and Known Risk Factors." In *Too Little, Too Late*. *See* Gordon-Bradshaw 1988.

Stimpson, Catharine R., and Ethel Spector Person, eds. 1980. *Women—Sex and Sexuality*. *See* Person 1980.

Sumner, L.W. 1981. *Abortion and Moral Theory*. Princeton: Princeton University Press.

Szasz, Thomas. 1961. *The Myth of Mental Illness*. New York: Harper & Row.

Szekely, Eva. 1988. *Never Too Thin*. Toronto: The Women's Press.

Tallon, James R., Jr., and Rachel Block. 1988. "Changing Patterns of Health Insurance Coverage: Special Concerns for Women." In *Too Little, Too Late*. *See* Gordon-Bradshaw 1988.

Taylor, Charles. 1985. *Philosophy and the Human Sciences: Philosophical Papers*. Vol. 2. Cambridge: Cambridge University Press.

Thomson, Judith Jarvis. 1971. "A Defense of Abortion." *Philosophy and Public Affairs* 1(1): 47–66.

Todd, Alexandra Dundas. 1989. *Intimate Adversaries: Cultural Conflict between Doctors and Women Patients*. Philadelphia: University of Pennsylvania Press.

Tong, Rosemarie. 1989. *Feminist Thought: A Comprehensive Introduction*. Boulder, Colo.: Westview Press.

Tooley, Michael. 1972. "Abortion and Infanticide." *Philosophy and Public Affairs* 2(1): 37–65.

Trebilcot, Joyce, ed. 1984. *Mothering. See* Ruddick 1984a.

———. 1986. "Conceiving Women: Notes on the Logic of Feminism." In *Women and Values. See* Pearsall 1986.

———. 1988. "Dyke Methods." *Hypatia* 3(2): 1–13.

Tuana, Nancy. 1988. "The Weaker Seed: The Sexist Bias of Reproductive Theory." *Hypatia* 3(1): 35–59.

Valverde, Mariana. 1985. *Sex, Power and Pleasure*. Toronto: Women's Press.

Van Wagner, Vicki, and Bob Lee. 1989. "Principles into Practice: An Activist Vision of Feminist Reproductive Health Care." In *The Future of Human Reproduction. See* Colodny 1989.

Warren, Mary Anne. 1973. "On the Moral and Legal Status of Abortion." *The Monist* 57: 43–61

———. 1989. "The Moral Significance of Birth." *Hypatia* 4: 46–65.

Warren, Virginia L. 1989. "Feminist Directions in Medical Ethics." *Hypatia* 4(2): 73–87.

Weaver, Jerry L., and Sharon D. Garrett. 1983. "Sexism and Racism in the American Health Care Industry: A Comparative Analysis." In *Women and Health. See* Brown 1983.

Weeks, Jeffrey. 1987. "Questions of Identity." In *The Cultural Construction of Sexuality*, ed. Pat Caplan. London: Tavistock Publications.

Weitzman, Lenore J. 1985. *The Divorce Revolution: The Unexpected Social and Economic Consequences for Women and Children in America*. New York: Free Press.

Wendell, Susan. 1987. "A 'Qualified' Defence of Liberal Feminism." *Hypatia* 2(2): 65–93.

———. 1989. "Toward a Feminist Theory of Disability." *Hypatia* 4(2): 104–24.

Wertheimer, Roger. 1971. "Understanding the Abortion Argument." *Philosophy and Public Affairs* 1(1): 67–95.

Whitbeck, Carolyn. 1973. "Theories of Sex Difference." *Philosophical Forum* 5(1, 2): 54–80.

———. 1984. "A Different Reality: Feminist Ontology." In *Beyond Domination. See* Gould 1984.

White, Evelyn C., ed. 1990. *Black Women's Health Book. See* Battle 1990.

Williams, Bernard. 1973. "Integrity." In *Utilitarianism: For and Against*, ed. J.J.C. Smart and Bernard Williams. Cambridge: Cambridge University Press.

———. 1982. "An Inconsistent Form of Relativism." In *Relativism: Cognitive and Moral. See* Foot 1982.

Williams, Linda S. 1989. "No Relief until the End: The Physical and Emotional Costs of In Vitro Fertilization." In *Future of Human Reproduction.* *See* Colodny 1989.

Wong, David. 1984. *Moral Relativity.* Berkeley: University of California Press.

Worcester, Nancy, and Marianne H. Whatley. 1988. "The Response of the Health Care System to the Women's Health Movement: The Selling of Women's Health Centers." In *Feminism within the Science and Health Care Professions: Overcoming Resistance,* ed. Sue V. Rosser. Oxford: Pergammon Press.

Wright, Barbara Drygulski. 1989. "Introduction." In *Healing Technology.* *See* Beck-Gernsheim 1989.

Yanoshik, Kim, and Judy Norsigan. 1989. "Contraception, Control, and Choice: International Perspectives." In *Healing Technology. See* Beck-Gernsheim 1989.

York, Geoffrey. 1987. *The High Price of Health: A Patient's Guide to the Hazards of Medical Politics.* Toronto: James Lorimer & Company.

Young, Iris Marion. 1988. "Five Faces of Oppression." *Philosophical Forum* 19(4): 270–90.

———. 1989. "Polity and Group Difference: A Critique of the Ideal of Universal Citizenship." *Ethics* 99(2): 250–74.

Zambrana, Ruth E. 1988. "A Research Agenda on Issues Affecting Poor and Minority Women: A Model for Understanding Their Health Needs." In *Too Little, Too Late. See* Gordon-Bradshaw 1988.

Zita, Jacquelyn N. 1988. "The Premenstrual Syndrome: Dis-easing the Female Cycle." *Hypatia* 3(1): 77–99.

Index